THE "LOST"

GROUP THEATRE

PLAYS

VOLUME 1

Dedicated to Arlene Stites

INDEX

Plays listed in order of production

FOREWORD

The creation of the Group Theatre, on Broadway from 1931-1940, which led to the creation of the Actors Studio in 1947, is the most important event in American Theatre history. Harold Clurman, Lee Strasberg and Cheryl Crawford, all working in the Broadway Theatre, had a vision of what theatre could be: an ensemble of actors doing plays that expressed America. The vision was articulated by Harold Clurman in a season of Friday night talks to the Broadway community. The direction and training were provided by Lee Strasberg who was heavily influenced by the Russians and Europeans and who probably knew more about the art of acting being done all over the world, past and present, than any other person. He was a prodigious, voracious reader. Cheryl Crawford found the money. Twenty-seven actors were chosen, boarded the bus to Brookfield, Connecticut, and seventeen weeks later opened on Broadway in *The House of Connelly* by Paul Green. There were twenty-two curtain calls on opening night.

Eventually the troops revolted. Some went to Hollywood. Some started their own acting schools. Elia Kazan and Bobby Lewis became Broadway's star directors. In 1947, they, with Cheryl Crawford, created the Actors Studio, a community of actors inspired by the Group Theatre "method of work" and the necessary sense of community. Lee Strasberg, Stella Adler, Sandy Meisner, Bobby Lewis, Elia Kazan and Cheryl Crawford changed acting worldwide. These people, four men and two women, are all gone. The Group Theatre plays remain. Many of them are a testament to "in the details you see God, Art, Beauty and the Devil."

A word to the wise: all plays, including those by Shakespeare, are conceived to be experienced, not read. The words are for the actors who, in turn, share them with audiences and a communal experience is created. The words on the page are a framework. Nonetheless, they're often a delight and offer their own experiences.

Estelle Parsons

Introduction to 1931-

In the year 1930, they were called simply "playreaders" not "literary managers" as they are in large Theatre companies today. Two of these young readers, Harold Clurman and Lee Strasberg, were firebrands who talked ceaselessly when they were not reading about their ideas regarding contemporary theatre. Both worked with Cheryl Crawford who was also on the staff of the highly regarded and adventurous Broadway new play producing company called the Theatre Guild.

As social turmoil and tumult gripped the Western Industrial nations in the early Twentieth Century, it inspired a complete renovation and innovation of Theatre making methodology everywhere. Notable leaders rose to the occasion, Erwin Piscator in Germany, Meyerhold in Russia, The Workers Theatre and the Documentarians in the United States. Theatre artists everywhere saw themselves as missionaries and messengers of social reform. Suddenly the ordinary working man was the center stage hero. Directors, playwrights, designers and the actors themselves created innovations in how to best rouse their audiences to leave the theatre and become a living part of change. Expressionism, Constructivism, Documentaries, and Heightened Realism were now added as the tools to increase audience awareness and experience; passion and compassion were used to intensify the urgent call to a suffering nation.

Finally, the 3 passionate individuals at the Theatre Guild decided it was the moment to form a new company. The name was the Group Theatre and was made up of actors, playwrights, directors, and designers with a totally American perspective reflecting only the social struggles unique to the American Depression experience.

It is hard to imagine a better choice of a play to represent these ideas (written in the moment, by and for the moment) than one of their first choices for this birth of a new, significant, exciting American Theatre company than Paul & Claire Siftons' epic, aptly titled *1931-*. It opened December 10, 1931 at the Mansfield Theatre on Broadway and was performed by the entire company of 29 actors playing over 45 roles.

Brooks Atkinson, young eminent Theatre critic for *New York Times,* didn't think it was a good play, though he acknowledged "the balcony cheered and the rest of the audience was stunned." In this case, "good play/bad play" is an irrelevant judgment since the play transcends these categories by delivering the intended effect with surprising power and strength. The stylistic choices of the writing and structure of the play are those typical of radical, populist documentary Theatre. In this kind of Theatre, there is no literary pretense; simplicity of language intends to give added power to just telling the facts as they are experienced by the man in the street. There is no subtlety in the depiction of character, but there is an epic sweep of societal character types leaving the specific humanity and individual subtleties to be added by the humanity and passion of the actor. Foremost is the depiction of the full suffering and redemption of the central character, center stage for 2 hrs. It is the cumulative effect of all these elements which creates a catharsis for the audience that lasts long after the curtain has fallen. Unquestionably, for Broadway audiences, this was a first time experience. Underneath all this, of course, are the playwrights' unique passions, compassion and sense of urgency. The Siftons borrowed the best techniques from their predecessors and contemporaries. To this end, their own instructions to the director:

> *1931-* is concerned with an individual in the tidal movement of a people caught in a situation which they can neither explain, escape nor exorcise. As the play develops, the contrapuntal design of the ten interludes suggests a ground swell that is bearing Adam, his group, and the audience itself, on to revolution of one sort or another. The fourteen scenes comprise one line of action, the drama of Adam; the ten interludes, occurring as flashes between the scenes, comprise the drama of the group to which he belongs. The two lines converge, slowly at first, then more rapidly, as Adam is beaten down and down while the group grows, stiffens, rises, welded together by the blood, heartbreak, blind hatred, despair and desperation of its million atoms. The alternating rhythm of the scenes and interludes is progressively accelerated, as a wave seems to race when it nears the crest, then curls and breaks.

> George Bartenieff

THE GROUP THEATRE, INC.

presented

1931-

by CLAIRE & PAUL SIFTON

UNDER THE AUSPICES OF THE THEATRE GUILD

Opening at the Mansfield Theatre, December 10, 1931

Production directed by LEE STRASBERG

Setting designed by MORDECAI GORELIK

CAST

FORMEMAN	J.E. Bromberg
ADAM, A TRUCKER	Franchot Tone
POLICEMAN	Morris Carnovsky
LOBBYGOW	Clifford Odets
BOSS FOREMAN	Clement Wilenchick
LOBBYGOW	Harry Bellaver
OLD WOMAN	Virginia Farmer
THE GIRL	Phoebe Brand
LEAN MAN	Grover Burgess
NEWSDEALER	J.E. Bromberg
DRUNK	Sanford Meisner
POLICEMAN	Clifford Odets
AGENT	Philip Robinson
AGENT	Clement Wilenchick
LANDLADY	Mary Morris
LITTLE GIRL	Gertrude Maymore
FRED	Walter Coy
FIRST PEDEESTRIAN	Friendly Ford
NEWSBOY	Robert Lewis
SECOND PEDESTRIAN	Lewis Leverett
THIRD PEDESTRIAN	Morris Carnovsky
A LADY	Ruth Nelson
A GENTLEMAN	Gerrit Kraber
STEEL WORKER	Art Smith
MUSICIAN	Sanford Meisner
CLERK	Friendly Ford
COLLEGE BOY	Walter Coy
REPORTER	Lewis Leverett

SECTION MANAGER	Grover Burgess
ACTOR	Morris Carnovsky
BUM	Philip Robinson
ITALIAN	J.E. Bromberg
CHECKER	William Challee
AGENT	Clifford Odets
MANAGER	Morris Carnovsky
EDDIE	Harry Bellaver
TOURIST	Sylvia Fenningston
TOURIST	Stella Adler
TOURIST	Eunice Stoddard
TOURIST	Gerrit Kraber
BOSS	J.E. Bromberg
BOY	Robert Lewis
POLICEMAN	Clement Wilenchick
COUNTERMAN	Philip Robinson
COUNTERMAN	Byron McGrath

WORKERS AND UNEMPLOYED: Clifford Odets, Walter Coy, Gerrit Kraber, Grover Burgess, Harry Bellaver, Philip Robinson, Lewis Leverett, Art Smith, Friendly Ford, William Challee, Sanford Meisner, Robert Lewis, Herbert Ratner, Margaret Barker, Dorothy Patten, Morris Carnovsky, J.E. Bromberg, Stella Adler, Eunice Stoddard, Mary Morris, Sylvia Fenningston, Robert Rather, Gertrude Maynard, Paula Miller, Ruth Nelson, & Franchot Tone.

STAGE MANAGER	Alixe Walker
ASSIST STAGE MANAGER	Robert Lewis
ASSIST STAGE MANAGER	Marvin S. Borowsky

THE RE:GROUP THEATRE COMPANY
presented
1931-
as a staged reading
8/9/10
The Irish Rep Mainstage Theatre
New York, NY.

SCENES

Scene 1. A warehouse, morning.

Scene 2. Another warehouse, night.

Scene 3. A public square, noon.

Scene 4. The Bowery, 10:15 PM.

Scene 5. The hall of a rooming house.

Scene 6. Outside a factory door, 6 PM.

Scene 7. A street, 5 PM.

Scene 8. Outside an apartment house, Park Avenue, 4 AM.

Scene 9. A furnished room, night.

Scene 10. Lower Fifth Ave, 4:30 PM.

Scene 11. A downtown street, dusk.

Scene 12. A basement off the Bowery, night.

Scene 13. Outside a restaurant, morning.

Scene 14. Inside the restaurant, afternoon.

Finale. A street, sometime.

1931-

Scene I

The interior of the shipping-room of a wholesaler of heavy goods. The twilight of the place is accentuated by spots of light at the checker's high desk at lower right, over the time clock at lower left, and the block of dirty daylight seen through the door to the loading platform at upper right.

The truckers move in line from lower left to the door at upper right, going through it to deliver their loads to the auto trucks outside and returning, empty, through the door at right upper. They use big flat trucks with two large wheels in the center and smaller castors at each end; a few use the two-wheeled kind, carrying the lighter end in their hands. They handle the trucks with careless expertness. The steady rhythm of their passage across the floor is subtly syncopated by slight outbursts of more speed, a swirl of the castors as the trucks are straightened out for the door, all indicating the unquenchable pulse of strength, life and spirit, and emphasizing the ebb of weariness, despair, blind pointless boredom and subconscious desperation.

The movement of the loaded trucks across the stage and the return of the empties farther upstage are as steady as the tides, fretted though they may be by winds or rocks or shallows.

At the checker's high desk are two high chairs. In the left chair is a boy of eighteen, checking bills of lading, item by item, as they are taken by on the trucks with a hardly perceptible pause before his desk.

The work goes on. The reiterated melody of movement is saved from monotony by the little variations in detail, the different shapes of the goods on the trucks, the varying effort in pushing them, the sluggishness of some workers, the restrained liveliness of others, the furtive flashes of spirit in the way some flirt the trucks up to the desk and on to the door, the glances at the checker, the skill with which some discharge a stream of tobacco juice into the sawdust just inside the door. It is work, heavy work, round and round, apparently to some purpose, unseen.

The checker concludes a set of bills, shuffles them together. The foreman comes in through the door/ He wears a derby hat and a coat.

He goes to the desk, followed by a truck driver with an aluminum book. The foreman riffles through the bills, stamps them in a clock on his part of the desk; the driver offers his open book; the foreman puts in the bills; the driver shuts the book, turns and goes out as the boy starts work on more bills, checking rapidly while the foreman looks on.

The foreman sits motionless a little while, staring over the heads of the passing workers. He leaves his chair, goes round in back of the checker's chair. A heavily loaded truck stops on the slight incline near lower left. The trucker behind it lets it roll back a few inches, turns and puts his back against the push bar, bracing and pushing powerfully up through his calves, his thighs, his back and shoulders. As he heaves it up and over the slight hump in the floor, the front castor catches the fore-man's foot, as he is crossing in front of it. The foreman pulls his foot free, at the same time ramming the truck back down the hump, dislocating the straining trucker.

FOREMAN Why the hell don't you look where you're going!

ADAM [*Stopping his truck and glaring over the load at the foreman*] How the hell can I! [*They stand glaring at each other. The other truckers gather around, at a timid distance.*]

FOREMAN None of your lip. Get moving.

ADAM Yeah?

FOREMAN [*Indicating the loaded truck*] Move, damn you, move!

TRUCKERS [*In low timid friendly chorus*] Better move.

ADAM What-d' you think I am... a mule?

TRUCKERS Mules!... Whoa mule. Giddap, mule!

FOREMAN Jackass! [*Whirling on the others, who resume work at once*] Keep moving.

ADAM [*Bending to the truckrail and giving his truck a final shove that sends it spinning through the door*] Yeah, keep moving. Hey!

FOREMAN You're fired. [*The others pause again to watch and listen.*]

ADAM [*Laughing*] Fired, hell! I quit.

TRUCKERS [*In low awed chorus*] Fired, he's fired; he's fired. Hasn't got a job. Fired, fired, fired. He's been fired.

FOREMAN [*Through the chorus*] Fired!

ADAM Free!

TRUCKERS Don't be a fool, kid. Don't be a fool. You gotta eat.

FOREMAN [*Crossing to the desk*] Get your time. I've got to cut down one man anyway.

ADAM [*Following, laughing, mostly to the other truckers*] Ok, by me! Mule, jackass, fool; that's you. Me... I'm free! [*Suddenly catching the foreman and spinning him by the shoulder, thrusting his face close to him.*] A man!

FOREMAN [*Handing him a slip*] Get out!

ADAM [*Sobered for a moment by the time slip, then resuming his ruddy confidence*] All right. I'm going, but listen, you pasty-faced slave driver. Here's my ticket; I get my say. You ain't big enough to have real guys working here. You like 'em runty and easy to handle. Me... I can beat your time at anything and you know it... why, damn you, I could even do a better job of licking the superintendent's boots than you do.

FOREMAN Get out.

ADAM When I get ready... [*Flexing his muscles*] Me... look at that. That's beans, that's ham-and. That's women, that's gasoline. That's *everything.* I got it. I can lift more boxes, more iron, more sacks, load 'em faster, check 'em better, make more trips, do more work, than any of your damn...

TRUCKERS [*Cutting in with a sardonic bark*] Mules.

FOREMAN [*Whirling on them*] Keep moving!... Move!

ONE VOICE [*Far back, mocking*] Giddy-yap, mules.

ADAM [*Striding into the doorway and turning*] Whoa, whoa, mules. [*They pause.*] A flat-footed dope, a lousy paddle-footed yes-man steps on his own feet in front of my truck and I'm fired! [*Flashing on the foreman*] Fired, huh? Fired! You make me laugh! I quit!

15

FOREMAN [*Almost shrieking*] Fired! Get the cops.

TRUCKERS [*Warningly*] The cops!

ADAM [*After hastily glancing down the platform. Resuming his parting sound-off*] Me – I can get mine, anytime. I can walk across the street and get a job. Any place, factory, foundry, road, mine, woods or water – they'll take a look at me and say, "Come to mamma!" [*He laughs.*] Any city, any state, wherever I go there's a job... Fired; hired! Like that, seven come eleven, that's me. I eat when I feel like it and I sleep in a bed... Money, I got what it takes to get it...

AN OLD VOICE I said that once myself.

FOREMAN [*Shrieking*] Get the cops! [*He stealthily gets out a nightstick from behind the desk.*]

ADAM [*Looking out along the platform again and preparing to leave*] Here comes the cop – old Popgut himself! [*He laughs and turns again to the foreman and the others.*] Take your lousy job, you and your hand-shaking, you double-quick time, your overloads and - [*To the truckers*] You, playing hooky out of an old ladies' home... [*Throwing out his chest*] Me – I'm going to get me a job that is a job... Plenty of jobs...

FOREMAN [*Raising nightstick to hit Adam*] Damn you!

ADAM [*With gentle irresistible precision planting the flat of his hand on the foreman's face and sending him reeling back ten feet*] Bye, bye, fish-face. [*Turning and waving his hand to the others*] So long, saps!

TRUCKERS [*Their teeth shining in smiles*] Haw-heee!

ADAM [*His teeth shining in a smile*] Mules!

TRUCKERS So long.

ADAM [*Turning and yelling suddenly in the face of an old fat special po-liceman, who jumps back, flustered and confused*] Hey! Popgut! [*Adam disappears down the loading platform. The foreman rushes to the cop.*]

BLACKOUT

SCENE II

Inside a warehouse. Night. A row of hand trucks parked at back. An irregular string of men is lined up, waiting for the foreman to come out to hire. The men are silent, nervous, watchful, as every moment their number is augmented by other men who look just like themselves. They shuffle softly, all looking the same way. Several hold cigarettes, unlighted, touching them to their lips as if to light up. A lobbygow watches, riding herd on them. One youngish man strikes a match and lights up, taking a deep drag on a cigarette.

LOBBYGOW [Barking at him] Hey! You! Douse that! Can't you read! [He points to a large sign "No Smoking." The youngish man pulls the coal off his cigarette. The lobbygow looks up the line.] Here comes the boss. [Instantly the crowd shifts, straightens, moves forward.]

BOSS FOREMAN [Big, fat, powerful, cigar in mouth, followed by another lobbygow, pushes through the men as if they were canebrake. He speaks to the FIRST LOBBYGOW cheerfully, condescendingly.] Say, Joe, what's the idea? Letting all these stiffs in... We only want five.

FIRST LOBBYGOW Better pick them quick, Boss. They's a lot more outside. [More men shuffle in.]

BOSS FOREMAN Tell Mike not to let any more through. [To SECOND LOBBYGOW as he turns to examine the men, while the FIRST LOBBYGOW shouts outside.] How about a little more light? [SECOND LOBBYGOW pulls a cord, clicking on one large bare electric bulb which lights up the men pitifully, making their faces pallid, haggard. At the same time, ADAM rushes in from the outside door, quickly, breathlessly going directly to the BOSS FOREMAN.]

FIRST LOBBYGOW [Harshly, to ADAM] Hey, you! Outside! Who told you to come in? ... Too late. Beat it!

ADAM [Brushing by the LOBBYGOW] Yeah? Are you the boss?

BOSS FOREMAN [Faintly interested] You're a fresh kid... Ever do any freight handling?

ADAM Sure, plenty.

BOSS FOREMAN Heavy freight, hand trucks?

ADAM Steel castings.

FIRST MAN [*Crashing in*] Say, boss it ain't fair... He busted in after you said... We... I been waiting all afternoon.

CROWD [*Swirling in*]

Me too.	Say!
Tain't fair...	Say, boss...

I've been here since *morning*...

BOSS FOREMAN [*To the last man*] That's too damn bad! [*To* ADAM] How long since you worked?

ADAM To-day.

BOSS FOREMAN Where?

ADAM [*Surly*] Ajax Machinery...

BOSS FOREMAN [*Walking over to* ADAM] Why'd you leave? Fired?

ADAM Hell, no. I quit.

BOSS FOREMAN Yeah? Why? ...

ADAM Why, I... I was through. That's why.

BOSS FOREMAN Yeah? They closing down, too?

ADAM [*Breaking out*] Hell, no. I just got through. That's all.

BOSS FOREMAN Trouble-maker, hunh? [*Turning away to the other men*] Nothing doing. [*Pointing to a husky man*] Hey, you! Stand out here.

ADAM [*Quickly*] Say. Listen...

BOSS FOREMAN [*Pushing* ADAM *aside as the man selected comes forward, stands, grinning. The* FOREMAN *looks quickly, expertly, at his shoulders, back and legs. Then, crossing* ADAM *quite deliberately, he points to another.*] You, Hunkie. Out here! [*A big, bovine Slovak comes out and joins the first man picked.*]

ADAM [*Taking a step after the* FOREMAN] I'm no trouble-maker. I work. All I want is a job.

BOSS FOREMAN [*With sarcasm he intends as light humor*] Oh, yeah! [*Indicating the other men*] What do you think these stiffs are here for, shipping for a Mediterranean cruise... [*The men laugh obligingly, the two* LOBBYGOWS *uproariously.*] Beat it! Ain't your organization paying lately?

ADAM Say, if you think I'm a lousy radical, I'll paste you one in the nose.

BOSS FOREMAN [*To* LOBBYGOWS] Get him out...

FIRST LOBBYGOW [*As he reaches for* ADAM] Outside, fellah! Get t'hell out.

ADAM [*Smacking the man's hands aside*] Keep your mitts off of me. [*He starts for the door with dignity.*]

BOSS FOREMAN [*Picking more men*] You, squarehead! Out here! [*Indicating a big Negro*] All right, Sambo... Front and center... [*Passing down the line*] You, Big Guy, out here. [*The five men chosen stand together. The unchosen start straggling away.* ADAM, *drifting toward the door, turns as a middle-aged, solid man goes up to the* BOSS FOREMAN *and speaks.*]

MIDDLE-AGED MAN [*Quietly imploring*] Say, boss... I got a sick wife. Three kids...

BOSS FOREMAN [*Cutting him off*] Sure, and you want a job! ...

MIDDLE-AGED MAN I'll do anything, boss... Chees, give me a job!

ANOTHER MAN [*Coming in between them, speaking desperately*] Take me, boss. I'll work for... for half what you pay... I'll work overtime... anything... No kicking... I ... I've got...

BOSS FOREMAN A Sick wife and *five* kids, hunh! ... Beat it.

ADAM [*Addressing the other man as he slinks, shamefacedly, toward the door*] Of all the goddamn lousy tricks... [Abruptly, with no warning, the man desperately swings on ADAM. They fight, clinch, roll, get up and slug again.]

BOSS FOREMAN [*After a moment of amusement, calling to a* LOBBY-GOW] All right, get the cheater. [*He turns to the man he called* SQUAREHEAD, *the smallest of the five.*] All right, you! Nothing doing... [*The* SQUAREHEAD *does not quite understand. The* FOREMAN *makes it simpler.*] Get out! [*To the man who offered to work for half, as* ADAM *stands pantingly watching*] Come on, you. [*Then to the other four*] Four bucks a day, no extra for overtime. [*To the* CHEATER] Three bucks a day... Anything over... is mine! [*The* SQUAREHEAD *understands now. He makes a snarling noise. The two* LOBBYGOWS *jump for him.*] Raus mit 'em. Bum's rush.
[*The* SQUAREHEAD *is seized and rushed out by the* LOBBYGOWS. *The* FOREMAN *relights his cigar and goes out the other ways as the newly-hired men turn to the hand-trucks, take one apiece, and follow him.* ADAM *and the other start out.*]

BLACKOUT

SCENE III

A city square. Noon of a sunny day. A walk runs in a curve across the stage. Benches line the walk, following the curve of the asphalt. Directly behind is the iron spike fence protecting the city's sparse grass. Beyond, a single lean tree offers scant shade to a squat drinking fountain.

Beyond, visible only as a threat, is a line of men waiting for a traveling soup kitchen. Nearly every seat, each of which is partitioned from its neighbor by an iron bar, making it impossible for tired men to stretch out and sleep, is occupied. The occupants are mostly middle-ages, or old men, roughly dressed; tramps, bums, panhandlers among them, and, here and there a younger man, not so slack, a little dazed to find himself with the others. Nearly every man is reading a soiled newspaper.

While they sit, reading or not reading, better dressed men and women, girls in couples, occasionally a child on skates and a mother with a baby carriage, go by. A cigar stub that is discarded is immediately pounced on by the nearest old man. A paper thrown carefully into the trash can at lower right is promptly retrieved.

ADAM appears at lower right, looks up and down the walk, sees that the GIRL has not arrived, crosses over to the drinking fountain, looks around, takes a drink, spruces himself up a bit, looks around, drinks a little more, rinses his mouth and spits.

While his back is turned, the GIRL appears lower right, stands a moment, half-glancing up and down the benches, walking quickly, intent. She is pretty in a gay obvious way. She is think, but healthy, except for possible undernourishment. About her is a checked eagerness, compounded of wistfulness and fear. She is just a little afraid that ADAM may fail to keep the appointment. She loves him.

ADAM, wiping his mouth with the back of his hand, turns, sees her and walks eagerly toward her.

ADAM I thought you weren't going to make it.

GIRL I lied to her… [*They saunter across the trash can and stand a moment looking at each other.*] I don't know what for…

ADAM Now don't get sore. Something happened yesterday… I didn't want to tell you over the phone…

GIRL [*In spite of herself*] I got you the first time.

ADAM It's the truth. I had to see somebody…

GIRL Yeah, I know…

ADAM Are you going to listen to me, or aren't you?

GIRL I'm listening.

ADAM [*After a pause*] You see… yesterday…

GIRL Go on...

ADAM [*Exasperated*] What's the use of pretending you don't give a damn...

GIRL Maybe I don't.

ADAM Maybe you do.

GIRL Maybe you don't hate yourself!

ADAM All right. Have it your way! [*Softening, blurting out*] Aw, looky here, baby. The reason I couldn't come out was...

GIRL ... you had to see... [*Insinuatingly*] a sick friend.

ADAM Will you keep your mouth shut for a minute!

GIRL Why didn't you say you had to work overtime? That's a good one too. [*He'd like to shake her.*] Why didn't you say so over the phone last night? Instead of keeping me awake half the night, wondering what it was that was so important you couldn't tell me. You could have said "You see, it's this way, baby, I was planning to come out like I said, but, well, just at the last minute, I remembered I gotta see some-body..." I understand English. I don't have to be hit with a truck to tumble... Maybe I'm sort of in your way right now. Maybe...

ADAM [*Seizing her arm roughly*] Damn you, shut up, will you! [*She stops, managing a tight defiant grin at him, full of pride and hurt.*] Are you going to keep still?

GIRL Sure, unless you break my arm. Then I'll holler for a cop. [*He drops her arm, stares hard at her, a moment.*]

ADAM [*Seeing that she will listen, he speaks, fumbling slightly for words.*] It's this way... I ... well, I'm looking for a job.

GIRL [*Startled, her pique gone*] Adam! Fired!

ADAM Naw. I quit.

GIRL "Quit!"

ADAM Sure. [*Defensively*] Why the hell not! That paddlefooted fore-man got his dogs caught under my truck...

GIRL And he blamed you...

ADAM Yeah. [*Brightening, as if to dismiss the incident*] But what the hell. There're plenty of other jobs.

GIRL [*Appalled*] Gee!

ADAM Before I left I told him where to get off... It was worth quitting for the chance to tell that yellow-livered son of a be just what I thought of him. Oh, well, what the hell, let's forget it... [*Turning to look for a couple seats, two seat together*] Let's grab a coupla seats... [*Bubbling over with pure joy of living*] What a day! Boy!

GIRL That's right... I've got to eat. [*She indicates the package she carries in her hand.*]

ADAM [*Leaning over an old woman who is sitting between the only two empty seats that are anywhere adjacent.*] Say, lady, do you mind mov-ing over?

OLD WOMAN [*Looking up contemptuously*] Yeah, I do!

ADAM [*Ingratiatingly*] Well, how about doing it anyway? [*Indicating the GIRL*]

OLD WOMAN [*Unmoving*] I'm setting here.
[*ADAM and the GIRL exchange meaningful glances. They move toward another monopolist, but a man drops into one of the two separated seats. The only vacant places near each other are those on each side of the unobliging OLD WOMAN. They decide to take them while they can. They sit. They look at each other across the OLD WOMAN's head, back of her, across her nose. They make faces. The GIRL giggles while she unwraps her sandwich and starts to eat. ADAM's hand goes over the back of the bench and touches the GIRL's shoulder. She lifts one hand to meet his.*]

GIRL [*Across the* OLD WOMAN's *nose*] Want some?

ADAM [Laughing] Gwan! Eat! [*They sit, glancing at each other, basking in the sun, now and then smiling to each other, pressing each other's hand. After a while*] Do you blame me?

GIRL What for?

ADAM What I was telling you?

GIRL Oh, no.

ADAM You'd a done the same thing, wouldn't you?

GIRL Me?

ADAM Unh, hunh.

GIRL I don't know. I guess so. But... [*She can't state the "but".*]

ADAM What?

GIRL You know.

ADAM [*Slowly*] Us?

GIRL Unh-hunh.

ADAM [*Largely*] This don't make any difference. Me, I'll get a job, a good job, damn sight better than that one.

GIRL [*Believing it*] Sure, I know.

ADAM That's why I didn't come out last night. I heard about a job down on Varick Street...

GIRL And...

ADAM [*Lying*] Too late. He took my name and everything. Said something might open up in a coupla days. But it wasn't so hot. Electrical machinery warehouse... Just as well. There's lots better jobs I can get.

GIRL If I'd lose my job... I wouldn't know where to look first.

ADAM Sure. With girls it's hard, but *me*... [*Pats her hand, alternating between speaking to her in front of the* OLD WOMAN, *or back of her. The* OLD WOMAN *sits imperturbably.*] Listen, hon, you just rest easy. I ain't never been out of work a week in my life. [*There is just a shade too much assurance.*] Me, I haven't tried... I been resting, soaking up the sun and some back sleep I been missing on account of you... [*Seeing that his banter isn't sufficient*] Say, I can walk right out of the park this minute and pick up a job. Just look at these mitts! [*He draws up the muscles.*] My legs... I can start two thousand pounds on a truck any day. What I want is a man's job, I got what it takes to pull down that kind of pay. It's no good getting stuck with a bum one... What's more, I ain't going to... [*The* OLD WOMAN *snorts briefly.*] See? [*A little girl flies by on roller skates, chased by a little boy who scurries after her.*]

GIRL [*Her eyes and mouth are tears and honey*] Gee!

ADAM [*Back of the* OLD WOMAN's *head*] What is it, kid?

GIRL [*Looking away from him*] Nothing. [*She meets his eyes.*] It kind of spoils things, doesn't it? [*She tries to smile.*]

ADAM Gwan. This doesn't change things one bit. [*Seriously*] What's the big idea? I've only been out of work one day. I could have had something already, if I hadn't kinda taken it easy... come down here and all... [*She smiles to him.*] Say, you aren't worried, are you?

GIRL [*Shaking her head*] No.

ADAM [*Quietly*] And not sore any more, are you... about last night?

GIRL No!

ADAM All set, same as ever?

GIRL Unh, hunh.

ADAM [*Happily, forgetful of jobs, thinking only how good to be alive,*

loved, sitting on a sunny park bench near his girl] You said it! Chees, kid, coming over here, through the park, I kept looking at the Chrysler building, you know, that thin silver looking tower... It's a nice job, whoever did it... How'd you like to live up there, in the top I mean. They say there's such a wind, they can't open the window without the furniture getting blowed clear across the room. They got a theater up there and a classy night club, they say... everything. Chees, I don't know's I'd like to be so far off the ground. Supposing the elevators broke, or the guys that run 'em went on strike... But it sure is nice to look at, shining in the sun... [*Pause*]
[*Two office girls walk across, absorbed in chatter. They teeter along, walking very fast and jerkily on their high heels.*]

FIRST OFFICE GIRL ... And I said to him, I said, if that's the way you feel about it all right just like that so I gave it back to him and he...

SECOND OFFICE GIRL [*Perfunctorily, feigning deepest interest*] Oh yeah, and what did he say then? [*They are off.*]

ADAM [*Watching the GIRL eat, soaking up the sunlight and leisure*] Don't the sun feel good, though! [*He looks up toward the sky as if it were a novelty.*] God, I don't know when I've seen such a day! It's like when I was a kid... [*The OLD WOMAN sniffs.*]

GIRL [*Leaning forward*] It'd almost be worth getting fired... to have a whole day... to sit in the sun, like this... [*Pause*]

SIMULTANEOUSLY

GIRL What have you been doing all day?

[*Two worried, pudgy jobbers hurry across the stage.*]

ADAM [*Laughing*] Sitting, mostly.

FIRST JOBBER Two hours he gives us! ... By two o'clock I should have the money there or he'll take out a judgment... Thirty thousand on the books! In one day, two days, we could get it...

GIRL [*Disapprovingly, even though she take it as a jest*] Oh, Adam!

SECOND JOBBER Business is business.

ADAM [*Trying to suppress a defensive tone, making it seem merely informatory, humorous*] Well, I set the alarm clock for four this morning... No use... Chees! Must have been a hundred men wanting that job... They musta stayed up all night.

FIRST JOBBER [*Fiercely*] From now on I am a Socialist...if I can get in again...

SECOND JOBBER Why not an anarchist... and I'll go with you. [*They exit.*]

MAN What job? [*He's at the other side of ADAM, speaking unexpectedly, not moving nor looking at him. The little girl flies by on skates again, the little boy still chasing her. Their noise cuts through all other sounds.*]

ADAM [*After the noise has died away, turning to notice the questioner*] B. & O. freight shed, North River.

MAN [*Mildly, positively*] Five hundred.

SIMULTANEOUSLY
[*Two gentlemen, much agitated cross the stage.*]

ADAM How the hell do you know?

GIRL But what'd they *say?* Didn't you tell 'em...?

FIRST GENTLEMAN I told him to sell at forty... I had a tip... I told him as plainly as I'm telling you... Now I'm wiped out!... [*As they exit*] All I have left is my inheritance.

ADAM [*Slightly sardonic*] Me! And five hundred! [*Indicating the MAN*] You heard him!

GIRL [*After a pause in which she contemplates the OLD WOMAN*] Don't you get scared? S'posing you... [*Her staring eyes complete the question.*]

ADAM Say!

GIRL [*Lightening, buoyed up by his spirit*] All right! [*After a pause, leaning toward him*] Anyway... we're pretty happy... now!
[*The look the* OLD WOMAN *gives her is compounded of envy, pity and venom.*]

ADAM [*Huskily*] Nothing else!

SIMULTANEOUSLY

ADAM ...I've been thinking... You know... If we could get a second hand car cheap, go some place where it don't cost so much to live... or else hit for Detroit... How'd you like that? Traveling round?

> THIRD OFFICE GIRL [*As she and friend hurry across the Stage*] ... Yeah, he wanted me to stay after the others had left and I   said to him I said, "You're married, ain't you?"

GIRL It's be wonderful... [*Trying to smile*] But where'd you get the money for a car?

> FOURTH OFFICE GIRL [*High pitched, excited*] And? [*They exit.*]

ADAM [*Largely*] They don't cost much... I got a little saved... something down...

GIRL You may need it... now. [*He looks at her, for the moment not catching her allusion.*]

ADAM Gloomy again?

GIRL No... Gee, that was going to be the first payment on the furniture for the house, wasn't it?

ADAM Yeah... soon as it got big enough. [*Laughing, recalling*] But, well, here or any place, a house's a house, isn't it? It doesn't make any difference whether it's in Detroit or Queens? ... It just depends where I can line up something steady, with plenty cash at the end of the week...

GIRL [*Softly, only half minding his words*] Any place is all right with me... with you.

ADAM [*Studying her intently, passionately, as a woman pushes a baby carriage across the stage*] Sure? [LITTLE BOY and GIRL *clatter by again.*]

GIRL [*Looking steadily into ADAM's eyes*] Sure.

SIMULTANEOUSLY
[*Two executives saunter across the stage.*]

ADAM I guess a car's a bum idea... after you get it, you got to find a place to park it... [*He stops to hear the two men who stand pointing almost directly at him.*]

OLDER EXECUTIVE There's no unemployment except among men who don't want to work. [*Noticing the men on the benches, stopping and pointing with his stick*] Look at those men!

YOUNGER EXECUTIVE [*Nervously*] Yes sir... I see what you mean.

OLDER EXECUTIVE All of them strong, healthy, fit to work. Lazy. They're simply lazy. [ADAM *makes a gesture as if to answer him. The* GIRL *touches his arm. The* OLDER EXECUTIVE *continues, with unconscious envy.*] I've never had a chance to lie around in the sun all day. Nobody who has a sense of responsibility towards society, toward life, toward one's family... [*Walking on*] They ought to starve... sprawling all over a public park.

YOUNGER EXECUTIVE Yes, sir... [*As they exit*] I was going to tell you about the factory division report. It came while you were in Florida... [*Both exit.*]

ADAM [*Relaxing, laughing*] I'd like to give a fellow like that a sock on the jaw... Lazy. Hunh! ... Oh, well, what the hell! [*Turning to the* GIRL] How about getting a radio, instead of a car, or a player piano or... [*Suggested by the baby carriage being propelled across the stage again*] a baby? ...

OLD WOMAN [*Checking out precipitately*] Where'd you think you'd park *that!* ... My Gawd!

ADAM [*Sarcastically, to the* OLD WOMAN] What! Leaving! Don't let us hurry you! [*The* OLD WOMAN *snorts and shuffles off.* ADAM *quickly slips into the vacated seat and leans toward the* GIRL, *close, so that their arms touch from shoulders down.*] Hello, kid. This any better? [*A pause. Her upturned face is eloquent beyond words, so much that* ADAM *is stirred, tender, fierce.*] Don't you worry, kid... You and me... we're on top of the world. Ain't we?

GIRL [*Softly*] Sure.

ADAM [*Fiercely*] God, I'd like to kiss you.

GIRL [*Trying to repress a nervous giggle*] What's stopping you?

SIMULTANEOUSLY
[*Two bums mosey slowly across the stage, talking.*]

ADAM [*Leaning toward her, telegraphs a kiss with his fingers*] That's one. [*With her lips she indicates the return of the kiss.*] Here's another for your nose... Here's one right between your eyes. [*A pause, more softly*] Here's another... and another... [*He touches the hollow at the base of her throat, her ears.*]

> FIRST BUM [*Acting out his idea as he talks*] See, it's like this... if you was crossing the street and kind of didn't see the car and it'd hit you... like this... you could fall down and act like you was hurt bad and then... there you'd be! Hospital, food, damages... easy the rest of you life.

GIRL [*Husky voiced*] Gee! [*A pause*]

> SECOND BUM S'posing you get killed? What good would that do you?

ADAM Chees', kid, I'm going to get a job right away. Something... We gotta get married quick. How about it?...

FIRST BUM That's just a chance you gotta take. Of course, you gotta study your car, so's you'd know what chance it'd have to hurt you. Pick one that's slowing down... just enough to knock you down. Of course, if you break a leg or some   thing... Goldern it, you'd have a case then!

GIRL [*Looking up, shyly, frightened*] All right. [ADAM *repeats the kissing, via finger, for a moment, then draws away, laughing shortly.*]

SECOND BUM [*Stopping to have it out*] Looky here, punk. Is this on the level or are you bulling me along?

ADAM Chees. I'm nuts about you!

FIRST BUM Honest to Christ! This is going to be me third time... Once in Chi... Once in Buffalo... The one in Chi was a lulu! Along comes the car... [*They exit. FIRST BUM recounting what happened in Chi.*]

ADAM [*Gruffly*] Why don't you say something?

GIRL What do you want me to say

ADAM Well, how about you?

GIRL [*Laughing*] I'm nuts about you, too.

ADAM [*Takes hold of her shoulders, speaks roughly*] Chees, do you know how it feels! [*The two children clatter by on skates.*] Do you?

GIRL [*Nodding, frightened*] Sure! [*Then as his face softens, she laughs happily. He looks long and steadily at her.*]

ADAM [*Seriously*] Whatever happens, kid, it's you and me, from now on. [*A pause*] It won't be more'n a day or two until I get a job again, but if it should be longer, say a week or so... it won't make any difference.

GIRL [*Unsure*] On our floor they aren't taking on anybody. They say... They let ten men go last week.

ADAM I'll get on! Those old bums and high school kids, maybe they

31

can't get jobs easy, but me, I'll get something… There's lots of things I can do. I used to drive a truck… good pay, too. I've got lots of chances… [*She is looking tenderly at him.*] Say, what'd you say we make it now… to-night… Saturday. What's the use of waiting? Huh? … Me and you… We could get a room, a coupla rooms, maybe. What the hell, I'll probably have a job by Saturday anyway. What d'say, Baby? To-night?

GIRL [*Softly, leaning toward him*] And if you… shouldn't…?

ADAM Well!

GIRL [*Diffidently*] All right.

ADAM Chees! [*They look at each other. He's aware of her trepidations. His voice is husky, soft.*] God, kid, I couldn't… Nope… Not unless I was sure. S'posing… of course it ain't going to happen, but s'posing I don't get on? S'posing you'd have a baby… you'd lose your job… and then… I heard those fellows down there this morning, talking… If it was any other time… Gee, I'm nuts about you, Baby… [*She sits, waiting.*] We'd be saps! Let's wait till Saturday. Then if I'm all set, all right. We'll mosey down to city hall…

GIRL [*A little relieved*] All right.

ADAM And we'll stick to that… [*Anxiously*] Even if it takes, say a week, a coupla weeks, even?

GIRL Yes… [*They're desperately in earnest. Suddenly she realizes the time and jumps up from the seat.*] Oh, my Golly, I got to be going…

ADAM [*Rising too*] Me, too. [*Indicating the folded newspaper in his pocket*] I got a coupla more places to hit up… Maybe I'll have something when I see you to-night…

GIRL That'd be swell! [*She starts off.*] Good-by. Come early if you can.

ADAM [*Heartened, cocky, tender, but almost condescending*] Sure. If I can. G'by! [*They rush off in opposite directions.*]

CURTAIN

FIRST INTERLUDE

*As the curtain falls on the preceding scene, a crowd of men sifts out
along the forestage in front of the flat entrance to a factory. Half an hour
before daybreak- Only a queer ground light- The men are surprisingly
quiet, considering their numbers. But they become silent and motionless
as death, tense as a loaded gun, when the gate swings open and a man,
flashlight in hand, halts their immediate eddying toward the entrance.*

EMPLOYMENT MANAGER Back up, youse, back up! What's the big
idea! We sent out a call for three. Three! [*He points to three good-sized
men who are near him.*] You, and you, and you. Youse fellows step up.
[*There is a surge forward, a small murmur of defeat.*]

AN OLD MAN [*Trying to step forward in the crowd*] Give me a chance,
Mister!
[*The crowd closes in and balks his attempt at a separate hearing.*]

EMPLOYMENT MANAGER [*To the three men selected*] You guys come
in here. [*To the others, as the gate closes*] The rest of you get going!
[*They swirl about, melt away, hurrying off in both directions because
other jobs are still available elsewhere.*]

BLACKOUT

SCENE IV

A few days later, 10:15 P.M.

*A street, the main stem of the labor market. In the uncertain light of
the arched street lamp are seen only the sidewalk, the curb and, back
near the building line, a newsdealer's set-up of boxes.*
*Standing on the sidewalk, leaning against the lamp-post, sitting on
the curb, are men who want jobs. They cluster vaguely about the bare
boxes. They are waiting for the first edition, for news printed in small
type in the back of the paper, news of jobs, of money, of food, of shoes,
clothes, liquor, love, news of life. ADAM comes along from across the*

street. He is still confident. The slightest perceptible edge of worry, fore-runner of a distant and impending fear, shows in his rather casual in-quiry.

ADAM [*To a tall lean stooped man at the lamp-post*] This the place to get the papers first?

LEAN MAN [*Limply jealous of ADAM'S fitness and assurance*] Yeah.

ADAM When'll they get here?

LEAN MAN If you'll give me your card, I'll take it over to him [*Indicating the news-dealer*]…and find out. [*Bowing toward the curb*] Have a seat!

ADAM [*Laughing and taking out a cigarette*] I get you.

LEAN MAN [*Taking one of ADAM'S cigarettes*] Don't mention it.

ADAM [*Striking a match and holding it for the LEAN MAN*] What do you do…beat it to the job right away?

LEAN MAN Some do. Me, I buy the paper for information, to cultivate my mind.

ADAM Oh, yeah?…Do you eat regular?

LEAN MAN Listen, kid. If you want a job, hustle right up to the place quick. [*Abstractly*] We have the good fortune to be living in what is known as the competitive system. [*His cigarette has gone out.*] Have you gotta match? [*He relights the cigarette.*]

ADAM [*Enjoying his advantage in the race for a job*] All these guys wait-ing?

LEAN MAN Very few of them, I regret to say, have ever cultivated a taste for the lighter reading you find in the front part of the paper.

ADAM [*Drawing away, instinctively*] What the hell!
[*Others draw around, half listening to the LEAN MAN.*]

LEAN MAN [*Conscious now of his audience*] Even the financial pages fail to interest them. Now *I*...

ADAM Are you trying to kid me?

LEAN MAN On the contrary. I was simply going to ask you...

ADAM "A nickel for a cup of cawfee." No... [*The others laugh.*]

LEAN MAN [*With dignity*] Certainly not. I'm a victim of charity as it is. What I was going to say is...would you mind letting me have the first section of your paper when you get it. I'd buy a copy myself, but if there's anything I hate it is waste. Now, if I...

ADAM Yeah, I know. If you was John D. Rockefeller.
[*He walks away and stands at the curb, waiting. The* LEAN MAN, *having lost his audience, shuffles off a little way. A wretched gray man, sodden with "smoke," comes along the sidewalk. He walks rigidly, eyes bulged out, staring blindly. The men, including* ADAM, *make way for him. Abruptly, without a stagger, he falls to the sidewalk, limp, out. The men, except* ADAM, *look at him with dull curiosity, then away. A youngish workman lights a cigarette. An older man, somewhat like the man who fell, bends over to see if he knows the prostrate one. He doesn't.*]

ADAM [*After first making an instinctive gesture to go to the man, checks himself in dislike of being conspicuous, then, as no one moves, speaks*] Say, why don't somebody do something?

YOUNGISH WORKMAN Aw, lay off. The cop's coming. [*A pause. A* COP *comes along from the opposite direction. He bends over the prostrate man, raps the soles of his feet with his nightstick, leans over to see if he is breathing, straightens, looks around toward the building at back, considers whether to lift the man and carry him away, get the wagon, or have someone else work for him. The men have gathered around him, looking at his clean uniform and shining insignia with dull curiosity, envy and dislike, some of them glancing down again at the prostrate man.*]

COP [*To the men about him*] Smoke...Where'd he get it? [*No answer. The men's faces are wooden.*] Jerry's, probably...Get him out of the way...[*No one moves. He points to the unseen building upstage.*] In there. The hallway. [*No one moves to obey. ADAM lights a cigarette. The COP barks at him.*] You! Pick him up, under his arms. [*Picking out another man*] You, his feet!

[ADAM *and the other man obey. With difficulty they half drag the drunk back through the crowd, which immediately closes in behind them. The COP prepares to resume his beat. The NEWSDEALER, a pudgy man in a snappy topcoat and soft hat, comes along, walking briskly.*]

NEWSDEALER [*Seeing the COP, speaking to him anxiously*] What's the trouble.

COP [*Cheerfully, wrapping the thong of his stick about his wrist*] Too much smoke. I moved him in there, out of your way.

NEWSDEALER [Relieved, chummy] Thanks, Tom. Much obliged. [*As he turns to go through the men to his boxes, taking off his tight gloves*] Too damn many of them lately. Bad for business.

COP [*Starting off*] See you later.

NEWSDEALER [*Pausing as he is about to take off his topcoat to change for a sheepskin reefer he has taken out from the locked box*] O.K.

ADAM [*Coming back through the men, speaking to the COP*] He needs a doctor.

COP [*Nettled, but trying humor*] Yeah?

ADAM Why don't you do something?

COP You askin'?
[*He stops, looks hard at ADAM, daring him to continue.*]

ADAM But—

COP Let him sleep it off.

ADAM What about an ambulance?

COP [*Closer, bullying*] Are you trying to give me an argument?

ADAM You going to let him croak?

COP Where do you come from?

ADAM Here. I live here.

COP How long?

ADAM I was born here.

COP What's your address?

ADAM [*Pointing at random to an unseen street number on a building*] That's it. [*The men laugh, timidly.*]

COP A vag. Do you know I could run you in?

ADAM [*Friendly, smiling suddenly*] Sure, why don't you?

COP [*Thrown off*] Because to-morrow's my day off. [ADAM *laughs. The* COP *starts off.*] You win, kid...But you better keep your lip buttoned up.
[*With the* COP'S *departure, the crowd subsides, resuming its dull incurious waiting. The* NEWSDEALER *has taken off his topcoat, folding it meticulously and stowing it in the locked box. He has put on his sheepskin reefer and a short canvas apron with coin pockets at the bottom. From time to time he looks at a gleaming watch on his thick wrist, then down the street. He rearranges the boxes, lights a cigar, contemplates approvingly a large diamond ring on his hand before flicking out the lighted match. He keeps shooing the men off his boxes, seeing to it that the space just in front of his stand is kept clear.*]

The crowd begins forming a queue along the building line. ADAM *falls in.*

The men stir restlessly, following the NEWSDEALER'S *every slightest movement, looking expectantly down the street.*

From the upper end of the street and crossing it, come two rather well-dressed employment agents. The men stiffen in the queue, then it swings out toward the agents and breaks as the men cluster about the newcomers.]

FIRST AGENT Ten men. Construction job. New Hampshire. Who's going?

VOICES

    How much?   What's the pay?

SECOND AGENT Four dollars a day.

VOICES

    And grub?   Bunk, too?

FIRST AGENT Everything. Free shipment. Leaving at two o'clock.

SECOND AGENT [*Rushing in*] Who's going?

VOICES

    What's the job?   Where is it?
    What's the charge?   How long does it last?

FIRST AGENT [*Tough*] Say, youse bums want a job or don't you? Who's going?

ADAM Me. [*He puts his hand in his pockets, then crosses to the AGENTS*] What is it?

FIRST AGENT New Hampshire.

ADAM What's the work?

VOICES [*Crowding in*]
    Yeah, who is it?   Me, too.
    I'll go.   How much does it cost?
    What's the fee?

SECOND AGENT [*To ADAM*] You'll do. [*To another husky young man*] You, too. Come along.

FIRST AGENT [*Looking the crowd over for more strong ones*] Anybody else? [*He ignores several applicants and turns to his partner. The LEAN MAN is back, looking on.*] All right, Lefty. That's two here.

ADAM [*Standing fast*] What's the job? Who is it?

SECOND AGENT [*Grudgingly*] Road work, out of Portsmouth.

LEAN MAN Lavarini, eh?

FIRST AGENT [*Like a flash, crowding the* LEAN MAN] Yeah, Lavarini...
What's it to you, stew-bum?

LEAN MAN [*Laughing in warning to* ADAM *as he gives ground*] Watch
your step, big boy!

VOICES [*As the Crowd subsides again, lining up as before*]
    Lavarini!   To hell with that!
    Three days!   The foreman's splitting with those guys.
    You gotta buy his "smoke."
    ...And his syphilitic women.

ADAM [*Wavering*] How much you charge?

SECOND AGENT [*As his partner crowds in*] Five dollars.

VOICES
    Five spot!   Gone to hell!

ADAM [*Hand in pocket*] When?

FIRST AGENT [*Eager for the kill*] Now. When you get your ticket.

VOICE Three days!

ADAM [*Slowly*] Three days! That's twelve dollars. I'll make seven.

VOICES
    If you're lucky!   Like hell you will!

ADAM [*After looking into the* FIRST AGENT'S *eyes, razzing him, backing
away, taking his hand out of his pocket*] Gwan. Five dollars don't grow
on trees. [*He turns away toward the newsstand, laughing.*]

YOUNG MAN [*Miserably, desperately, after a hesitant consideration of* ADAM'S *refusal to go*] I'll go.
[*He takes out a five dollar bill and looks at it.*]

ADAM [*Quickly turning, putting a hand on the boy's arm to stop him*] Hey! Kid! It's a gyp. Save your money and buy whisky.

FIRST AGENT Can you beat these guys...broke and they turn up their noses at a job. [*Blustering up close to* ADAM] You want to get jugged for thirty days?

SECOND AGENT Bust him one, Joe.

ADAM [*Talking over them to the boy*] Think it over, kid.

YOUNG MAN [*Desperately*] I've got to have a job.
[*A paper handler crosses with a big bundle of papers and dumps them on the newsdealer's boxes as the crowd swirls in to buy.*]

ADAM So've I. [*Offering the boy two cents*] Here's two cents...Find *yourself* a job. Like me. [*He starts for a paper.*]

YOUNG MAN I tried that...there ain't much chance...I'm going.
[*He goes out with the two* AGENTS. ADAM *crosses, buys a paper, opens it to the Help Wanted ads, reads.*]

VOICES [*Meanwhile as the Men read intently*]

The goddam gyps!	Five dollars!
Three days' work!	God help him in New Hampshire!
Portsmouth's tough.	Twelve dollars...try and get it!
Company store!	Lousy flops.
Crummy grub!	Rotgut booze!
Jawbone whores!	The goddam gyps!

LEAN MAN [*Sidling up to* ADAM] Could I trouble you for the first part of the paper? That is, unless you...
ADAM [*Hardly looking up from the page*] Aw go to hell. I can read, too.
[*Still reading, he starts walking away. The* LEAN MAN *watches him go. Meanwhile, as each man bought a paper he carefully but quickly folded the first section and pocketed it, then opened the second section to the*

Help Wanted pages, reading rapidly, then quickly, quietly, almost stealthily disappeared up and down the street, until only the LEAN MAN and the NEWSDEALER with his diminished stack of papers are left. Then the limp body of the drunken man who was dragged back through the crowd is seen again, propped up against the building.
A man comes down the street, almost at a run, puts down two cents, opens the paper and hurries away, reading the ads.]

LEAN MAN [*Crossing to the newsstand*] I should like to make a small buy on the open market.

NEWSDEALER How many?

LEAN MAN [*As if it were a hundred*] One. [*He puts down his two cents. The* NEWSDEALER *ceremoniously lifts and folds the paper for the* LEAN MAN, *who accepts it, returns to the lamp-post, seats himself on the curb and comfortably leans back against the post, settling himself. He unfolds the paper and scans the first page headliners, much in the manner of the Union League window-sitters. Still reading, he addresses the* NEWS-DEALER *in a conversational tone.*] How's business?

NEWSDEALER [*Counting his money*] Rotten.

LEAN MAN [*Tapping the paper, speaking in gentle reproof*] In the words of Frank Sullivan It beHoovers us to be thankful!
[*Silence. The drunken man stirs, tries to rise, slips, falls forward on his face, unnoticed.*]

BLACKOUT

SECOND INTERLUDE

The sacred ground where jobs exist is enclosed by a fence topped with overhanging barbed wire. In the center is a high iron and wire gate, with a smaller door in the center.

The crowd of men that swirls about the gate is a little less quiet than in the First Interlude. They are just a bit more desperate, a little more frightened, a little hungrier, a little more anxious about the opportunity, a little less considerate of each other.

This time the man who hires step out of the gate aggressively.

EMPLOYER What the hell!...The ad said *two*! [*After a deliberate pause in which they stand still, silent, while he looks them over as if they were cattle.*] You over there with the blue shirt...and you, there, Curly. [*The two men selected are almost mauled as they attempt to reach the gate. The EMPLOYER is pressed and cornered by the crowd...a pleading, desperate, rather than menacing crowd.*]

VOICES [*In the crowd*]

I'll do anything...	I got a wife and...
Sugar! ...	Give me a chance to work!
Cheater!	Job!
Work!	Job!
Work!	Wages!

EMPLOYER [*Near panic as the men press in upon him, pushing them away*] Get back... Get out of my way! Get the hell out of my way! [*The newly-employed men form a wedge and take the EMPLOYER through to the gate.*]

VOICE [*In a high despairing wail from a thin man who stretches out his arm in appeal... It is a thin, knotted arm and hand*] For Christ's sake! ... Give me a job!
[*The gate swings shut. The crowd is slower, more reluctant in leaving, eddying away with backward looks at the gate. One or two of the men hurry off, still hopeful the others are unable to decide where to go next.*]

BLACKOUT

Scene V

The hall of a rooming house. ADAM, cap in hand, is at a public pay telephone on the wall.

ADAM [*Simulating good spirits*] Yeah... Yeah! [*A little sag*] Well, no, not exactly... Naw, that was the boloney... Three days... I just got back... walked, mostly. Oh, well, what the hell... How about to-night? Chees, kid, I been thinking about you a lot... [*Eagerly*] How's that?... Yeah. Well, that ain't nothing to what I think about you! ... What? ... Unh... hunh... How's the job? Chees, that's tough... Too bad you can't bust her once... Me? ... Oh, I'm all right. Naw, I'm all right... Listen, kid, don't take it like that. I'll get along... Sure... [*Landlady appears, listens, unnoticed*] Say, listen, baby, that's a date for to-night, ain't it? ... Okay. Well, kid, I'd like to talk to you some more, but I gotta see that bird about starting to work to-morrow morning... Yeah, he's waiting for me down to the corner now... You see, I kinda stalled him off until I gave you a buzz and, anyway, there was that other proposition I told you about... [*Much confused*] Listen, baby! Everything's okay... No... Hell, no... I mean, listen, I'll tell you about it later... Sure... Well, not exactly... [*Brightening, indicating that the GIRL has guessed*] Yeah, that's the idea! ... See you at eight... Okay... G'by. [*He hangs up and turns to go, stops, confused on seeing the landlady, speaks.*] Hello.
[*She acknowledges his salute, lets him go almost the length of the hall. He is on the threshold of escape when she speaks.*]

LANDLADY [*Gently, quietly, but commandingly*] Adam.

ADAM [*Halting, half-turning*] Yeah? [*Completing the turn*] Want me?

LANDLADY Where have you been?

ADAM Out on a job.

LANDLADY Can you pay me something?

ADAM It was a gyp. Free shipment, my ear! They held out for commission, bus-fare, grub... I got a buck and a quarter out of it.

LANDLADY You're four weeks behind.

ADAM I haven't got any money... [*Holds out a little to show*] Seventy-three cents.

LANDLADY I have to have the room.

ADAM Chees!

LANDLADY [*Kindly*] I've got to pay rent, too.

ADAM [*Acting*] Listen, give me another week. Chees, I know you been carrying me along for a hell of a long time, but, well, I'll probably be all set inside a week. [*Smiling at her*] I leave it to you... you gotta get the breaks sometime... don't you?

LANDLADY Are you telling me or asking me?

ADAM I'm asking you to have a heart. Give me a little credit... that's a good girl.

LANDLADY [*Stopping him as he is about to slide out*] Until Saturday... Saturday morning... [*He turns on her, his teeth bared in a fit of animal ferocity. She explains, but does not draw back.*] We gotta live! [*Fiercely*] What'll become of me—what'll become of the kids—if you fellows don't pay up... ?

ADAM [*Scornfully, to appear unmoved*] What with?

LANDLADY I'm sorry for you, Adam. [*Pleading*] But you can make out... Anywhere. They got places for men to sleep...

ADAM Flophouses!

LANDLADY Sure, flophouses! [*With* asperity] Furnished rooms's for them that can pay for them.

ADAM "Furnished rooms!" The cockroaches make such a noise on the wallpaper you can't sleep!

LANDLADY If that's the way you feel about it, you can get out right now.

ADAM All right, I will. [*Pause. But he doesn't want to.*]

LANDLADY Go on... Who's stopping you?

ADAM [*Hesitating*] And if I get a job to-morrow... It ain't so easy to find paying roomers now.

LANDLADY Since when have you been so thoughtful!

ADAM [*Turning and going left toward the stairs*] All right. Kiss good-by to four weeks' rent. [*Exits*]

LANDLADY [*Miserably hugging herself, sick with indecision, stands waiting for him to come back downstairs*] Oh, gorry... gorry... gorry... [*A thin, emaciated little girl, who might be six or twelve years old, comes quickly to her mother.*]

LITTLE GIRL Mummy . . . mummy . . . The ice man's here. Says he won't leave any unless you pay him something.

LANDLADY He did, did he! I'll... [*As she disappears, yelling*] Tell that Adam, when he comes down, to give you seventy-three cents... [*She goes out. The* LITTLE GIRL *stands at the foot of the stairs. After a moment* ADAM *descends, carrying a paper suitcase.*]

ADAM Hello, kid...

LITTLE GIRL Hello, Adam. Mummy says for you to give me seventy-three cents.

ADAM [*Flabbergasted, then angry*] Tell her to go to hell.

LITTLE GIRL [*Getting on to more important matters*] Say, Adam, got any candy or something?

ADAM [*Trying to be angry*] Hell, no. [*He fumbles through his pockets.*] How about some gum?

LITTLE GIRL Gee! [*He searches his pockets and can't find a thing. He looks at the* LITTLE GIRL, *so wide-eyed, expectant.*]

ADAM What the hell! [*He counts his silver again, hands the girl three cents.*] There, go buy yourself some gum—G'by, kid… if anybody comes looking for me— [*He jingles the money in his hand as he pockets it and picks up his bag.*] I'll be at the Ritz— [*He stares hard at her, suddenly overwhelmed by the fact that he is homeless.*] Me—on the street! [*A pause. He senses the landlady's return and he recovers himself as he goes to the door.*] Tell your Ma I'll pay her when I get some money— plenty of money!
[*He goes out. As he disappears, the* LANDLADY *reappears, breathless.*]

BLACKOUT

THIRD INTERLUDE

Light goes up on the flat front of a building job. A solid board fence protects it and passersby. In the center is the superintendent's shanty, raised three feet above the sidewalk level.

A mob of sullen shivering men crush toward the shanty from both sides of the stage.

A face appears at a window in the shanty, looks out. The window is slid open.

EMPLOYER [*In the window*] One! [*A pause. The crowd swirls toward him, jamming up to the side of the shanty, holding up hands, each man trying to attract attention to himself. The* EMPLOYER *takes his time.*] You!

[*He points to a tall, broad-shouldered man. The man hitches up his pants, swaggers through the crowd. The Crowd, after one snarl that is cut off by the closing of the window, falls back, in upon itself, sags and breaks into individual hopelessness, unable to think of or plan the next move.*]

BLACKOUT

Scene VI

The exit door of the factory. Evening. The workers are streaming out, going home. ADAM *stands at the side, scanning each man's face, looking for one he knows. He sees it, steps forward and speaks.*

ADAM Hello, Fred.

FRED [*His face lighting, then quickly going under a veil of distant blackness as he is drawn out of the stream to the curb.*] Hello! ... Hello, Adam.

ADAM How's everything.

FRED [*Non-committal*] Oh, so-so. I ain't kicking. What the hell. [*Indication the factory*] It's better'n nothing. [*A very slight pause*]

ADAM Say, Fred...
[*He stalls, fishes for a cigarette.* FRED *takes out his own.*]

FRED Want a smoke?

ADAM [*Taking it*] Yeah, thanks... Say, Fred... Doing anything to-night? How about bumming around like old times?

FRED Chees, I ain't done that in a long time... My wife...

ADAM I get you... [*Again trying to get it said*] Say— [*He balks.*]

FRED [*Seeing it coming, but wanting to get it over with, somehow.*] Yeah?

ADAM [FRED*'s "Yeah" helped. Now he can say it.*] How about letting me have five dollars... a coupla bucks, for a little while... You know me... I'll pay you...

FRED What's the matter? ... Wimmin!

ADAM Hell, no... Just busted... [*Very low*] ... out of a job.

FRED [*Slightly more remote*] Chees! you mean you ain't working!

ADAM Just this week... I'll get something... in a day or two, inside a week anyway. But, Chees, how about it? ...

FRED That's tough... [*He puts his hand in his pocket.*] But, hell, I ain't got that much... Honest, I ain't.

ADAM Make it two...

FRED Nit even that much, kid. Just carfare... My wife holds out...

ADAM [*Terribly put to it to ask it*] How about to-morrow? ... I'll meet you... hunh?

FRED Chees, honest, if I could, but we ain't got more'n enough to run out the week, ourselves.

ADAM [*Hesitates. He is miserable with shame and desperation.*] Okay... Okay...

FRED You ain't sore, are you? ... Say... [*He thinks desperately.*] Here's a quarter... [ADAM *looks at it.*] I wish I could make it more... see, that leaves me a nickel to get home on... see! [*As* ADAM *looks from the coin to* FRED*'s face and back down again,* FRED *stiffens.*] Well, do you want it?

ADAM [*Almost snatching it, harshly, turning away*] Sure. Why the hell not! Thanks. [*He walks up the street.*]

●

BLACKOUT

FOURTH INTERLUDE

As an ominously silent crowd of men seeking jobs comes out on to forestage and reaches the factory gate, higher, stronger, blanker, than before, a sign is lowered over the post at the side of the gate. It reads NO HELP WANTED.

There is a silent, frustrated movement in the crowd, then a yowl of protest... then a blind instinctive surge against the gate, to force it. It holds.

As they swirl and turn away, in upon themselves, aimless, bewildered, there is an accompanying groan.

BLACKOUT

Scene VII

A quiet side street, night. A street lamp gives some light. ADAM *is standing near the lamp-post, hugging himself. It's a cool autumn evening. Several persons walk past, more hurriedly as they come abreast of him. He makes tentative moves toward accosting them.*

Finally, a tall, middle-aged man comes along, smoking a cigar, carrying evening papers home. ADAM *takes a half step toward him. The man gives him a sidelong startled glance.* ADAM *walks at his side a couple of steps.*

ADAM [*Mumbling*] How about a nickel for a cup of coffee, Mister? [*No answer.* ADAM *speaks almost threateningly, because it's difficult to say anything.*] I never did this before, Mister, but I gotta eat.

MIDDLE-AGED MAN [*Looking at him scornfully*] "Eat!"
[ADAM *gives up, stands at the curb. A woman hurries by from the other direction, clutching her fur coat tightly at the throat. She feels his eyes on her. He looks for another pedestrian and takes a step to meet him.*]

ADAM [A little more entreatingly. He has gone two days without a thing to eat. He is almost desperate.] How about a nickel for a cup of coffee, Mister?

SECOND PEDESTRIAN [*Stopping*] What's that? What did you say?

ADAM   [*Withdrawing, almost shamefacedly*] I've been out of work three months, Mister. I can't find anything. I gotta get some money, somehow. I gotta eat!

SECOND PEDESTRIAN [*Precisely, ethically offended*] I don't believe in it.

ADAM   [*Not understanding*] I don't get you.

SECOND PEDESTIAN I don't believe in charity.

ADAM [*He hadn't thought of it that way before.*] Oh!

SECOND PEDESTRIAN Why don't you do something? There must be lots of jobs for big, strong fellows like you.

ADAM There just isn't, Mister.

SECOND PEDESTRAIN [*Walking away*] Well, don't get downhearted. Just keep after it. Something'll turn up.

ADAM [*Raises his hands, clenches them as if he'd like to wring the man's neck*] Gawd! [*His gesture startles a couple of old gentlemen who are walking over to their club. They hurry quickly by. To* THIRD PEDESTRAIN, *now commandingly because he's sore*] Say, Mister, how about a nickel for a cup of coffee? This ain't charity. I'm hungry.

THIRD PEDESTRAIN Why... why don't you go to the breadlines. The city...

ADAM [*Harshly*] I told you I ain't looking for charity.

THIRD PEDESTRAIN [*Frightened, searches through his vest pockets for small change. He finds a dime and with hasty trembling fingers, offers it to ADAM and starts to back away.*] Here! [*The dime falls to the street and rolls to the gutter.*]

ADAM [*Thoroughly angry now*] Too good to hand it to me, are you?

THIRD PEDESTRAIN [*Terrified*] It...it...just...slipped...

ADAM [*Recognizing the man's fear and gloating perversely in it*] Git!
[THIRD PEDESTRIAN *scampers out of sight. ADAM stands surlily looking
after him. He starts for the dime. A small urchin, teetering along the curb,
circles the lamp and catches the gleam of the coin in the gutter. Like a
flash he is upon it. ADAM beats him to it, spins the kid around and throws
him against the lamp.*]

KID [*Crying*] That's mine...I saw it first!

ADAM If that's yours...I'll...I'll cut my throat!

BLACKOUT

FIFTH INTERLUDE

*Another gate, not unlike the one in the Fourth Interlude. Hanging on
it, high up, and larger than before, the same sign NO HELP WANTED.*

Two private policemen are on guard before the gate.

*The crowd, advancing slowly this time in two solid blocks, converg-
es on the gate.*

*The crowd bears down on the policemen. They try to hold the
crowd back. The crowd forces them up against the gate. As the crowd
pins them against the gate, then starts to ease them away to the sides so
that it may be opened, one policemen blows a whistle.*

*Instantly a great siren starts at the bottom of a terrifying trajectory of
sound, rising and rising. The men look up, over the wall, then around,
then slacken and fall back. The crowd falls apart. The men disperse
quickly, in terror, running for cover and escape.*

BLACKOUT

Scene VIII

The walk before the entrance to an expansive apartment   house.

A few hours before daybreak.

A woman in evening dress, ermine wrap, bareheaded, trips up to the door, half turns to her escort, as yet unseen, signals to him that she will wait for him inside, and goes within. She is in high spirits, laughing— a little lit with this and that.

Her escort, a tall slim young man as much like Clifton Webb as money can buy, elegantly dressed, comes on, putting change from the taxi fare in his pocket as he, too, trips across the entrance. As his hand goes in and out of his pocket a gleaming chain catches the light from a nearby street lamp. The head of his stick, his high hat, his dancing shoes, the shirt studs, his white silk muffler and the silk braid on his trousers all reinforce the impression of careless plenty left from the flash across the scene of the bundled-up ermine wrap, red lips and sparking eyes.

As the ESCORT trips toward the entrance, echoing the Woman's tinkling laugh, ADAM, shabby, collar up and cap down, steps out of the shadow at the side of the entrance.

ADAM [*Right hand in his coat pocket*] Put up your hands!
[*Quickly, but as he glances up and down the street, the ESCORT puts up his hands. A pause. He waits to be robbed. ADAM looks him over, taking in the details from hat to shoes, including the man's willingness to sacrifice his money for his safety. ADAM is stalling, against his conscious will. The departure from the orthodox scenario for such affairs adds to the ESCORT's terror.*]

ESCORT [*Visibly shaking*] I say—[*A pause. ADAM can't bring himself to do it. The ESCORT is unable to stand in suspense.*] It's in my pocket, breast pocket, coat—the money, you know... [*A pause*] Why don't you do something?
[*ADAM puts up his hand, to take the money. His hand stops six inches from the coat, hesitates. He looks at the ESCORT's strained face, then up and down the street, then back to the coat pocket.*]

ADAM [*As his hand falls to his side*] Aw, go to hell! [*His shoulders slump as he turns and disappears. A pause. The ESCORT keeps his hands up a moment longer, then cautiously lowers them, staring in amazement after*

ADAM. *The door opens, the* WOMAN *looks out inquiringly, annoyed.*]

ESCORT [*Bursting into speech*] I say! I've just had the most amazing experience!...

BLACKOUT

SIXTH INTERLUDE

Higher, stronger walls and gate. At the top, iron spikes laced with barbed wire. Every few feet along the wall and gate are the signs NO HELP WANTED.

Painted on the wall, diagonally, by an unpracticed hand, is the legend BUY NOW, *with the* N *reversed.*

The private policemen have been reinforced by city police who are strung out in front of the gate, nightsticks swinging idle from their wrists.

Facing them, the crowd of unemployed stands quiet, but holding their ground, waiting, watching the largest NO HELP WANTED *sign at the top of the gate.*

POLICE SERGEANT [*Trying to be friendly diplomatic*] Go on, move along. There ain't a job going to be open here for a year!...

[The crowd remains, silent, waiting, its numbers constantly augmented.]

BLACKOUT

Scene IX

The Girl's Room

She is washing out her stockings.

There is a soft knock at the door. Startled she turns as ADAM enters, wildness in his manner. He is much shabbier. He has just shaved. He is pale, almost haggard.

ADAM [*Very high*] Hello, Baby.

GIRL Adam! [*Shocked to rigidity, neither move for a moment. Their eyes fuse. They are drawn swiftly together. They embrace, kiss passionately, then draw apart, remembering the facts of their life.*] You shouldn't come up here.

ADAM Nobody saw me. [*Trance-like, soaking in the room*] A room, a bed... God-damn the luck!

GIRL It's been ages...

ADAM [*Half-turning to the door to look at it*] Door... a lock

GIRL I waited...

ADAM ...It's warm and dry...

GIRL ...Almost a month...a month Friday...

ADAM Alone...Nobody...

GIRL You look awful. What happened?

ADAM No noise, no smell, no damn bells...

GIRL It's been terrible...

ADAM ...I'll say!

GIRL ...Without you.

ADAM [*Somehow as from a distance in the impersonal elevation of delirium or desperation*] Still got a job, haven't you?

GIRL [*Not answering, just telling, almost as if she were singing a song of her loneliness*] I thought you'd gone...

ADAM [*Continuing*] ...Eating regular...

GIRL [*Continuing*] ...for good...

ADAM   Something to do...

GIRL Every day I looked for you...

ADAM People to work with...

GIRL Every night...

ADAM People to talk to...

GIRL ...I kept thinking...

ADAM Money in your pocket on Saturday.

GIRL ...You'd call up...

ADAM   A place to sleep...same place. Every night.

GIRL Or come... [*In growing terror*] Adam!

ADAM A place to sleep!

GIRL What's the matter with you!

ADAM You're lucky, Baby...

GIRL You talk so...queer.

ADAM ...If it was anybody else...

GIRL Tell me!

ADAM [*Suddenly wild*] God-damn, damn, damn, damn... [*He turns toward the door, then back to glare at her.*] Wish to God I hadn't come!

GIRL [*Hurt, miserable*] Oh!

ADAM [*Seeing her, softening, crossing and taking her in his arms. She buries her face in his shoulder.*] Don't pay any attention to me. [*He starts to caress her, then abruptly lets her go. She doesn't quite know what to make of it, as he crosses over and tries to speak in an everyday tone.*] What you doing? [*He indicates the bowl of water.*]

GIRL [*Watching him*] Washing out my stockings.
[ADAM *looks at her legs, then quickly away.*]

ADAM Been going out a lot lately?

GIRL [*So simply as almost to disarm him*] Who with?

ADAM [*Sharply*] Say, you haven't any strings on me...I never said I'd marry you, did I? I never asked you to stop going out with other fellows, did I? [*Then casually, as if to trap her*] How's Tony?

GIRL How should I know?

ADAM [*Awkwardly trying to make it seem joshing*] If you think you're going to make me believe you've been sticking around here... every night...

GIRL I kept hoping... [*Pitifully*] Why didn't you come before?

ADAM [*Turning abruptly and walking away from her*] Hell I don't know... [*A long pause. Then, not looking at her*] I thought about you enough...sitting on a park bench...riding freights and trucks...God, how cold the nights get!...The flops are worse...Bugs...Old men... Drunks...[*He leaves out something.*]...I hope to die before I get like that.

GIRL [*After a long pause*] You didn't find anything...any place.

ADAM [*Slowly, huskily*] Baby, there just ain't any jobs...[*A pause. He looks around.*] Gee, this place is quiet...It looks clean.

GIRL 'Tisn't much. [*A pause*]

ADAM ...I was talking to a steamfitter the other day...He says they've got a small house...kids...They're getting put out Saturday... Four months, no work...

GIRL Couldn't *she* do something?

ADAM Guess not...[*A pause*] I tried to stick up a fellow a coupla nights ago...

GIRL [*Horrified*] Oh, Adam!

ADAM [*Fiercely*] A guy's got to eat! [*More quietly*] But I didn't do it... [*A little ashamed*] He was scared green...begged me to take everything he had...

GIRL [*Panicked*] What if you'd been caught?

ADAM Hell, I could stand a few months in a nice warm jail, eating regular...a place to sleep with your shoes off, without getting them stolen...

GIRL [*After a pause*] They why didn't you? Oh, I don't mean...I'm glad you didn't—

ADAM A sap, I guess. I knew it all the time we was standing there. Him with his sissy white hands up in the air...I kept telling myself Go on, you poor fish, it's a cinch...It was dark and I'd seen the cop walk by on his beat...Take it, I said, and what the hell...But...I couldn't...Not yet... Chees! Me, thinking what's right and not a square meal for a week!...

GIRL [*Going quickly to the closet, opening the door and taking out a box of characters on which his eyes fasten at once*] You're hungry!

ADAM [*Laughing once, shortly*] I'm getting used to that...[*Half heartedly*] Keep your crackers, you may want them some day...

GIRL It's all I've got... and these sardines...

ADAM [*Humorously, but as he takes the two boxes and opens them quicker than she would have*] Is this a handout?

GIRL Go ahead and eat... I'll see if I've got some milk...[*She opens the window and lifts in a can of condensed milk, shutting the window again quickly. She watches him open the sardines and devour them and the crackers. A pause.*] They've got breadlines...There's one down by the park...Why didn't you...when you're hungry...I mean...

ADAM   [*Trying to be leisurely and offhand about eating, but he is hungry*] Hell, I haven't got down as low as that—standing in line ... three hours ... they show you off like animals in a zoo, so's they can get more dough. [*A pause*]

GIRL One day I tried to telephone your landlady ... you know ...

ADAM I haven't seen her since I left ... [*Between crackers*] I've been everywhere ... Detroit ... Cleveland, Chicago ... Indianapolis ... [*He looks at her.*] I'm thinking of going to California ...

GIRL California!

ADAM The oil fields ... It's tough, they say, but good pay if you get on ... [*He eats a while. She stands, looking at him, terrified by what his departure may mean to her.*] ... Anything's better than Detroit. That's the toughest town for jobs in the whole United States. Everybody figures like I did ... hit for Detroit; that's where the work's going to open up first. Maybe it will ... but *when* ...They treat the guys out of work like cattle in the stockyards. Herd them around, give them slum and flop ... Me, I talked to men that's lived there ten years, so I checked out ... It's a lousy town ... [*He eats and then drinks some of the milk, which she has thinned and poured into a cup.*] The South's just as bad ... I got a job driving a new truck clear through to Alabama. Thought maybe I'd land something there. Not a chance. They got niggers doing most of the heavy work, and there isn't enough to go around. Anyway, they don't like northerners. If you haven't got a job you'd better blow ... and fast. They got a trick of putting you to work on the road gangs for six months if they find you haven't got a dollar on you ...

... I've covered a lot of territory ... been seeing America first ... only trouble is you do your traveling at night, mostly, so you don't get an idea what it looks like ... [*He looks at her.*] How things been going?

GIRL [*Slowly*] They fired one of the girls off our table last week ... Mame and I do most of the work ... [*Because she can't help it*] What are you going to do?

ADAM [*After a pause*] A fellow's gotta get the breaks *some* time ...

GIRL [*After a pause*] If I lost *my* job!

ADAM [*As a warning to her*] The way I feel now, I'd let twenty foremen get their damn paddle feet under my truck and throw me halfway down the hump to start and I'd say nothing ... [*A short pause*] Boy, how I'd like to get hold of a truck, one that was working right ... anything that was steady and not a goddam gyp ... Get up at seven in the morning, grab a cup of coffee, bust through the subway crowd, check in, and get to work ... every day ... money in your pocket ... At night ... [*He breaks off, gets up, turns, then back to her, his voice shaky and harsh.*] Aw, but what the hell! It's a hundred-to-one shot, a kiss off the nine ball on the bank into the side pocket ... [*After a hard pause*] Listen, Baby, you and me ... we got to call it off ... [*A pause. The GIRL makes a movement of distress.*]

GIRL [*She says it simply.*] I love you.

ADAM [*Harshly, to cover up his own feeling*] That's out now.

GIRL [*Slowly*] What will become of me!

ADAM [*More to himself*] Or me! ... That's *it.*

GIRL [*Takes a step toward him, imploringly*] Together ...

ADAM It's every man out for himself ... alone.

GIRL I don't want much ...

ADAM You will want more.

GIRL Oh, no.

ADAM It's something you can't help ... or me ... [*A pause*] Or the human race ...

GIRL Don't talk so funny!

ADAM Funny! Me! Now! Oh, God!

GIRL [*Going to him, importunately*] Tell me, tell me, tell me!

ADAM What's there to tell?

GIRL You love me?

ADAM You know that.

GIRL You *do*, then!

ADAM [*Taking her face between his hands*] Love! Love what's that got to do with us—you and me—people like us? ... It's a sucker's game! ... [*In a wave of passion*] Yes, I love you, I love you, do you hear! God, how much! [*Remembering*] We're going to let it go at that ... No more ... [*In spite of himself*] I love your face, your forehead, your eyes ... Oh, Honey ... don't ... [*He kisses her eyes shut, to block out the look in them.*] Love, love what a word for a bum to use! ... [*He kisses each feature, hungrily, tenderly, yet with a suppressed savageness.*] I love the smell of your hair, your lips ... [*They kiss and cling. Her arms go round his neck ... His head pulls back and away. He looks down into her eyes.*] It's all over and done with—with me, Baby, and you ... Try again ... maybe ... somebody else ... It'll be better for everybody ... You'll see ... If I'm lucky, maybe I'll be back, but don't wait ...

GIRL I couldn't stand your going away again ... I was so lonesome ...

ADAM [*After a pause*] Don't, Baby! Have a heart! ... That isn't for us ... Not us. We can't live like regular people and be happy ... Try for it; make a pass like you was going to have some of it—and they catch you for the works ... Mules—I called those guys mules when I quit ... Hell, we're less'n that! Nothing, nothing that has a right to do what I'm doing now, hold a girl's pretty face in his hands, like this ... So much beauty! That's what they call it—and if I, if you, do what we'd like to—if we go on from here—Wham!—in for life ... and what a life! ... See, Baby, that's the way it is!

GIRL Other people take a chance. I could ... I could.

ADAM [*Bitterly*] You will! You'll find another fellow ... But be a better picker next time ... Oh, somebody that ain't hard to look at, somebody that has a job ...

GIRL I can wait!

ADAM Wait! It's like being in a tunnel with the lights out ... With you—thinking how'd you'd 'be—it'd be hell.

GIRL [*Tight*] Damn you, don't you ever lie awake at night wishing you were dead! What did you come back for? ... Just to go away ... It's not right ... I hate you. I hate—

ADAM [*Holding her tight, trying to calm her*] Don't say it.

GIRL I hate you!

ADAM [*Quietly*] And I love you ... I ... I just don't want any bastard kids ...

GIRL Marry me, then.

ADAM Same thing.

GIRL There won't be any ...

ADAM [*Accounting for everything*] Furnished room ... you work ... I don't ... scared to death ...

GIRL What of?

ADAM Babies ... Oh, sure, I know ... You think you can beat it ... But you can't, not for sure... Not us ... You'd be scared; I'd be scared. It'd be hell, either way. You gotta have money to be safe ... You'd get to looking seedy, sick, one way; tired out from trying to do all the work if we had 'em ... that's not love; that's just a life sentence ... We're saps to think we got love coming to us ... me. [*The GIRL breaks down, sobs uncontrollably against him.*] Christ, why do they make us want what we can't afford, why do they make us love and have kids ... when we can't get the money to make them decent ... [*A pause. He caresses her, trying to quiet her, but losing command of himself.*] I wanted you to have it easy ... to give you ... everything ... [*His arms tighten about her. He kisses her hair.*] I can't let you go ... I can't ... Oh, what the hell ... [*They kiss.*]

BLACKOUT

One minute interval, curtain down, house lights one-third up, indicating the passage of a couple of hours.

As the house lights go down and the curtain rises, ADAM is sitting on the edge of the bed, looking at the GIRL, who is standing, half turned away from him, at the mirror, straightening her hair.

THE GIRL You've got to go now.

ADAM Gee, Baby, how I love you!

GIRL [*Crossing to him, holding his head against her, running her hand through his hair, over his neck, the tips of his ears*] Me, too. [*A short pause. She looks at the alarm clock.*] Please go ... I'm afraid ...

ADAM [*Looking up, quickly*] Sure, I know.

GIRL If they'd find you here ... in the house ... I'd get put out. There's a girl on the fourth floor, she works at the same place. See? ... Please ... It's awful late.

ADAM [*Standing up*] What do you want to do?

GIRL [*Frightened, wistful*] I don't know.

ADAM Want to get married?

GIRL [*Looking at him uncertainly*] I don't know.

ADAM *I* don't want to ... [*He tries to soften it.*] unless we have to.

GIRL [*Slowly*] If you'll just keep coming out ... I can stand it if I see you once in a while.

ADAM Nothing more?

GIRL ...Unless you find something... ?

ADAM That's wishing for ... Heaven. [*He leans toward her in a wave of tenderness, putting his hands on her shoulders.*] Good-by, kid, you're something to remember ... [*He kisses her.*] I'll try to stick around. If I have to get out of town, I'll let you know where I am ... so's if anything happens ... I'll stick around anyway ... long as I can ... just to make sure.

GIRL You ... you better go ...

ADAM God damn it! Seven come eleven! ... You got to get the breaks some time ... somehow! [*He laughs shortly, turns for his cap.*]

GIRL Not so loud...

ADAM [*Picks up his cap and turns to the* GIRL] Okay. Bye, baby ... Don't forget ... I love you ...

GIRL [*Putting her hand to the knob of the door, then lifting her face to his*] Good-by.

ADAM Bye. [*He kisses her, tenderly, passionately, breaks down, caressing her, kissing her again and again.*]

GIRL [*Finally, after a kiss, as she opens the door behind her*] Bye. [ADAM *goes out. She closes the door. Then through a growing trance, opens it a crack and listens until he has gone down the stairs and out the door. She closes the door, locks it, looks at the alarm clock, crosses to it and winds and puts on the alarm.*]

BLACKOUT

SEVENTH INTERLUDE

At rise of curtain, the same as at the end of the Sixth Interlude. It is darker, about 4 P.M. of a winter day.

The crowd of men seeking work is strengthened by two great clots of new arrivals who come from each side of the stage.

The crowd is pressed toward the line of police. The police heave the crowd back, then, in the same rhythm, the crowd swings up toward the gate.

The police bunch and charge, still not using their clubs, break the crowd down through the middle and turn the two parts back toward both corners of the forestage.

Abruptly, the two parts of the crowd stiffen and hold fast …

BLACKOUT

SCENE X

Lower Fifth Avenue, twilight of a winter day. Snow shovelers are at work. It is still snowing.

ADAM is among the workers, an oddly assorted crew: an actor in an expensive tailored suit, no overcoat, a worn Borsalino hat, torn gloves, spats and worn patent leather shoes. A broken down clerk. An unemployed musician. An Italian laborer. A former floorwalker in a dry goods store, with striped pants and spats and a sack coat. A bum. A college boy in a gay sweater. A newspaper reporter wearing a wide loose coat with raglan sleeves. A steel worker. A few are properly dressed for the work, overcoat, overshoes, rubber boots or rubbers, and mittens. ADAM has no overcoat, overshoes, nor mittens.

They all work with varying degrees of enthusiasm and skill. The AC-TOR, the CLERK, and the FLOORWALKER try hard, but fight themselves in handling the snow. The COLLEGE BOY works exuberantly, by fits and starts. Like the FLOORWALKER, he is conscious of the passerby, turning away constantly to avert his face, then drawn again to look at the people unseen on the sidewalk. ADAM *works slowly and with difficulty. It has been several days since he has eaten. The* STEEL WORKER *has the best shovel, but, on the rare occasions when he uses it, he handles the snow as if it were expensive ice cream, dicing it meticulously into small bits before dropping it down the manhole.*

They have been working since early morning. They are tired, wet, cold and hungry. More than anything hungry, most of them. Pitiable though they are, there is something cruelly ludicrous about the scene.

COLLEGE BOY [*After a time*] Say what time is it, anyway?

ACTOR It must be six o'clock ... Don't we stop at six? [*A pause. The* ACTOR *straightens his back, leans on his large scoop on wheels, looks up and down the street, at his wet feet, beats his hands together, looks at the other men. The* STEEL WORKER *is looking at him with sardonic amusement. Embarrassed, the* ACTOR *addresses him.*] I beg your pardon, have you the time?

STEEL WORKER You mean, have I got a watch?

ACTOR Yes.

STEEL WORKER No.

ACTOR [*To the* CLERK] Have you?

CLERK Not *with* me. [*They all straighten and rest.*]

FLOORWALKER [*To* ITALIAN *railroad worker*] We get paid, don't we, to-night?

ITALIAN [*Smiling, friendly, at home*] After we quit ... six, seven, eight, maybe nina clock ... You gotta stand in da line ...

FLOORWALKER Nine! ...God, my feet are frozen ...

ITALIAN Sure, you gotta take your turn ...

FLOORWALKER [*To* COLLEGE BOY] What time is it?

COLLEGE BOY I don't know …

FLOORWALKER Why don't you ask somebody? …

STEEL WORKER [*Indicating the sidewalk*] Some of your friends …
[*The* COLLEGE BOY, *fussed, looks up at the sidewalk, turns, goes back to work.*]

REPORTER [*Unbuttoning his overcoat, looking at his watch furtively, putting it back and buttoning up again before speaking*] It's half past four.

ACTOR Four—nearly two hours more… [*Quietly, as in surprise*] I don't think I can stand it … [*Suddenly*] I wish I had a cup of coffee.

ITALIAN [*Helpful again*] Coffee Pot, Sixt' Avenue … Warm like hell.

ADAM [*Stops, sways and tries to focus his mind on the* ITALIAN] Coffee … ?

ITALIAN [*Looking at him curiously*] Say, you ain't … sick, or something?

ADAM [*Taken aback, self-conscious, stubbornly proud*] Naw … Just … thinking …

STEEL WORKER [*Looking at* ADAM] Take it easy, buddy.

ADAM [*Fiercely*] I'm all right.

ACTOR [*In the meantime, to* REPORTER] Isn't there some place near … I mean … around here …

COLLEGE BOY Subway station, three blocks over.

REPORTER There's a comfort station in the park.

BUM Closed … just in summer.

ACTOR [*To* COLLEGE BOY] I wonder if I may ask you to lend me a nickel … until … we get paid?

ITALIAN Tell de guy you for da city. [*Then quickly as he sees someone coming.*] Hold it!
[*All look up, then fall to their work at double quick as a portly uniformed checker, with brass buttons and a badge, comes to look them over.*]

CHECKER [*To ADAM, who is the only man not working effectively*] Better get a move on, you ... [*More generally, as he turns to go on*] This is the slowest gang on the street ... [*Fixing on the ITALIAN to explain*] We gotta get this block cleaned ... quick ... Savvy. There's important people lives on the corner ... See!

ITALIAN [*Smiling as usual*] Okay, boss.
[*The CHECKER leaves.*]

REPORTER [*Edging over to ADAM*] Pretty tough, eh? [*Then kindly, but curiously*] Say, I didn't see you eat lunch, did I?

ADAM [*The words sticking in his throat, slowly*] I'm saving up for a hell of a big supper.
[*That's familiar to the BUM. He giggles. The STEEL WORKER looks at ADAM, then with eloquent care picks out a piece of snow, chops it up and puts it down the manhole. At the same time the COLLEGE BOY pushes up a big pile of snow and is about to dump it when the STEEL WORKER slice through it with his shovel.*]

STEEL WORKER [*To the COLLEGE BOY*] You get some more ... I'll put this down ...

REPORTER [*Laughing, trying to be chummy with the STEEL WORKER*] Take it easy, huh?

STEEL WORKER Why the hell not?

CLERK [*Looking form the REPORTER to the STEEL WORKER, seriously*] That's sabotage.

STEEL WORKER Nerts! [*Note: This is the intimate Brooklyn version of the Bronx cheer. It requires careful practice to obtain the full values of contempt, doubt, healthy vulgarity and defiance.*]

ACTOR [*Trying to catch up with the conversation*] What was that you said?

STEEL WORKER Me? Nothing ... I'm conducting an individual revolution against the established order and ... [*Indicating the* CLERK] Mr. Morgan here doesn't like it.

REPORTER Say, that's swell! [*Crossing to the* STEEL WORKER *eagerly*] Where'd you get the idea? [*He takes out a crumpled piece of paper, starts to write down.*] "Individual revolution" ...

STEEL WORKER [*Swooping on the* REPORTER *and snatching away the paper, looking at it*] Who are you, baby face, a stool from the Department of Justice?

REPORTER [*With dignity*] Certainly not ... I'm a reporter.

STEEL WORKER [*Deliberately*] Nerts.

ITALIAN Yeah? What you doing here?

REPORTER You don't believe me?... Here... [*He pulls a limp police card from the inside pocket.*] My police card...

STEEL WORKER [*Examining it curiously, laughs, shortly*] The World!

BUM Aw, let the kid alone... [*To the* REPORTER] I used to be a newspaperman myself...

REPORTER [*Still with dignity*] I... I freelance.

CLERK What's that?

REPORTER I figure I can write a story about this... and sell it to the papers... The Times... or the Herald-Tribune.

STEEL WORKER [*Sardonically*] Try it on the World-Telegram.

COLLEGE BOY [*With respect*] Then you're going to get paid twice!

REPORTER Maybe... if they use it...

STEEL WORKER [*Returning the police card*] Here, kid's your souvenir. [*A pause. The* REPORTER, *thrown off, moves away for more snow. The* FLOORWALKER *is near him.*]

FLOORWALKER [*Almost crying with cold and pain and hunger*] God, I can't stand it... I thought my feet could stand anything.

REPORTER Policeman?

FLOORWALKER No. Section manager... I was six years at Wanamaker's... two at Macy's, and then... [*Pain submerging pride*] If I quit now... do you supposed I could get paid.... Up to four o'clock?

REPORTER It's only about an hour longer.

FLOORWALKER [*Tears in his eyes and voice*] My feet... They're like ice... I can't stand it!

CLERK [*Pointing to the hardening slush*] It's freezing up... 'll be hard by morning.

FLOORWALKER [*Continuing, indicating the* ITALIAN] He said...

REPORTER Yeah, eight o'clock, maybe. It's a goddamn crime.

CLERK [*Looking at the* FLOORWALKER's *spatted feet.*] You ought to have rubbers... Why didn't you trade in your spats?

FLOORWALKER [*Starting to laugh hysterically*] Rubbers! "Don't go out without your rubbers, Willee!"

CLERK I don't see why the city doesn't provide them. Somebody ought to start a fund...

STEEL WORKER [*Interpolating*] Nerts!

CLERK [*Puzzled and annoyed*] I wish you wouldn't keep saying that all the time. What does it mean, anyway?

STEEL WORKER Don't you like it? It happens to be the way I feel about things generally.

MUSICIAN [*Suddenly, full of his grievance*] You're goddamn right. It's the banks... and the big corporations. They got people working day and night figuring out machines to throw men out of work... That's the whole trouble.

ITALIAN [*Kindly*] You in the needle trades? The cutting machines threw my brother...

MUSICIAN [*Frigidly cutting off the* ITALIAN] I'm a musician... I've been the first violin... Held a union card here for seven years... The squawkies put me on the bum. Look at my hands... [*Inarticulate at the sight of them.*] Look at them! [*He blows on them.*]

STEEL WORKER Nerts! [*The* MUSICIAN *looks at him once and starts shoveling snow with the same silent desperation he has displayed through the day.*]

ACTOR [*Toward the* MUSICIAN] They're ruining the legitimate stage.

REPORTER [*Alert*] Are you an actor?

ACTOR Yes. I've played all over the country... stock in Denver and Buffalo... I had a bit here last fall, but we closed out of town...

REPORTER That's tough. Did you get paid?

COLLEGE BOY You know... I've been thinking... there must be something wrong... I thought... You know... it had just happened to me; I mean that I couldn't scrape up enough money. But... an actor, a reporter, a musician... I don't know what all these other fellows are. But, you know, I think, there's something wrong. I mean...

STEEL WORKER Don't, kid, it's breaking my heart.

ACTOR [*To the* COLLEGE BOY, *ignoring the* STEEL WORKER] As I see it, the American public is losing its taste for the finer, nobler, the more poetic things of life... All this sordidness, this fascination with...

STEEL WORKER Nerts! [*Pause*]

CLERK The way I see it, everybody's got the wrong psychology...
[*That stops them.*]

REPORTER [*To the* COLLEGE BOY] What's your line?

COLLEGE BOY Going to school, college... Had to stay out this term...

REPORTER Columbia?

COLLEGE BOY [*Reluctantly*] Harvard.

ADAM [*Breaking in, his voice high, more as if he is trying to prove to himself that he's still one of them.*] I knew a guy once that could do a swell tap dance... Name was Campbell... His right foot wasn't so good though... [*As an afterthought*] Damn good electrician.
[*Pause. They all look at* ADAM, *conscious that he is not well. They work, spasmodically except* ADAM, *who is now almost unable to lift his shovel.*

A rather prosperous dapper man appears, stands at the curb, watching the men.]

BROKER [*To* COLLEGE BOY] Hey, Bud, want to sell your ticket?

COLLEGE BOY Me?... What'd you say?

BROKER I'll pay cash for your ticket... so's you can go home.

FLOORWALKER [*Crossing over, eagerly*] You mean... you'll pay now?

BROKER I said I'd buy your ticket.

STEEL WORKER Hundred percent profit.

FLOORWALKER How much?

BROKER Two dollars.

COLLEGE BOY For the whole day?

STEEL WORKER Sure. He's been resting his dogs all day in a Tammany speakeasy. Now he comes along, buys your ticket and makes as much as you do.

FLOORWALKER [*To no one in particular*] I couldn't stand waiting in line... It's so cold!

ITALIAN [*Of the broker*] The son of a bitch.

FLOORWALKER [*Plaintive and bitter*] But it's worth four dollars! Can't you give me more? Three?

BROKER Four. If you want to wait. Line up at six, stand in line until eight, nine, maybe ten... On the sidewalk. I'm giving you two bucks, cash, right now!

COLLEGE BOY [*Considering, blowing on his hands, looking up the street*] And I'd have to work the rest if the day anyway!

BROKER [*Cynically, since the boy is green enough to ask*] Sure, they got your name, haven't they? [*He is watching the FLOORWALKER, who had turned away to look at his ticket and consider. The BROKER picks out the ITALIAN.*] How about you, Joe? Want to sell?

ITALIAN [*Smiling, his teeth showing*] Me! I can use that four dollar. [*To the others, pointing up the street*] 's five o'clock. See!

BROKER [*Money in his hand for the FLOORWALKER, speaking to the CLERK*] How about it, brother? [*CLERK shakes his head and starts for more snow. The BUM silently crosses, hands the BROKER ticket, gets his money in his shaking hands and vanishes. The FLOORWALKER, again near the BROKER, watches the transaction. His eyes follow the BUM down the street. The BROKER points to the STEEL WORKER*] How about it?

STEEL WORKER You goddamn heel!

BROKER What'd you say?

STEEL WORKER You heard me.

BROKER [*After "mugging" him, that is, memorizing his face and general appearance for future reprisals*] You lousy Red. [*He turns to* ADAM.] How about you? You want to eat?

ADAM [*Staggers forward*] Eat? [*He stops, unsure of his feet. He is so sick he is about to fall. The* FLOORWALKER *comes between him and the* BROKER.]

FLOORWALKER [*Offering his ticket*] Here, give me the money. [*To the others, apologetically*] I've got to... I've *got* to, really...
[*Several others come along, sell their tickets and go off to eat. The* BRO-KER *turns for a last look around.* ADAM *is standing in a daze, unable to move, to make a decision.*]

BROKER Anybody else want a little action?... No?... [*As he walks off, another worker sells his ticket.*]

STEEL WORKER [*To* ADAM] A hell of a swell country *this* is, hey, bo?

ADAM [*Looking up, his eyes burning, unreasonably flaring, as much because the* BROKER *has gone as because of the* STEEL WORKERS's *idea*] Yeah!

STEEL WORKER That's what I said.

ADAM [*Thickly, but true to form*] ...If you don't like it, why don't you get the hell out...?

STEEL WORKER I'll tell you why... [ADAM *swings at him, misses, staggers, and falls in a dead faint. The* STEEL WORKER *goes to him quickly, lifts his head and shoulders up from the pavement to his knee, meantime speaking to the others.*] Starved, I guess... That's all... Been watching him all day... Here... [*He gives the* COLLEGE BOY *a dime.*] Here's a dime. Get him something hot, quick... coffee... [*Afar off is heard the clang of the ambulance bell.*]

BLACKOUT *as the bell comes close, loud.*

EIGHTH INTERLUDE

Outside the high wire fence and gate of a great oil plant with its storage tanks and stills. It is twilight. At rise of curtain, police are holding back two great blocks of unemployed from the gate and fence, men drawn there from all parts of the county in the hopes that there will be jobs. More police are inside the fence, in reserve. The NO HELP WANTED *sign is up, One man, madly hopeful, tears loose, gets through the police line, runs for the gate and the shed just inside. The line of police breaks, three turn and chase the running man. They club him; he goes on, reaches the gate, then they club him down to his knees. Meanwhile the fighting has become general. Nightsticks, blackjacks, fists, feet, knees and teeth are used... Scalps are torn, arms hang useless. As the reserves pour through the gate from the inside the sound of a police gong, deeper in tone than the ambulance gong of* SCENE X, *is heard approaching rapidly. Two swinging shafts of light from automobile headlights sweep the scene from the side.*

BLACKOUT

SCENE XI

A street and sidewalk in front of an abandoned excavation for a new building. Farther back, the soaring outlines of office buildings, windows lighted here and there. ADAM, *thin, shabby, drifting, comes along the sidewalk, stops, makes his way to the railing and leans on it, looking at the excavation.*

About him the sounds of the living, breathing, dying, constantly re-born city; purr of motors, horns, police whistles, faint roar of subway, occasional hum of talk, a woman's laugh; snatch of a hit song on the radio; a gun shot... with lulls of silence.

ADAM [*His back still to the audience. His words come through the city's noise in snatches.*] White... and warm... smooth... smother than... smooth... Door shut... locked... Nobody else. Her mouth... mine... [*A pause. He turns up the collar of his thin overcoat. After a while he goes on in the same tone.*] Four blocks over... long blocks... pork and beans... a million on the plate... bread and butter... ten cents... [*With growing intensity*] A dime! Ten cents!... Me... TEN CENTS!... [*He throws up his hands to the buildings behind and above the excavation in desperate, feverish supplication.*] Oh, God, give me a job... Let me have her... I'll work, work like hell... all my life... like a dog... I don't give a damn. Anything that pays wages... Anything so's I can live. Other guys get the breaks... Me... Give me a chance. I'll beat their time... Somewhere, any place, let me hold down some kind of a job... Please, please, for Christ's sake, have a heart... Amen!... [*A pause... he buries his head in his arms...*] To-night, to-morrow... make it soon!... [*He half turns around as if he thought someone had come up and was standing at his elbow.*] What happened, baby? Where've you been? I've been looking for you... all the old places... [*Harshly, putting out his hand as if to grab her wrist*] What happened? [*He stares a moment, his harshness fades. He explains.*] I was in a hospital... just got out... had a job... [*Laughs harshly*] ...passed out... couldn't stand the gaff... Me!... They put me to bed... When I came out they said you'd gone away... [*Irrelevantly*] I got some food out of it. What the hell... [*After a pause*] I've been up to your place twice, where you worked, too... Where you been keeping yourself, huh? Love me? Still love me?... [*Pause*] It sure is good to see you... [*He wavers uncertainly, perceiving that she is not there.*] ...to see you... To see... I thought... [*Pause*] Chees, that's funny as hell... [*He turns away, beating with his fist on the railing.*] I got to eat!... [*Fiercely*] No more fool proud!... Sure, I'll go and stand in line and beg for a bowl of slum... stand where they can come and look at me... A guy's got to live!... You got to get ready for the breaks... You got to eat. You got to feel strong! [*He laughs looking at his thin hands, checks himself, looks intently at the City.*] A thousand windows... a million maybe... a million people working. A million jobs. Christ, there must be a million jobs in this city. Isn't there one place... one job... a little job I can do! [*Passionately*] Listen, You! Loosen up, will you! You got me licked... I admit it, you hear! I'll take it... I'll take anything... Give me the chance!... [*A pause*] Me! Saying that! Chees, you can't help it. It gets you down, knowing you're no damn good... just a bum... No good... They can tell when they look at you... No pep. Can't talk back, you want the job so bad... can't look at 'em... No stuff on the ball... Chees, you think they're right when they look at you... like an ex-convict when they look at you. Me! N.G.! [*A pause*] God knows it ain't true... Gimme something to eat, some shoes, some decent clothes. I'm just the same as I ever was... God, if I ever get over this hump!... I'll [*Pause. Dreamily, fiercely, as if defying*] Me and her... She's game... lots of nerve... [*A pause*] We'd get along. Other guys... [*A pause*] They only got two hands and a head, same as me, and they ain't nearly as strong... when I'm eating regular... [*Again he turns to the City.*] Oh, God, what's the answer? There's gotta be one. "Whatever goes up must come down." I *know* there's Something... Someone... The sun, the tide that comes up the river and goes out again... everything's regular, ticking like a clock, back and forth... [*Higher, his face raised to the buildings in supplication and defiance*] I've swung far enough, do you hear! [*Hard, wheedling, cunning*] You could give me a job, easy... never notice it... Any kind, I don't give a damn... Anything... Make it dirty as hell, I don't care... It's money I want... regular. A wad of jack at the end of each week. Money. That's everything; eats, sleep, clothes, a woman... kids... everything you think about when you haven't got it; everything a fellow's got to have to stand up and look a man in the eye. Money, get me, that's what I want. Not a hell of a lot, but regular... regular as hell... [*Passionately*] I've got a right to live! I've got a right to work! Whaddeya say? [*He waits, face uplifted, for the answer.*]

BLACKOUT

NINTH INTERLUDE

The gate of a great iron works. The same sign in big letters. NO HELP WANTED.

Instead of police, a line of militia, long and short, thin and fat, sloppy and neat, is strung out along the wall and gate, bayonets fixed on rifles.

Under the eyes of a pot-bellied officer, they keep the trickle of silent, smoldering men moving from right to left, now and then shoving a reluctant man along with a gun barrel or butt.

The trickle collects at the left of the forestage, turning to look at the militia.

BLACKOUT

SCENE XII

A sub-basement in a building off the Bowery, dimly lighted by small electric lamps, two of which are above the steaming cans of "coffee" and the pile of stale bread at center right. Coming from the left is an open landing in a staircase used by visitors. It is ten feet above the cellar floor and is protected by a solid railing, reaching above the knees of the visitors. As the curtain rises, the last men on the line are being served with "coffee" and the bread. Each man is given a big tin cup of the liquid and a third of a loaf of bread. As they are served, they walk off into the murky place to eat. Some of them start to wolf the bread at once. Others wait until they have found a place on the floor to sit. Some eat alone, facing the wall. Others huddle in groups.

As ADAM takes his cup and bread, he turns and goes to the lower right corner. He eats ravenously, tearing at the tough bread with his teeth, washing it down with the "coffee."

FLUNKEY [*A washed-out man with a beery past, wearing a grayish white apron and cap, calls to another man at the door , unseen as he hands out the last few pieces of bread*] That's all, Joe. Punk's all gone. Shut the door. [*The men in the cellar look up for an instant at this, exchange dim glances of triumph at having landed inside.*]

VOICE That's all. No more...
[*An instantly swelling spurt of murmuring, cut short by the slamming of a door. JOE, another flunkey, appears, crosses in back of the "coffee" and a moment later is seen crossing the landing of the stairs. He opens a door, goes through it, shutting it after him.*

A short pause.

The same door is swung open. A big, husky, well-dressed man, stiff collar, iron gray hair, with a manner between a business executive and a Y. M. C. A. pep expert, with a dash of ministerial sanctity thrown in, enters, showing in the tourists from the sight-seeing bus parked in the street above.]

MANAGER ...And this, ladies and gentlemen...[*Parenthetically, to a timid elderly lady, taking her elbow and propelling her along the landing to make room for the rest of the party*] 'S perfectly safe, lady. Not the slightest danger...[*Resuming his spiel*] ...This, ladies and gentlemen, is one of the most touching sights of our great city... This is where we feed them. Every night, seven nights a week, winter and summer, these unfortunate men, the flotsam and jetsam of a great city, are fed good nourishing food, in addition to the lodging which is provided free through the charity and generosity of our many visitors from all over the world...

YOUNG GIRL [*Breaking in, in a high, almost adenoidal voice*] You mean they sleep there?

[*Pointing to the floor. The tourists, all on the landing now, crane their necks to see the floor below.*]

MANAGER [*Annoyed at the interruption, but unctuous withal, closes the door and comes to the railing*] Yes, my dear young lady, and they're only too pleased to be given a nice dry flood to stretch out on. [*He turns to the others and goes on quickly into the main body of the spiel.*] Practical religion, my friends...

YOUNG GIRL [*Looking down into the pit with interest and disgust*] How awful!

MANAGER [*Ignoring her*] Practical religion, my friends, is something more than mere words from a pulpit on Sunday morning, something more than prayers... "By their deeds ye shall know them"...That's what Jesus said, my friends. Just the good old time religion, friends, every night, upstairs in the main auditorium... and oh, how these men love to sing the old time gospel hymns... songs their mothers taught them years ago when they were innocent little children...yes, we give them the Word, the Blessed Word that still has the power to save. But we do more than that...We feed the body as well as the soul. "For the spirit is willing, but the flesh is weak."

YOUNG GIRL [*Breaking in again*] What do they eat? [*To her, they are animals in a zoo.*]

MANAGER [*Thrown off, tartly*] Bread and coffee, and they're glad to get it !

YOUNG GIRL [*Wide-eyed*] That all!

MANAGER [*Trying to dismiss the GIRL and recapture the attention of the tourists to the business at hand*] You'd be surprised how much it costs to feed these many hungry men just this simple, nourishing meal... [*Returning to his spiel*] As I was saying ...ah, how weak the flesh is! You, my friends, who come from good respectable families, comfortable homes where the word of God is not used only as an oath, you will never know, I hope, the depth to which a man who denies his God can sink. These poor souls, look at them! Grateful for a crust a bread and a cup of coffee given in Christ's name. These men victims of drink, victims of sin, victims of their own lusts and appetites and the foolish pride of their hearts... Men who'd be walking proudly this very minute on the streets of this earth, had they not denied Christ. Now, they're brought close to his blessed saving grace, ready to be saved, to be born again, and to find rest and comfort and new courage in His mercy and His everlasting arms.

ELDERLY LADY [*In the ensuing pause*] You do, of course, try to find work for them? [*At the word "work" ADAM and a few others stop eating, turn and stand motionless, listening.*]

MANAGER [*Controlling his annoyance*] Ah, my dear lady ... we wish we could do that, too, but our resources are so limited. Their souls, if we can save them; the rest ...They're always plenty of jobs for good Christian men.

ADAM [*Who has been hypnotized by the word "work" answers the EL-DERLY LADY'S questioning eyes*] Work...I can do anything...
[*The old-timers grab him and pull him down among them, as the MAN-AGER, incensed, tries to look into the pit and make out the man who made the disturbance. At the same time, the old lady, moved by some-thing in ADAM'S voice, has opened her purse and is about to throw a bill to him below. This electrifies the assembled men, who prepare to jump for the money. The old lady is detained from her kindly impulse by the manager who says, as he takes the money from her hand.*]

MANAGER Very sorry, Ma'am, but we don't allow this. It disrupts our organization. However, if you wish, you may help us. For twenty-five years this business of giving practical religion, day in and day out, night after night, without regard to race or creed, has been supported entirely by voluntary contributions...[He places the bill, without wait-ing for her consent, on the platter which seems to be conveniently at hand. He turns to the others.] Anything at all you may feel like giving will be appreciated by these homeless men. It will feed them, keep them from starving, give them new hope and courage, lead them to Jesus... [*The tourists start filing out past the MANAGER, putting coins and bills in the plate. At the same time, below, on the cellar floor, a man near ADAM is suddenly sick. He rushes out, leaving a hunk of bread. AD-AM and another man pounce on it at the same time. As the tourists file out the struggle between ADAM and the other man for the piece of bread can no longer be ignored. The MANAGER leans over the railing and bawls at the FLUNKEY.*] Hey, Eddie! ... Eddie!

EDDIE [Popping hastily out of the darkness] Yes, sir.

MANAGER [Pointing to the two struggling men] What are those men fighting about?

EDDIE Bread...a hunk of bread...

MANAGER [*As ADAM and the other man are parted, ADAM with the bread, the MANAGER turns eloquently to the tourists.*] God forgive them, they are hungry... Whatever you may care to give... [*The tourists file out, give much and little, some large bills. After the last tourist is out, the MANAGER closes the door a moment, bawls to EDDIE.*] Eddie, find

out who started that...put him out... [*To all the men*] You men will have to learn to be orderly if you want to come here... Understand...No fighting... [*Harshly, as if talking to dogs*] And any man caught smoking tonight will be put out and turned over to the police.
[*He turns and goes out the door.*]

BLACKOUT

TENTH INTERLUDE

The Factory Gate is now like the entrance to a great fortress, with watchtowers, armored slits, more militia on guard before it, a soup wagon in full blast before the gate, serving the soldiers.

A barbed wire fence now separates the patrolling militia from the crowd of unemployed, who are desperate to the point of daring the ultimate to madness. More men join the crowd, actually shoving the mass forward against the wire. Quickly, at an order, the militia don gas masks, the soup wagon is deserted.

Meanwhile, the men pushed against the wire surge back instinctively. The whole mass then throws them forward. The fence snaps, goes down. An officer jumps to the step of the soup wagon, blows a whistle. The militia set off the tear gas.

The crowd yells, surges forward another step, then falls apart as the gas rises, choking the men, who thrash about blindly, then run, stumbling, falling and picking themselves and each other up, through the men at the back who in turn go forward, get the gas, turn and flee.

BLACKOUT

SCENE XIII

A street outside a cheap restaurant. A boy, about nineteen, is washing the big window. Men, in varying degrees of shabbiness go by, some walking aimlessly, eyes drawn to the restaurant window. One stops, counts his money, then walks in.

Suddenly the boy, who has seen something inside, spurts in his work. In an instant the BOSS is out the door.

BOSS Say, you going to take all day! ... Been out here an hour...

BOY [*Suddenly, but in a low voice*] Like hell I have.

BOSS [*As ADAM comes on the other side of the stage, walking aimlessly, dejected, worn*] What's that you said?

BOY [*Still sullen*] I said, like hell I have.

BOSS You're fired.

BOY [*Cocky*] All right! ... Take your lousy job. You know what you can do with it... And try to get somebody else to stand for all your...

BOSS [*Cutting him off*] Yeah? I can stick out my hand and get ten men better than you. [*At random he points to ADAM.*] Hey, you! [*ADAM starts, looks up.*] Want a job... twelve dollars a week... and meals...

ADAM [*Simply, but in a daze, now that the break has come*] Sure, where?

BOSS [*Pointing to the BOY and the window*] Here, start now. [*To the BOY*] Give him that apron. [*To ADAM*] Put it on. Finish that window. Make it snappy. Lots of work inside. [*To BOY*] You, come inside... if you want what's coming to you.

BOY [*Swaggering*] That's just swell... [*With a side swipe at ADAM as he and the BOSS go inside*] And don't forget ...I got fourteen bucks a week! [*ADAM hears that, pauses the fraction of a second to look after the two, then goes on with his work*]

BLACKOUT

SCENE XIV

Inside the restaurant. Self service, white glass-topped tables; a tiled steamy hole in the wall. The door to the Street is at upper left. A big window on the street runs the rest of the back. ADAM, wearing a dingy apron, is working, taking out dirty dishes, wiping off tables, bringing in racks of clean cups, tumblers, silver and stacks of dishes for the counter and the water fountain.

The BOSS sits at the cashier's desk, watching the windows outside, keeping his eye on ADAM, the two fly-blown countermen inside the food counter and the two customers who are finishing their coffee and strudel.

ADAM loads up with dirty dishes from a table, swabs off the top, takes the load out to the kitchen, through the swinging door at lower right.

The GIRL comes in, goes to the counter, gets doughnuts and coffee, takes her punched check, goes to the table and sits down facing the window. The countermen are friendly in a sly sidelong way. She is flashily dressed, but tawdry, jumpy, furtive, miserable.

ADAM comes in, sees a woman at the table, walks by with a side glance, but does not recognize her. He returns to his dish-stacking at the next table beyond her, wipes off the table, picks up his dishes, and starts toward the kitchen. Their eyes meet. They remain motionless for a minute.

GIRL [*First to speak, her voice husky with emotion*] Adam!

ADAM Baby!

GIRL [*Pause*] Where'd you go?...You said...

ADAM [*At the same time*] Where you been? I went to your place...

GIRL I waited ...

ADAM I passed out... sick... the hospital, six weeks.

GIRL [*Slowly*] I was sick, too.

ADAM [*Constricted*] What happened?

GIRL [*After a pause, trying to pass it off*] I lost my job.
[*Pause*] [*The countermen look on and snigger noiselessly, directing the BOSS'S attention as ADAM, stepping close, is standing over the GIRL, looking down into her face.*]

ADAM Chees! It's been a long time!

GIRL [*Like a cry*] Yes.

BOSS [*Crossing, speaking in a loud blustery voice, sore at ADAM, unconsciously showing off to the GIRL, at the same time humiliating her*] Hey, hey, nix on that stuff! [*He steps in front of ADAM, indicates his work.*] Take these dishes out. Get to your mopping. That's what you're paid for.

ADAM [*Pauses only a moment as he goes by the GIRL, to say, out of the side of his mouth, almost as convicts do*] Wait...
[*The GIRL turns to watch him go out to the kitchen. A police SERGEANT comes in, crosses directly to wall telephone.*]

POLICE SERGEANT Spring 7-3100

BOSS [*Loud enough for ADAM to hear*] Looky here, girlie, you can't pull that stuff in here...
[*The GIRL lowers her head so as not to attract the cop's attention, as he waits to get his call through. ADAM comes in from the kitchen door, carrying a mop and a pail. The BOSS, who has gone to the desk, watches him. ADAM sees that the BOSS is watching him, understands that he may lose his job if he speaks to the GIRL. He starts to work, keeping his eyes away from her. She does not look up, though she knows ADAM is back in the room, because the cop is still there.*
    The two customers pay their bills. The BOSS rings up the change. They go out.]

POLICE SERGEANT [*Hastily looking around, then turning to transmitter and trying to hold down his voice*] Lieutenant Delaney... Sergeant di Campolo talking ... Listening, Lieutenant ... they're going to do it...Yeah...They're starting now... No, not for City Hall...the warehouses...Gansevoort market...Huh? From that stool...you know...Yeah, that's his name... Huh?...I don't know...Ten thousand maybe and they keep coming...Yeah...Better send over some more men...guns...Yeah.
[*He looks around. The BOSS and ADAM, who have been listening, shift guiltily.*]

BOSS [*To ADAM, covering the fact that he has been listening*] Come on, now, pick up that pail and get going.

ADAM [*Quietly*] Yes, sir.
[*The BOSS turns back to the telephone, but the SERGEANT is just hanging up. He meets the SERGEANT and anxiously goes with him to the front door, asking*]

BOSS Is it going to be bad?

POLICE SERGEANT [*Pausing at the door, where ADAM is swabbing up, to speak to the* BOSS] You keep your trap shut, get me. [*Unable to do the same himself*] They got a new racket...pulling the line they've got to eat! [*Struck by a humorous idea*] They'll be coming in *here* next... You better look out!

[*He laughs and goes out, the* BOSS *watching him.* ADAM *gives the* BOSS *a fleeting glance as he wrings out the mop and swabs up more floor. After a moment the* BOSS *hurries back to the desk, opens the cash register excitedly, takes out the bills, trying to be casual and unnoticed, puts them in his pocket, goes to the front window, watches up the street.*

ADAM *watches him, as do the countermen.*

The BOSS *sees something, feels in his pocket, starts out the front door, hesitates, comes back, hurries to the kitchen door, through it.*

At once ADAM *makes for the table where the* GIRL *is.*]

SIMULTANEOUSLY

ADAM

Quick, now, tell me...

GIRL [*Quickly, telescoping*]
Mame told me about a
woman...I don't know...she
said I could go right back to
work...but...I was in bed a
month...Her all the time
scared to death I'd die on
her hands...When I got
back...they'd given my job
to somebody else...so I
couldn't keep my room...

ADAM [*Fiercely*] Well...

GIRL I tried to find you...I tried to get another job...I didn't have much money...

ADAM Go on...

FIRST COUNTERMAN

[*In a low flat monotone*]
He can't get out that way.

SECOND COUNTERMAN
[*In the same tone, eyes on the
kitchen door*] He's hiding it.

FIRST COUNTERMAN Where?

SECOND COUNTERMAN [*With
ratlike fierceness*] Say!...How
the hell should I know!

GIRL Christ, I couldn't starve, could I? They don't have flophouses and places like that for...girls, do they?

ADAM [*Slowly, understanding*] Chees!

GIRL [*Unstrung, near tears*] I wish I had died...I wish...
[*The swinging doors are pushed open. ADAM hushes the GIRL. The BOSS appears as ADAM returns to his work. The BOSS is breathless; frightened, suspicious. He stands in the open doorway a moment, looks at the two countermen, who make themselves busy. He goes to the front windows again.*]

BOSS [*Impatiently*] Anything happened yet?

ADAM [*Still mopping*] Nothing...
[*The BOSS stands at the window, watching tensely. Outside the window the crowd blackens, begins to flow in one direction slowly. Men's heads are lined up just outside the window. The countermen hang back, one of them edging toward the door to the kitchen.*]

BOSS [*To ADAM, indicating the nearby front door*] Shut that door.
[*ADAM obeys. The BOSS looks back at the countermen, pausing a moment, then, signaling them to come up front.*] Hey, you guys, turn off the lights and come up front here...[*A pause. They obey, switching off the lights, leaving only one overhead light up near the window, where the BOSS is looking out.*] Chees, this is terrible for business...How can anybody get in here—even if they did have the money...And that cop making cracks...[*He stands on a chair to see better and looks out anxiously. The two countermen stand a little behind him, their passive, limited cunning ready for any little break of luck. ADAM is working along with his mopping, back toward the GIRL.*

From outside is heard, faintly, quavering, the first notes of the Inernationale. ADAM pauses, listens, then goes on mopping, but listening, too, to the song, to the cries that follow the verse, to the sound of the passing crowd. The BOSS'S hysteria rises.] Lookit 'em!...Chees, I didn't know they was that many...No-good bums...They look tougher'n hell...[*Speaking to the countermen, as if contradicting them—some one*] But they ain't'...Yellow, that's what's the matter with them. They ain't got the guts to work...They're no goddam good at anything...Rats... Thinking they got a *right* to get something for nothing...

ADAM [*Close to the* GIRL *again, speaking out of the side of his mouth*] Where are you staying now?...[*Watching the* BOSS] Your address, quick!

GIRL I don't want you to come there...

BOSS [*Looking out the window, almost shrieking with joy*] Look at that guy run, the cops after him!...Chees, this is going to be good...
    [*The crowd outside is singing again.*]

ADAM [*To the* GIRL, *speaking low, passionately*] I'm getting twelve a week...we could get a room...Nights I could bring home something to eat...[*The* GIRL *starts to sob.*] Twelve a week...twelve hours a day...but if you got somebody...waiting for you—you could keep going...

GIRL [*Shaking her head, sobbing*] Not now! [*Trying to tell him*] Not now!...
[*The noise outside suddenly swells. The* BOSS *jumps off his chair.*]

BOSS [*Calling to* ADAM] You! Lock the door...Quick!
[*He runs and does it himself.* ADAM, *wary of being noticed, gets to work twice as hard with the mop. He souses the floor and swings the mop back and forth. In one wing it wraps a strand of smoking wetness around the* BOSS'S *leg, nearly tripping him up as he is running back to his chair.*]

BOSS [*Venting all his accumulated fear and spleen*] Look out, you clumsy dummkopf! [*With scorn and contempt*] Why the hell don't you look were you're goin'.

ADAM [*Quietly, after a pause*] Yes, sir.

BOSS Get to work...No lip... [*The* BOSS *hurries back to stand up on his chair again.*]

ADAM [*After warily working his way back close to the* GIRL] It ain't worth it...nothing's worth it. I can keep eating, just drifting around... You got to have somebody...You got to want to live a hell of a lot...to... take this. [*Indicating the mop, the boss and all*] Twelve hours a day, seven days a week...year in and year out...

GIRL Not now! [*He looks at her hard.*]

ADAM You can' be making such a hell of a lot yourself...

GIRL It isn't that...Oh, Adam...[*Her tone changes.*] I'm *sick*...[*Then, tenderly*] Don't you understand! That's why. [*A pause*]

ADAM [*Slowly*] That makes it perfect...a hundred per cent...[*A pause. Then he straightens, drops the mop. Another pause. He speaks as if to himself, adding things up.*] Rock bottom...there ain't any more down to go...[*Hazily including her*] Might as well see what those guys outside are after...[*Intensely, as a prayer before battle*] Christ, I hope it's something I get hold of with my hands! [*The BOSS turns quickly, hearing ADAM above the sound of the thousands in the street. He watches ADAM go to the kitchen, quietly, smoothly, unhurried, taking off his apron, coming back through the doors in a moment with his cap and coat, putting them on as he walks toward the street door. As he passes the GIRL'S table, he commands, not taking his eyes from the street door.*] Come on, Baby... [*She looks at him, but does not move. ADAM goes straight on toward the door. The BOSS anticipates him by grabbing the key out of the door, pocketing it. ADAM keeps on, speaking to the BOSS in a quiet, level tone.*] Open the door.

BOSS [*Hysterically*] No...I won't...[*ADAM looks at him a moment, leaning across a table.*] You goddam lazy bum...
[*ADAM straightens, his hands gripping the table top, which comes up, away from the frame. He looks at it, turns, raises it above his head and deliberately throws it through the door. The street noise spurts in. He steps through.*]

The GIRL'S head is buried in her arms. She is sobbing uncontrollably.

The crash electrifies those outside, there are shouts, men appear at the door, peer in, then enter, cautiously, like wild animals, drawn on by the scent of food. The BOSS starts forward, driven to protect his property; the countermen back toward the kitchen, driven to protect themselves. The GIRL'S face is still buried in her arms.]

BLACKOUT

FINALE

[*During the Blackout the singing and noise strengthen, come nearer.*

The lights go up on an empty stage. The song, which is more shouted or barked than sung, goes on without a break, draws nearer. Suddenly onto the stage spills a streaming crowd of men and women, ADAM among them. They are not singing. The singing continues offstage. The song is not the Internationale, it is that and more, a wordless battle hymn of ferocious desperation.

They walk steadily across, eyes ahead. Halfway across, gun-shots start. Two fall. Two waver, turn and run. The others go on; more shots; still they go on.

As they near the other side, machine-gun fire begins.]

CURTAIN

Claire and Paul F. Sifton

The Siftons wrote several plays including *The Belt* (produced by The Theatre Guild in 1927), *'1931-'* (produced in London under the title *The Age of Plenty* in 1933), *Fame and Fortune, The Doctors, In the Meantime, The Pift* and *Blood on the Moon*. When the latter was performed in London in 1933, the production was halted by Lord Chamberlain because it was deemed to be an unfriendly act toward Germany. Their 1930 play, *Midnight* became a film featuring Humphrey Bogart.

Mr. Sifton voluntarily enlisted for service in World War I in 1917 and served as a Private, first class, in the American Expeditionary Forces. The following year, he was on the front lines when the Germans launched their last ditch assault, and he was incapacitated during a gas attack. He contracted tuberculosis and, as a result, had to have part of a lung removed. He went on to attend the University of Missouri, where he met his future wife. Mr. Sifton later became the Sunday Editor of *The New York World* and was on the editorial staff of *New Yorker*. He then held a number of government jobs dealing with labor problems--first with the New York State Department of Labor and then with the Wage and Hour Division of the United States of Labor. He became a political writer for the National Farmers Union after World War II and met Walter Reuther, then U.A.W. vice president, during the 1945 strike at General Motors. The two men became fast friends and worked together, especially after Mr. Sifton became the Washington representative for Democratic Action. He joined forces with Mr. Reuther and such liberals as former Senator Paul H. Douglas, Joseph L. Raub, and Clarence P. Mitchell of the National Association for the Advancement of Colored People to outline strategies for civil rights and welfare bills. He combined writing skill and political acumen to argue for progressive economic and civil rights policies for more than 30 years before his retirement in 1962. After his retirement, Mr. Sifton and his wife spent summers at Bailey Island, Maine and winters in Oaxaco, Mexico, where he died in 1972.

Mrs. Sifton (born Claire Ginsburg in **Rio de Janiero**) was the daughter of missionaries and attended schools in Brazil before coming to the States to enroll at Stephens College. Claire and Paul were married in 1922 after meeting at the University of Missouri, where Claire received a graduate degree and became the first female instructor in journalism. Claire was also a specialist on children's education and was the author of *The Perfect Baby,* a book about child care. She belonged to the Daughters of the American Revolution but withdrew from the group in the dispute over Marian Anderson, the black concert singer, in 1939. During the 1940s and 50's, Mrs. Sifton was associated with the United States Children's Bureau in Washington. She wrote for Government publications on nutrition, education and family life. Mrs. Sifton passed away at their home in Oaxaca in 1980.

THE
JOHN HOWARD LAWSON
PLAYS

SUCCESS STORY

Introduction to the Lawson Plays

Maybe only children know when they're lost. Like grownups, old plays can go on and on, with years of earned patience, quietly waiting to become of use and importance. I knew something was "lost" in my artistic career, so I began a quest to find it. I committed to reading at least one play every day, for what turned out to be a period of over three years. I remember the day I finally sat in the 42nd Street library reading room, under the guard's watchful eye, and cracked the red cover of John Howard Lawson's *Success Story*. I'm not sure what was found that day: the play, a sorely neglected playwright, the artistic-director of the ReGroup Theatre Company, or a new movement by Theatre artists actively concerned with the state of the Theatre . Maybe it was all those things and much more yet to be discovered.

As I read Lawson's words, it instantly became clear how directly they informed the words of my favorite playwright, Clifford Odets, whose words shaped the words of Arthur Miller, whose words inspired the next generation of playwrights. Pieces finally clicked into place, and for the first time, I felt something I'd never felt in the Theatre before: roots!

By the time I got through Act I, I was so immersed in the world of Solomon Ginsberg that I knew that I needed to find my own copy of the play, immediately. Besides, it was too hard to focus with this new idea of Theatrical Roots bouncing around in my head. I returned the book to the librarian (to be locked away once again) and headed home. An extensive search of online antique booksellers finally turned up a copy of the play for $99. As I waited for it to arrive, I began exploring the ideas of roots and saw how interconnected the Theatre community had once been. It did not begin with the Group Theatre, though they planted most of the seeds that formed our American Theatre. What if we could plant a few of those seeds again? Would they still bear fruit?

Upon the play's arrival, I was hooked by Lawson's writing; his characters had a poetic ease and unique style with words that are typical of the best playwrights. As an actor, this type of dialogue is the most challenging and riveting to speak. This personal style is a skill that has been forgotten and even shunned as it isn't "realistic." (Having spent 2 years on a long subway commute to Brooklyn, I treasured the plays that took me into another world and away from the superficial, "real" conversation that was going on all around me. Half the plays I had seen on the NY stage in the recent years had merely mimicked conversations I had gone out of my way to keep from overhearing on that commute.) Not only were Lawson's characters articulate, and fully developed, but 75 years on, they were still relevant.

From there, I immediately ordered *Gentlewoman* and *The Pure of Heart*, published together under the title *With A Reckless Preface*. Again, I was not disappointed, and coincidentally, the week I first read it, the news of Bernie Madoff had hit the airwaves. The Madoff headlines and the parallels between plot points in *Gentlewoman* showed that crooked businessmen were not a creation of our time. Would anyone think to write a sympathetic stage composition exploring the struggles of Madoff's wife and her potential desire for escape with a young poet, or would it be easier to write her off as a one-dimensional villain? Lawson had taken a similar character in that of Gwyn Ballantine and showed us the complexities that make up any person.

Where had these plays been, and more importantly, why hadn't I heard of them before? As they were produced by one of the most esteemed companies, it is unlikely that their disappearance was due to an abysmal first production. Surely, the McCarthy trials were responsible for their lack of productions for a long while, but could that still be the cause 60 years later? With admirable Theatre companies specifically doing the works of "lost" playwrights, why hadn't I ever seen Lawson's *Success Story, Roger Bloomer* or even the amazing *Processional* on the New York stage? Had thoughtful, poetic dialogue really gone out of fashion? When plays by a master playwright, produced by the greatest Theatre Company that this country has turned out, can be forgotten maybe it is actually our Theatre that has gotten lost and not the plays. I hope that the main reason for their prolonged absence is simply because they were so difficult to find. With the publication of this volume, I hope we can help restore Mr. Lawson to his proper place amongst the other American master playwrights.

No matter where the ReGroup goes, or what it becomes, it started with a *Success Story*. Thank you, Mr. Lawson.

Allie Mulholland
Artistic Director

THE GROUP THEATRE, INC.
presented
SUCCESS STORY
by JOHN HOWARD LAWSON
Production directed by LEE STRASBERG
Setting designed by MORDECAI GORELIK

CAST
(*In the order of appearance*)

SARAH GLASSMAN	Stella Adler
DINAH MCCABE	Ruth Nelson
JEFFERY HALLIBURTON	William Challee
RAYMOND MERRITT	Franchot Tone
RUFUS SONNENBERG	Morris Carnovsky
SOL GINSBERG	Luther Adler
MARCUS TURNER	Art Smith
AGNES CARTER	Dorothy Patten
HARRY FISHER	Russell Collins
MISS FARLEY	Margaret Barker

THE RE:GROUP THEATRE COMPANY
presented
SUCCESS STORY
as a staged reading
June 21, 2010
The Neighborhood Playhouse School of Theatre
NY, NY.

SYNOPSIS OF SCENES

The scene throughout is a private office, in the New York headquarters of Raymond Merritt Co., Inc., Advertising and Sales Counsel.

Act One

A Summer Afternoon, 1928.

Act Two

A Morning in the Fall, 1930.

Act Three

Scene 1. An Afternoon in

Scene 2. Early the Next
Morning.

ACT ONE

RAYMOND MERRITT'S *private office, the Raymond Merritt Co., Inc.*

A Summer Afternoon, 1928.

A richly furnished office, suggesting the center of a prosperous and important business. The room is done in modern style, concealed lighting, the walls paneled in polished mahogany; the furniture is upholstered in heavy green leather. Most of the rear wall is occupied by big windows which look out on an uninterrupted expanse of blue sky. Since the room is on the fortieth floor, no other buildings are visible on the exterior. MERRITT'S *desk, left center, facing toward right, is a specially constructed desk, a circular affair made of bronze and glass. On the desk an ornamental inkwell, a bronze statue of a naked woman, an onyx clock, a French phone, a silver cigar box. Beside the desk, an inter-office dictaphone. Right rear a door leads to the office of* MERRITT'S *secretary,* MISS GLASSMAN. *Front right are files built into the mahogany woodwork of the wall. Also built into the wall right front is a panel which slides back to show a small safe where* MERRITT *keeps important private papers. There are two doors at left, the one at rear leading to a library which* MERRITT *uses as an accessory to his main office. The door front left leads directly to the corridor of the building, and is generally kept locked. Between these doors, a large map of the United States on the wall. The carpet is of rich neutral material which muffles every footfall. Across the windows rear is a transparent silken curtain which prevents the light from being too glaring, but at the same time gives the figures on the stage the effect of being seen in silhouette. There are heavy curtains which can be drawn across the big windows at night, but which are at present open.*

In addition to the big comfortable chairs, two other articles of furniture right center attract one's attention. These are two large models on metal stands. One is a detailed architect's model of a big manufacturing plant, the other a model of a piece of complicated and beautiful machinery; each is complete in every detail and a thing of considerable beauty.

When the curtain rises, the stage is empty.

The door at right is ajar, and through the opening can be heard the steady monotonous click of a typewriter. After a few moments, the typing stops and SARAH GLASSMAN *enters from right, carrying a*

*number of freshly written letters with envelopes, in a neat pile. SARAH is
a dark girl of twenty-six, handsome in an Oriental way. Sleek black hair,
olive skin, full bodied and vigorous.*

*She crosses to desk, sets the pile of letters neatly in center of desk. As
she turns away, the dictaphone on the desk buzzes and she turns back
and moves the proper key.*

SARAH [At *dictaphone*] Yes— [*A man's voice is heard roaring
indistinctly in the machine at the other end.*] I can't disturb him, Mr.
Turner, he's in a very important conference. [*TURNER'S* voice is heard
in the machine the words "Atlas Motor Company contract" being indistinctly heard.] All right, I'll tell him.

[*The male voice grumbles at the other end and the connection clicks off.
SARAH makes a note and puts it on the desk. While SARAH has been
speaking, DINAH MCCABE has entered right; DINAH is a thin girl with a
peaked face, inefficient, gossipy and unprepossessing. She tries to make
up in willingness what she lacks in good sense. She carries some sheets
of yellow typewriting paper held together by a clip. While waiting for
SARAH to finish she takes a piece of gum from her mouth and a fresh
stick from her pocket. She carefully wraps the used gum in the paper
from the new stick, puts it in the trash-basket under the desk and
proceeds to masticate the fresh piece.*]

DINAH This is terrible important, Miss Glassman— Mr. Halliburton
says Mr. Merritt must read it immediately an' talk to him about it.

SARAH [*Taking the yellow sheets and glancing at them*] Oh yes, the
Glamour Cream copy— [The *dictaphone buzzes again. SARAH turns to
it.*] Yes... Miss McCabe is here now, Mr. Halliburton. [*The voice is
heard at the other end, "got to see Mr. Merritt immediately..." SARAH
answers the dictaphone.*] It's impossible at present, Mr. Halliburton;
he's tied up— I'll tell him— [The *voice on dictaphone: "I'm coming right
in." SARAH clicks off, turns to DINAH. Looking at the yellow sheets of
foolscap.*] You'd better copy this decently, Miss McCabe, half of it's
crossed out and written in pencil—

DINAH He won't let me copy it, he says there ain't time—
[Confidentially, *chewing her gum vigorously*] He *likes* his copy to look
messy— he thinks he's a genius, that's what *he* thinks! He says I always
spell the words wrong— can I help it if he uses words that ain't in the

dictionary!

[JEFFERY HALLIBURTON *enters right. He is a very neat young man, dressed in perfectly fitting tweeds, rather handsome in a collegiate way. He has only been out of Yale two years, and is quite sure that he knows more than anybody in the business.*]

JEFFERY Where's the Boss, Miss Glassman?

SARAH [Indicating *door left rear*] He's in the library, Mr. Halliburton.

JEFFERY This Glamour Cream copy is very urgent; do you suppose I could interrupt him for a minute to explain about it?

SARAH You could *not;* he's with Mr. Sonnenberg.

JEFFERY Rufus Sonnenberg? [SARAH *nods;* JEFFERY *whistles.*]

DINAH Who's that?

JEFFERY Did you ever hear of Einstein, Miss McCabe? [She *shakes her head.*] What Einstein is to mathematics, Sonnenberg is to Wall Street. Do you get the idea? [Again DINAH *shakes her head.* JEFFERY *turns to* SARAH.] It's useless to tell her anything. [DINAH *looks tearful.*]

SARAH [To DINAH] He's a banker, Miss McCabe. [*Holds out the sheets of paper to* DINAH] Kindly make six copies of this and bring it back as quickly as you can.

JEFFERY I don't want it copied, that's just a rough draft; I want to talk over the general line-up and make the necessary changes. [DINAH *looks from one to the other helplessly.*] That's all, Miss McCabe.

DINAH Yes sir. [She *exits right.*]

SARAH [To JEFFERY *as she turns back to her own office right*] I'll call you as soon as he's ready.

JEFFERY I hope he won't be long; I do want to get away early today— [SARAH *shrugs.*] And another thing Miss Glassman— I want a

different secretary immediately— I hate to make a girl lose her job,
I've stood for her a long while because she means well, but she's hopelessly dumb, she can't spell the simplest words—

SARAH [Interrupting] I have nothing to do with that; you'd better speak
to Mr. Jones about it, he's in charge of personnel—
[The *door left rear opens and* RAYMOND MERRITT *walks into the room,
followed by* SONNENBERG. MERRITT *is a big man of thirty-five, blond,
good-natured, vigorous, a square jaw and sharp eyes. He offers a good
contrast to* SONNENBERG, *representing as he does the best qualities of
Nordic charm.* SONNENBERG, *on the other hand, is a grey-haired stout
Jew, a man of great culture and refinement; his silken voice and his
delicately expressive gestures make his suaveness a trifle artificial, but
his eyes are wise and kindly.*]

SONNENBERG [As *they walk into the room.*] Then we're in complete
accord. It simply remains for our lawyers to make our little
agreement as complicated as they can.
[HALLIBURTON *immediately becomes a different person; he is not
embarrassed but he is on his guard, servile, eager to make a good
impression.*]

JEFFERY I hope I'm not in the way, Mr. Merritt?

MERRITT Not at all, Jeff. [JEFFERY *casts an admiring glance at the great*
SONNENBERG, *and turns to go.*] Wait a minute— I want you to meet
Mr. Sonnenberg, Mr. Halliburton—

JEFFERY [Shaking *hands*] How do you do, sir. [SARAH, *seeing she is not
wanted has gone out right.*]

MERRITT One of our coming young men, Mr. Sonnenberg, he's
handling some of our important accounts in the fields of drugs and
specialties.

SONNENBERG Nothing like youthful vision in business—

JEFFERY I had the privilege of knowing your son at Yale, Mr.
Sonnenberg.

SONNENBERG From what I've seen of his friends, I can only hope that you were not one of them!

JEFFERY I... well, hardly— I— [SONNENBERG *is glancing at his watch, winding it absently.* JEFFERY *takes his cue, turning to* MERRITT.] I've got a great set-up on the Glamour Cream campaign, Mr. Merritt— see you later about it. [MERRITT *nods.* JEFFERY *bows to* SONNENBERG.] It means a lot to me to have met you, Mr. Sonnenberg.

SONNENBERG [Nods *vaguely*] Thank you. [JEFFERY *exits right, closing the door after him.*]

MERRITT Just a moment... I'll get you the data we were discussing. [He *is at his desk.* SONNENBERG *sits in easy-chair right of desk.*]

SONNENBERG Thank you... purely a formality; my banking associates insist on detailed figures.

MERRITT I'm glad the impression is favorable. [Sitting *at desk, he moves a key on the dictaphone— a male voice answers "Hello."*] Is that you Fisher? [The *voice answers, "Out for the afternoon— can I do some-thing for you?"— but before the voice has finished,* MERRITT *rings off, and presses a buzzer under his desk, addressing* SONNENBERG *apologetically.*] My statistician doesn't seem to be on hand.

SONNENBERG Oh that's all right; send it down by messenger in the morning.
[SARAH *enters right, note-book in hand.*]

MERRITT Where's Fisher?

SARAH He went to his wife's funeral—

MERRITT Too bad! [Rising] Will you excuse me for a moment, Mr. Sonnenberg? I'll go and dig up the information myself from the files.

SARAH Mr. Fisher's assistant can give you anything you want on a moment's notice, Mr. Merritt.

MERRITT Can he? I doubt it...

SARAH He knows the files from A to Z.

MERRITT Does he really? Then tell him I want the report of our operations for the last fiscal year ending May first— not the abbreviated form, but the full report; also the charts of advertising distribution and sales according to industry and according to territory; also the plans for development in California and Northwest— [*Turning to* SONNENBERG] I believe that will give you the authoritative picture your associates require.

SONNENBERG It sounds both exhaustive and exhausting.

MERRITT [To SARAH *who noted what he said in her shorthand book*] Tell him to have that here in two minutes and to have it right. [SARAH *nods and exits right.* MERRITT *continues to* SONNENBERG] I'm proud of my statistical department. This chap Fisher is a genius with charts and diagrams. [SONNENBERG *nods and rises, walking about the room.*] Statistics are the nerve center of a business such as ours.

SONNENBERG Oh quite... quite... [He *is looking at the models on stand right.*]

MERRITT The new type of merchandising service is entirely dependent on two sciences: In the first place, industrial analysis of sales appeal, density of market, buying power; in the second place, psychology, the knowledge of people's whims, desires, phobias... [SONNENBERG *nods.*] The sales counsel must have those two sciences in the hollow of his hand.

SONNENBERG [*Staring at model of factory right, interrupts* MERRITT *with a casual wave of his hand.*] You talk well, Mr. Merritt, almost too well!

MERRITT [Rises *and joins him.*] What does that mean?

SONNENBERG I am a great admirer of glibness, but in a close financial association I prefer candor.

MERRITT You're clever— that scientific talk is about seven-eighths bosh.

SONNENBERG And the remaining eighth is poetry. I am not giving you my support because you hold science and psychology in the hollow of your hand, you have sanity and good education; you've built up a successful business from a small beginning. By the way, how much did you start with?

MERRITT Fifty thousand.

SONNENBERG Where did you get it? These little details are always of great interest to me.

MERRITT An inheritance from my grandmother.

SONNENBERG Good! Now that you have millions to play with, don't lose your head; let science and psychology be your handmaidens, but don't be beguiled by their rather wanton charms.

MERRITT A word to the wise!

SONNENBERG [Studying *the factory model with great interest*] These industrial plants have a genuine aesthetic quality... not a bad substitute for the Gothic cathedral!

MERRITT That's the new works of the Atlas Motor Company at Great Bend.
[SOL GINSBERG *enters right, carrying several folders and charts. He is a handsome boy of twenty-five. He is tough, uncouth, somber; he bristles with East Side mannerisms, which he tries to cover up with an unsatisfactory seriousness. He is self-educated, sharp and imaginative, full of undigested ideas and impressions. He is egotistic and hot-tempered. His clothes are baggy and ill fitting, and his shirt rather dirty— he has absolutely no consciousness of personal neatness. This is the first time he has been called to* MERRITT'S *office and he is excited and annoyed at himself for being nervous or impressed.*]

MERRITT [Glances *at* SOL *good-naturedly.*] That's quick work.

SOL [Gives *a covert glance at* SONNENBERG *as he crosses to the desk*] I got everything here you asked for, Mr. Merritt. [Opening *one of the folders.*] Here's the report of operations—

SONNENBERG [Tapping *the pile of folders*] This is a regular encyclopedia. I'll have a boy carry it down to my car.

MERRITT You don't need all this truck— I'll assemble the important material in one folder for you—

SOL You asked me for the charts on the different industries, Mr. Merritt, so I brought the whole thing—

MERRITT [Looking *through the folders vaguely, while* SOL *stands beside the desk ready to butt in at the proper moment*] Your people are particularly interested in our plans for expansion in the West—
SOL [Picking *out the folder expertly*] Here's the stuff you want—

MERRITT [Glancing *through the papers and charts*] Yes, here's the map of population density— here's the distribution of our products and analysis of rival products—
SONNENBERG Very instructive. I'm amazed at how much detail you have here—

MERRITT It's kept up to date daily.

SOL Every week. ...

SONNENBERG [To MERRITT] It's very nice to have the information, but I wonder if any of your executives take the trouble to consult it?

MERRITT [For *the first time* SOL *grins, starts to speak, but holds his own counsel.* MERRITT *looks over the folders rather angrily.*] Why in hell isn't there a short summary of this material?

SOL [Producing *a small packet of filing cards from his pocket*] There is— in these here filing cards— I worked 'em out myself—

MERRITT [Thumbing *over the cards*] That's all you need, that's very satisfactory.

SONNENBERG Have you copies of all this data?

SOL Sure, the reports are mimeographed, and we make three copies of all the charts.

SONNENBERG [Looking *at Sol's eager, serious face with a flicker of kindly interest*] What's your name, young man?

SOL Ginsberg... Solomon Ginsberg.

MERRITT That's all, Ginsberg. Come back for the rest of this later.

SOL [Starts *to speak, thinks better of it, mutters*] O.K. [And *exits right*]

MERRITT [As SOL *goes, assembling the sheets and maps*] I think this will be quite sufficient for your needs.

SONNENBERG [Paying *no attention, absently looking after* SOL] A sharp young man, — [MERRITT *nods agreeably.* SONNENBERG *continues with thoughtful cynicism.*] The Russian Jews are the world's most gifted and most difficult people, Mr. Merritt—

MERRITT You don't say; I never gave it a thought!

SONNENBERG [Taking *the file of papers which* MERRITT *offers him*] These will do very nicely. [Turning *to door right*] Your lawyer can call mine and arrange the details.

MERRITT [At *door front left*] This way if you don't mind— this will spare you the walk through the office.

SONNENBERG Thank you. [He *shakes hands with* MERRITT.] From now on we are practically partners.

MERRITT I hope you'll never have cause to regret it.

SONNENBERG Win or lose, I'm sure our personal contacts will always be as delightfully cordial as at present. [They *both smile.*] Good day. [SONNENBERG *exits left.* MERRITT *closes the door. He walks tiredly to his desk, sits down, presses the buzzer under the desk.* SARAH *enters right, with her notebook. She approaches the desk.* MERRITT *is staring moodily at his hands, clenched on the glassy surface in front of him.* SARAH *waits patiently. After a moment, she enquires evenly.*]

SARAH You want me?

MERRITT [Looks *up at her, smiles*] Sure... I want to talk to you... talk to somebody human— bankers aren't human.

SARAH You look tired, Mr. Merritt.

MERRITT I am; going out and get a flock of drinks after a while, but first I need sympathy, a woman's sympathy— which I'm sure you'll be glad to give me, Miss Glassman.

SARAH I...

MERRITT I'm kidding you, Miss Glassman. I feel pretty good; everybody in this concern should feel pretty good. Do you realize what I just pulled off with Sonnenberg, Miss Glassman?

SARAH From what I overheard I supposed it was all settled at last.

MERRITT At last we've agreed on every point; it puts this concern right on top of the heap, unlimited backing, money to expand— [He *hesitates.*] I don't know whether I'm glad or sorry.

SARAH Why?

MERRITT It's a big change... this business has been my private affair. I made it... now it's going to be bigger than ever, but it's going to be a corporation with a lot of Wall Street gorillas pulling the strings... [He *shrugs good-naturedly.*] Sonnenberg and I keep a working control of the stock between us... I fought for two weeks to keep a majority of stock in my own hands, but Sonnenberg's a slippery old whale... [He *laughs.*]

SARAH Naturally... those bankers aren't in business for their health.

MERRITT Sure, but it's got me worried... what I mean is... sometimes I think I'm a great man, Miss Glassman. Other times I think it's all the bunk— I mean myself— it's not so much a great business brain that's put me where I am... it's just that I manage to put over my personality.

SARAH Honest... I think pretty near everything in this world is just personality salesmanship.

MERRITT I like to think of myself as a real thinker, get me? A wise guy! But I'm always afraid I'm just a smart mixer that talks his way into things.

SARAH But that's the whole game, talk people into buying things they don't want, in print, magazines, signboards, over the radio... sell, sell, make yourself believe that selling is a religion.

MERRITT Do you believe that?

SARAH No, but that's what all the dumb-bells believe— I guess you don't want too much brains around here.

MERRITT You're too bright yourself, Miss Glassman.

SARAH Honest, Mr. Merritt, I didn't mean to be fresh.

MERRITT Not at all, you're dead right... too much brains is no go... and you've got 'em. I'm not at all sure a clever girl like you isn't a misfit compared to the others. But don't worry, some way or other your head will get you a long way.

SARAH It hasn't got me much yet.

MERRITT You wait, we're growing up; no reason at all you shouldn't grow with us.

SARAH Thanks... you *are* feeling good. [She *glances at the pile of statistics left on the desk.*] Did Mr. Ginsberg bring you the right material, Mr. Merritt?

MERRITT Sure; who is that fellow Ginsberg?

SARAH He's been here four months— you probably don't remember but I recommended him.

MERRITT Oh, I recall... I told Fisher to do whatever you advised— a friend of yours?

SARAH [Nods] I've known him since we were children. We come from the same tenement.

MERRITT Really? ...

SARAH [Glances *at clock*] It's late, Mr. Merritt, and you have a lot of things to attend to—

MERRITT All right, don't rush me; first off I'll straighten out the legal end of this with Turner. [He *moves a key on the dictaphone. A male voice at the other end says, "Hello."* MERRITT *speaks over the dictaphone.*] It's all set, Mark, the Sonnenberg deal... absolutely... Sure it's good... There's a dozen points I want to take up with you... No, I'll come right over to your office; I want you to have your reference books handy... Right away. [*He clicks off, looks up at* SARAH.] Get me all your memoranda on the banking deal.

SARAH Yes sir. [She *exits right, leaving the door open.* MERRITT *rises and starts across to right.* JEFFERY, *who has evidently been waiting in* SARAH'S *office, appears right.*]

JEFFERY How about me, Mr. Merritt, I've been waiting?

MERRITT I'll get to you later, Jeff. [SARAH *re-enters right, with sheets of pink memorandum paper, which she hands to* MERRITT.]

JEFFERY I'm worried about this copy, Mr. Merritt, it's got to go out to eighteen women's magazines tonight.

MERRITT Don't get so het up about it; take his temperature, Miss Glassman, I think he's got a fever... [He *starts to go, turns to* SARAH *again.*] Sign my name to those letters and send 'em out.

SARAH You haven't looked them over.

MERRITT I don't need to— [Waving *a hand to* JEFFERY] See you later, Jeff. [*He exits right.* JEFFERY *picks up the yellow sheets of copy on the desk, looks at them— ruefully.*]

JEFF [To SARAH] I suppose he hasn't looked at this?

SARAH No, he's been exceedingly busy.

JEFFERY Well, I'm going to stay planted right here till he comes back. [He *sits on* MERRITT'S *desk, picks up the telephone.*] A line, please. [SOL *enters through open door right.* JEFFERY *is at the telephone, dialing.*]

SOL [To SARAH] Is it all right if I get my stuff from the files now? [SARAH *nods.* SOL *goes to the desk to get his papers.* JEFFERY *is talking over the phone.*]

JEFFERY Is that you, Edwards? Miss Estabrook, please... Miss Virginia Estabrook... this is Mr. Halliburton. [SOL *is trying to pull a set of maps from under the phone.* JEFFERY *looks up annoyed.*] Just a minute please, if you don't mind. [SOL *looks gloomier than ever and waits, listening to the conversation with a frown.*] Hello, sweet... yes, your voice sounds a little vague... is the whole crowd there?... no, I'm tied up in knots... Sure I can hear the ice tinkling in the shaker— I'll try to make the dinner party, but if I don't I'll turn up at the theatre... Cheerio! [He *rings off, rises, addresses* SOL *with pleasant but rather condescending courtesy.*] Sorry to keep you waiting.

SOL [Imitating *his polite manner*] Don't mention it, we enjoyed the cocktails! [SOL *is assembling his data on the desk.*]

JEFFERY [Turns *to* SARAH] I'm missing an excellent party... but it can't be helped! I guess big things are afoot around here, aren't they, Miss Glassman?

SARAH I really can't discuss it.

JEFFERY Sonnenberg gave *me* the impression he was going to take an active interest here.

SOL Yeh, he gave me an earful too— "Ginsberg," he says, "let's throw out the college boys an' get some real men in this lousy concern." [JEFFERY *looks at* SOL *angrily.* SARAH, *worried, puts her hand on* SOL'S *arm.*]

SARAH Please—

JEFFERY [With *an attempt to be very dignified and severe*] I've had enough from you, Ginsberg.

SOL I had plenty from you.

JEFFERY I'm civil and I expect other people to be civil in return.

SOL Yeh, you were civil yesterday when you bawled me out in front of the whole office. ...

JEFFERY I told you you'd given me a set of inaccurate figures and caused me a lot of trouble. ...

SOL Them figures was right an' your stenographer copied 'em wrong.

JEFFERY [Calmly *feeling quite master of the situation*] You're an assistant clerk here, Ginsberg: when a member of the staff criticizes your work you ought to take it in the right spirit and remedy the mistake— If you'll bear it in mind, I shall be entirely civil to you.

SOL [Trying *to control himself*] If you're not civil, I'll take care of it in my own way.
[DINAH MCCABE *enters right.*]

DINAH Mr. Halliburton, Mr. Rogers, from Ryan and Malevinsky is here to see you about the Sunday spread.

JEFFERY Good Lord! I'd forgotten all about it. [He *hurries through the door right, calling to* SARAH *as he goes.*] Call me the minute Mr. Merritt's ready. [He *exits.*]

SOL I'll show him.

DINAH What's the matter, Mr. Ginsberg? Did Mr. Halliburton bawl you out again?

SOL Never mind.

DINAH [Looking *around to see that no one is within earshot*] I don't like him either... every time I make a mistake he says he's gonna have me canned—

SOL Why don't you use your sex appeal, kid? Next time he calls you down, jump on his lap an' rumple his hair— that's Miss Glassman's system with the boss an' look how well she's gettin' on.

SARAH Oh, shut up, Sol! [SOL *has seated himself on* MERRITT'S *desk.*]

DINAH You got your nerve, sittin' on the boss's desk.

SOL It's my desk now, he give it to me— You see, I'm a fraternity brother of his, so he says to me, "Take this money-trap home, I'm gonna install a pool-table here for myself an' the staff!"

DINAH Gee, you're fresh... If I told on you, you'd get fired! [She *flounces out right, leaving the door open.*]

SARAH [Coming *to* SOL *seriously*] Don't you know she'll repeat every word you say? You couldn't pick a better way to lose your job!

SOL I know it... I know what I'm doin'!

SARAH If you feel that way, why don't you tell Merritt to his face, instead of making silly jokes behind his back?

SOL I will! I'm gonna walk in here and spill some things to Merritt that will make his hair curl!

SARAH You'd better think twice.

SOL I thought a hundred times.

SARAH It's a big step to quit.

SOL [Shrugs *uneasily*] Sick of it, that's all.

SARAH Wait... [Speaking *as she crosses to open door right*] I want to ask you something... [She *shuts the door. During the following scenes, both* SARAH *and* SOL *speak in rather low voices.*] What are you going to do if you quit here? Have you got any plan, or are you going to be just as confused as you are now?

SOL I ain't confused— this place don't suit me— there's nuthin' in it for me.

SARAH You're getting more money than you ever got in your life before.

SOL Yeh... twenty-five a week, an' you get seven bucks more than I do—

SARAH At least it's nice for us to work in the same office.

SOL It's nice for *you* — you're in a soft spot— you're a swell secretary locked in here with the boss— everybody yeses you 'cause you're on the inside— you don't get kicked around an' spat at by loafers like Halliburton—

SARAH Why don't you have a frank talk with Mr. Merritt? Maybe he'd give you a raise and put you in another department.

SOL Yeh! Maybe he'd make me vice-president an' general manager— when I come in here a little while ago, he didn't even know my name— treated me like an office boy—

SARAH He asked me who you were—

SOL Did he?

SARAH [Nods] He tries to be nice to everybody— I worked for three other concerns before I came here and he's the only human being I ever had for a boss.

SOL Oh, I got his number all right— he's a lazy smartaleck— he gets big accounts 'cause he's a hand shaker an' he belongs to a lot of nifty clubs— all he's gotta do is sit here an' rake in the dough— [*He opens a drawer of* MERRITT'S *desk.*]

SARAH I wouldn't do that if I were you.

SOL Cards an' cigars— I'll bet he sits here playin' solitaire. Where does he keep his liquor?

SARAH In the library— Please stop looking through those drawers— I know more about Mr. Merritt than you do... he *does* waste a lot of time, but that's his way of working; I take his dictation and I ought to know; this is a complicated business and he's got his finger on every part of it—

SOL He's got his finger on you all right.

SARAH He's decent and he's intelligent—he makes money because he's got a lot of personality and a nose for business—

SOL What about my nose? Does it look bad to you?

SARAH What's the matter with you, Sol—what have you got against Mr. Merritt?

SOL Go on, sleep with him!

SARAH Sol—

SOL That's what your raving about his personality amounts to—He's soft on you an' you eat it alive— Personality, bah! Don't you know where he keeps his? Go on, I don't blame you... maybe he'll raise our salary two bucks a week!

SARAH So that's what you think? That's what our love amounts to?

SOL Why don't you set that to music?

SARAH I can't stand your going on like this—I'm the one you hurt—you like to hurt me, you like it. ...

SOL No... I don't mean to hurt you. ...

SARAH You and me are the same... we're everything to each other... I hope. ...

SOL [Gruffly, *very much touched*] We said so enough times!

SARAH couldn't live without you, Sol; I mean the future for us
together. I'd die without you.

SOL Yeh, we dreamed about the future, but it don't get any nearer.

SARAH That's up to us, if we care enough—

SOL [Interrupting *her*] Don't now... you hurt me... [He *kisses her,
pushes her away roughly*.] There's no future without money, I must get
it... I been waiting for a break ever since I was born!

SARAH We had one good break, each other.

SOL What good is that? When you're in bad with life, two is no better
than one.

SARAH Two people can stand together, protect each other.

SOL Protect!... thicken your skin, kid, you need a thick skin, you're too
soft.

SARAH So are you; you're soft and emotional as a woman.

SOL Aw hell!

SARAH You don't look it, but I know.

SOL Maybe I was soft, but I'm gettin' over it fast.

SARAH You have changed some, Sol.

SOL Sure I'm changin'. I had enough watchin' other people rake in the
money, people like that fool, Merritt— [He *points to the desk, derisive
and defiant, as if* MERRITT *were actually sitting in the empty chair*.]
Sometime I'll get my mitts on that bozo an' when he comes up for air
he'll be all bloody, an' then I'll bust up the whole place 'cause it smells

of money... break up these little partitions that shut off one fool from another fool... to Hell with 'em, yours for the revolution, signed, Solomon Ginsberg!

SARAH That would be a big help for the revolution, wouldn't it? [*Pleading*] You and me have learned a lot together, we've studied and read and gone to meetings. ...

SOL Sure, we're chock full of Marx and Lenin, but when you come up against a cheap capitalist grafter like Merritt, you fall for him.

SARAH That's childish, Sol... why don't you grow up and see things straight?... we both know there's crazy social injustice... that's no reason for gettin' sore at *people*...

SOL What does all the talk mean? It means we ain't got a look-in on the cash, an' we're sore at them that's got it.

SARAH It means a great deal more than that to me.

SOL I'm sick to death of radical meetings an' sour-faced people an' cheap gab. ...

SARAH We can't help being part of a system, but we can keep our heads clear.

SOL On twenty-five dollars?

SARAH But your spirit, Sol, your spirit?

SOL My father had a spirit too, him an' me used to sit in his newsstand under the El at Houston Street till his spirit went up one night an' he froze dead under my eyes.

SARAH You're exaggerating as usual.

SOL Oh it's near enough... anyway the old man died two weeks later an' he caught cold in the stand, didn't he?... When I think a' the old boy... [*Shaking off the idea*] Oh what's the use?... You an' me ain't even workers, we're white collar slaves in a business built out a' smart lies.

SARAH I'd rather be here than working in a factory for eight dollars a week like most of the girls I know.

SOL I can't help seein' that the revolution ain't gonna happen next week... Say, I wouldn't be surprised if it didn't happen all summer.

SARAH Can't you look just a little farther ahead?

SOL Sure, but when's my pay-day?

SARAH That's cheap—

SOL You're the cheap one; you get such a kick out of your own ravings, you don't look at facts... I'll spend my life waitin' for a break, an' never get it... You know how hot the sand is on your bare feet down at Coney? Them's the years I see, walkin' with blistered feet over them hot years, nuthin' but the sky ahead, till the pearly gates open in the sky an' there isn't any more.

SARAH You must forget yourself and worry about other things.

SOL Not me, I got myself on my mind!

SARAH That's unhealthy.

SOL Who, me? Unhealthy? [The *door opens right, and* MERRITT *enters with* MARCUS TURNER. *The two men are walking arm in arm chatting and laughing as they come.* TURNER *is a heavy-jowled sensual man of forty-five; he might have been a prominent member of the bar, but has preferred to devote himself to women and liquor. He now has a comfortable berth as counsel for the Raymond Merritt Company at twenty-five thousand a year. He is invaluable to* MERRITT, *who likes him and understands him.*]

TURNER [As *they walk in, evidently telling a long anecdote*] The old hens were furious, said I had no right to bring a woman like that to the country club.

MERRITT Did you leave?

TURNER I'll say we didn't; we got tight and Myrtle nearly wrecked the place. [Neither *of the men pay any attention to* SOL *and* SARAH, *who stand waiting.*]

MERRITT [*Turning to door, left rear*] Come in here, we'll have a little thirst quencher.

TURNER That's exactly what I'm looking for, R. M. [*They walk into the library left, shutting the door.* SOL *looks after them with bitter disgust.*]

SOL Saps... gold-plated saps!

SARAH It's up to you? Are you going to stick here and adjust yourself— or are you going to wear out shoe leather looking for another job?

SOL I dunno... I want somethin' real—either make real money, or else... work for somethin' I believe in.

SARAH But you've got to be practical—there's a real chance here—

SOL One chance in a hundred.

SARAH Sure, it's one in a thousand anywhere else. Do you want to go back to being a waiter in that kosher quick lunch?

SOL It's with my own kind at least. I got no place in this genteel racket—I wisht I had the nerve to learn to be a gunman like my brother—

SARAH You were called to something else, you got to be true to what you're called to.

SOL What— [TURNER *and* MERRITT *re-enter left rear.*]

TURNER Excellent, I must have a few cases sent up to my place.

MERRITT [*Going to his desk*] It's the smoothest rye I've been able to find.

TURNER I think I'll duck... I'll have a conference with Sonnenberg's attorney in the morning, and then we'll know where we stand.

MERRITT You're convinced that the set-up is O. K.?

TURNER With the proper legal safeguards, it's magnificent, R. M. Cheerio! [*He turns away, nodding genially to* MISS GLASSMAN.] Good night, Miss Glassman.

SARAH Good night. [TURNER *exits right.* MERRITT *looks at* SOL *who is waiting sullenly*.]

MERRITT What are you hanging around for?

SOL I came in to get that stuff from my files, Mr. Merritt. [*Approaching the desk*] But that ain't all... I want to talk to you.

MERRITT [*Looking up at* SOL *with friendly interest, sizing him up*] Is that so? All right, stick around a while; if I don't get to it this evening, I'll see you tomorrow. [SOL *nods and starts to take the folders from desk.* MERRITT *puts his hand on the folders*.] Leave them here—I'll look 'em over. [SARAH *is watching nervously*.] Your name's Ginsberg, isn't it?

SOL That's right.

MERRITT You seem to do good work on this stuff.

SOL That ain't the half of it.

MERRITT Huh!

SOL I mean I do better than that.

MERRITT You Jews are a funny lot, you beat the Dutch.

SOL Every time.

MERRITT Sometime I'm going to give you a big chance.

SOL Why not today?

MERRITT It's too hot today, you wouldn't want a chance— [*Dismissing him with a wave of his hand*] I'll send for you later, Ginsberg.

SOL I'll be waitin'. [He *turns and exits.*]

MERRITT I told you to sign these letters and send them out.

SARAH I know it... frankly, Mr. Ginsberg and I have been talking ever since you left.

MERRITT Really? I appreciate your frankness. If people said what they meant, business would be cleaner.

SARAH I'm afraid there wouldn't be any advertising, Mr. Merritt.

MERRITT I begin to value you very highly, Miss Glassman.

SARAH You mean you're trying to value me, you're not sure yet.

MERRITT No, when I get the value settled I'll make my offer.

SARAH Below market figures?

MERRITT That's sagacious, isn't it?

SARAH You'll have to bid pretty high, Mr. Merritt.

MERRITT Tell me, Miss Glassman, what are you after?

SARAH I'm after keeping my job, it means a lot to me—without getting in any more disagreeable talks with you—

MERRITT I don't mean that—I mean what do you want in life? Everybody's got some key that they're after—that's the secret of advertising.

SARAH Oh... what about yourself?

MERRITT I'm pretty much at sea—that's why I ask you... If you knew me, you'd like me and maybe feel sorry for me—

SARAH You!

MERRITT I don't get much out of life, in fact I make rather a mess of it... I'm not even as rich as people think I am... you ought to know that, you handle all the money. ...

SARAH From my standards, you're disgustingly rich.

MERRITT Am I? What sort of people do you come from?

SARAH Very poor... East Side... You can't picture it.

MERRITT Funny the way we're caught together way up here in a tower. A lot of queer fish in a money net. [Telephone *rings.* SARAH *answers it.*]

SARAH Yes, Mr. Merritt will speak to him. [Handing *phone to* MERRITT] Mr. Albert Flannigan.

MERRITT [*On phone*] Hello, Flannigan... yes, that's substantially correct. You're damn right, we'll sell it at twenty-eight dollars. Ask your own stenographer if she won't pay twenty-eight dollars for a cream made out of alligator glands—genuine eighteen karat alligator glands—I've seen the alligators myself! There's big money behind it and I advise you to get on the bandwagon... you've never lost money by taking my advice yet... Good for you, Flannigan—give my best to the missus. [*He rings off, sits back amused.*] Glamour Cream is driving the beauty trade crazy.

SARAH It sounds swell. I wish I had some.

MERRITT I'll give you a few jars, but you don't need it... Glamour Cream for you is just painting the lily.

SARAH I think it will sell, Mr. Merritt, just because it is so expensive... women are all alike... they want anything that costs a lot and looks showy.

MERRITT Are *you* like that?

SARAH A little. ...

MERRITT [*Glances at clock*] It's after six now—we'll go and get some cocktails at a little place on Forty-fourth Street.

SARAH No thanks.

MERRITT Afraid?

SARAH Don't be ridiculous. Afraid of you! That is, I just mean you're a gentleman, and you're very nice to work for; it's great here but you see I was expecting this.

MERRITT Are you a mind reader?

SARAH You're easy. I can tell how a man looks at me, besides you raised my salary; it's not much, but it means something from you; you wouldn't do that for no reason. Then again you never held my hand or touched me, which is so unusual it makes a girl expect the worst, that's how I knew it was coming. Now if I got enough breath, I'll tell you why I gotta say no... First 'cause I got brains, that's a big enough reason right there, but second cause you'd despise me.

MERRITT Not a bit of it.

SARAH Well, maybe not, I guess I'm bright enough to keep you guessing, but anyway I got another fellow.

MERRITT I'll say you cover the ground, but reasons don't count in these matters; I might be able to make you happy a little.

SARAH That's Christian of you, but you see I'm Jewish and miserable.

MERRITT Score one, I have no answer... But give me credit, I don't do this sort of thing often.

SARAH Oh yes you do, I'm your secretary and I ought to know.

MERRITT Score two... but my interest in women is just nervousness... I'm so bored: nothing I want outside this office— now you haven't told me what you want? The inside thing that makes you so sure of yourself?

SARAH If I told you, you'd think I was crazy—a kind of ideal you couldn't dream of.

MERRITT You haven't much respect for my character, have you?

SARAH You're nice but you don't go very deep.

MERRITT Ideals, huh. [*He walks around the room, nervous and depressed.*] Maybe that's what I need. Funny, isn't it? We work together for years without any human contact—

SARAH I'm sorry for you now I know you a little better.

MERRITT I won't bother you this way again... I don't want to lose you— [*He stops short as* AGNES CARTER *enters right. She is a delicious blonde, beautiful and slightly artificial, expensively and charmingly dressed. A creamy complexion, and large melting eyes*]

AGNES I just dashed in; can I see you for a minute, Raymond?

MERRITT For a minute only, Aggie.

AGNES Don't look so sour, Raymond, Miss Glassman wasn't in her office so I just walked in... it's late and I thought you were all alone.

SARAH [*To* MERRITT *as she turns to leave*] You won't forget about Mr. Halliburton, will you?

MERRITT There's nobody I'd rather forget.

SARAH And Mr. Ginsberg?

MERRITT Miss Carter will only be here two minutes.

AGNES Don't you believe him, Miss Glassman; I'll stay as long as I like.

SARAH I'm sure you will. [*She exits.*]

MERRITT [*Marching about the room nervously*] You're really impossible, Aggie; you have no sense of proportion.

AGNES What's the idea? Are you having an affair with Miss Glassman?

MERRITT I'm simply thinking of appearances. You sweep in here as if you were bringing a message from the Pope; this is my office.

AGNES [*Rising*] Shall I go back and do it all over again? [*Turning to the door*]

MERRITT Don't be absurd. What do you want?

AGNES Money—money—money—

MERRITT Charming, you're so nice and subtle about it.

AGNES I'm much too nice to be subtle and you know it... I don't know how to be coy, and you wouldn't like me if I were... If I'm not satisfactory, you can kick me off the payroll.

MERRITT You're one of the most annoying women the devil ever created. The way you get rid of money is simply delirious. What do you do with it?

AGNES It burns my fingers. Every time you give me a check I feel so immoral I run out and buy a dozen new gowns!

MERRITT You're crazy. [*He rings buzzer on desk.*]

AGNES A little... but I'm honest... I know you, and I know myself and I have no girlish illusions.
[*SARAH enters right.*]

MERRITT Will you make out a check please... the usual amount?

AGNES I'm sorry to trouble you, Miss Glassman.

SARAH Oh, it's no trouble at all. [*She exits.*]

MERRITT [*Calling after* SARAH] I'll sign it for her as she goes out.

AGNES I wonder what she thinks of it?

MERRITT She thinks it's shockingly indecent, and she's damn glad she's an honest woman.

AGNES That's where I'm right with her.

MERRITT What? Want a job in the office, Aggie?

AGNES No... I haven't got the character. ...

MERRITT Then don't be so morbid; everything between us has been square and on the level. We trust each other, we're good pals, and we have an exceptionally straight-forward understanding.

AGNES Sure, as far as it goes it's swell—

MERRITT What's really on your mind? Sore at me?

AGNES Not at you, you big slob... I'm sore about money, because you've got it and I haven't and it's so damn important—

MERRITT I notice you take it freely.

AGNES Sure, that's what makes me so mad.

MERRITT You're a scream, a pathetic little thing who simply can't make both ends meet on a thousand a month.

AGNES You're generous, in fact you're rather a fool to be as generous as you are.

MERRITT Then why complain about your tragic fate?

AGNES It isn't tragic. It's undignified—

MERRITT And what do you suggest to give it dignity?

AGNES Why don't we make it nicer? Why don't you marry me, Ray?

MERRITT Is money the chief consideration?

AGNES I'm too honest to pretend it's not, but money in a big clean way!

MERRITT You don't love me?

AGNES No, but I might get to, if I had plenty of leisure to concentrate my mind on it!... and you must consider, you're pretty crazy about me.

MERRITT No, I'm not.

AGNES Oh, be yourself, Ray... you know how you feel!

MERRITT I've given it considerable thought, Aggie; I have a lot of respect for you.

AGNES That's a funny thing to say—

MERRITT Why not? You're hard boiled and wise and a hundred percent decent—you're an unusual girl, and you could probably make some man very happy.

AGNES But not you?

MERRITT Not me. ...

AGNES How do you figure that out?

MERRITT You've got no soul—

AGNES Neither have you, you old codfish, that's why we're so well suited.

MERRITT Maybe I want a soul.

AGNES Good Grief, are you getting mushy on someone else?

MERRITT I don't know—

AGNES Oh—but you don't see anything wrong in going on the way we are?

MERRITT Why not? What's a little sex among friends?

AGNES It's fair enough... but it's not very romantic.

MERRITT Your marriage suggestion isn't very romantic either.

AGNES No, but you see, I want either one thing or the other—one side a' me wants security an' comfort—I've always figured I'd marry somebody dull, rich and kind—

MERRITT And I'm the type?

AGNES Yes you're that and more—you're a great pal. I suppose that's all you can ask for—no use looking for anything better.

MERRITT Better?

AGNES It's no good chasing after something mad and wonderful that doesn't exist— men are all soft-brained mahogany ninnies, like you— aren't there any romantic people in the world?

MERRITT Try Spain.

AGNES People who can squeeze a girl breathless, and go mad with adoration!

MERRITT Find some young kid if you want that.

AGNES I don't like 'em young.

MERRITT Is that so? Well you won't make a dream daddy out of me... I advertise every preparation that goes to make you wonderful—

AGNES Then you admit I am?

MERRITT You do a good job on your carcass, it's the way you fix it up that makes men go crazy—if they're a little cracked to start with! I'm still sane and I'm busy, so that's that. [*He leads her towards door right.*] Go around to Giovanni's and get a Tom Collins, I'll be over as soon as I get through.

AGNES Half an hour?

MERRITT Maybe less, go on now.

AGNES All right, but I don't mind telling you you're a pig.

MERRITT Thanks, why?

AGNES Just your nature... nothing gets you, talk about soul, my foot! You're just a nice good-natured pig doing a big business in slops. [MERRITT *opens door right, bows to her politely.*]

MERRITT Just for that I'll see you to the elevator!

AGNES [*Laughing as they exit right.*] And the check? Don't keep me waiting more than half an hour, Ray; I'm likely to get tight. [*They are off scene right, leaving door open. Outside the windows, the twilight has deepened to grey. The lamp on desk left makes half the room bright, the rest in partial shadow.*]

JEFFERY [*Entering room right*] Now I'll see him or bust.

SARAH [*Following JEFFERY into the room*] I presume he's ready for you now, Mr. Halliburton.

JEFFERY If I had women wasting my time in business hours, I'd be fired.

SARAH No doubt. [SOL *enters right.*]

SOL I seen him taking that Jane to the elevator. What's the chances a' getting in now, Sarah? [*She shrugs non-commitally.*]

JEFFERY You'll have to wait, I have an important conference with Mr. Merritt—

SOL It's up to him to tell me whether I wait or not, not you!

JEFFERY Are you going to start this again, Ginsberg?

SOL That's up to you.

JEFFERY I don't like to be talked to in that tone of voice, and I don't like to be threatened— [SARAH *looks on very worried.*] I'm willing to drop the matter if you are—if not. ...

SOL If not, what?

JEFFERY If not, you can go straight to hell— [SOL *suddenly walks up to* JEFFERY *in a furious temper, seizes his necktie and pulls him violently to his feet by it.*]

SOL You little college shrimp— I could shake the stuffings out of you with one hand. [JEFFERY *starts to shake himself loose, pounding* SOL'S *side with his fist.* MERRITT *enters briskly right.*]

MERRITT What the hell is this? [SOL *releases* JEFFERY.] This isn't Madison Square Garden— what's the idea?

JEFFERY [*Arranging himself*] This tough guy threatened to shake the stuffings out of me.

MERRITT Did you indeed? Why?

SOL Just to see the sawdust fly!

MERRITT [*Looks* SOL *over sharply, turns*] Get out!

SOL I'm on my way— you and your high hat fraternity brothers from Yale are all of a piece to me, Mr. Merritt. You don't want any one around here with brains enough to stand on their own feet— you got a lot of saps in this office that don't know their jobs— all they know is how to go down on their knees and pray every time you look at them— I don't like the place, I don't like the way it's run and I don't think so much of you.

MERRITT You're fired.

SOL You can't fire me, I've quit.

MERRITT Be out of the place in ten minutes. [SOL *turns on his heel and exits right.* MERRITT *turns to* SARAH.] Make out a slip to the cashier to send him his pay to five o'clock this afternoon. [SARAH *nods and exits.*] Sit down, Jeffery.

JEFFERY [*Sitting*] Well done, Mr. Merritt.

MERRITT Don't be so cocky— I imagine it was your fault as well as his— [*He chuckles.*] I rather like his nerve.

JEFFERY [*Holds out the yellow sheets of copy that have been lying on the desk*] Have you had time to look this over?

MERRITT No... [*He glances at the sheets.*] I'll tell you one thing at first glance— the types you indicate simply aren't practical— they won't fit with the layout of the page.

JEFFERY I tried to get something novel, use imagination—

MERRITT What do you think you're doing? Writing a story for the Yale monthly? [*He tosses the sheets on the desk disgustedly.*]

JEFFERY You're not fair; I've given deep thought to this Glamour Cream proposition and you don't take the trouble to read it—

MERRITT No, and there's a hundred million people just like me! No woman's going to plow through this essay— it would have to be set up in midget type to squeeze it on the page— you use three bad adjectives instead of one good one— [*Presses a key on the dictaphone.*] No answer, Dennis has gone home for the day. [*He rings the buzzer under his desk.*]

JEFFERY You don't have to hand it over to Dennis; I'll sweat blood to get this right.

MERRITT Your blood won't sell Glamour Cream and neither will your goddamn copy— what's the deadline on this?

JEFFERY It ought to go tonight, it can be taken by special messenger at nine o'clock tomorrow morning. [SARAH *enters right, notebook in hand.*]

MERRITT See if you can get Dennis at his house— if he's not there, leave word he's to come to the office any hour he gets in. [*She nods and exits.*] Dennis and I will have to spend the night dishing up this stuff... [JEFFERY *starts to speak* , MERRITT *stops him with a wave of his hand.*] That's all, Jeffery. ...

JEFFERY You're not fair, Mr. Merritt.

MERRITT I'm so fair that I'm giving you another chance. Go out and get drunk, maybe that'll make you forget you're a bright young man.

JEFFERY All right, sir. [*He exits.*] [SARAH *enters right.*]

SARAH Mr. Dennis won't be home till eleven; they're trying to trace him, but they don't know where he is.

MERRITT Christ alive, I'd like to kill that sap.

SARAH Which one?

MERRITT Halliburton.

SARAH Yes sir, Ginsberg felt the same way.

MERRITT Don't kid me, Miss Glassman, I'm in no mood for it. [*She says nothing, he starts to look at the Glamour Cream copy, but he can't keep his mind on it. He mutters between his teeth.*] Am I running a business or a nut-house? [*Throwing the copy on the desk*] I'd better get some dinner and some drinks before I tackle this. Can you work tonight?

SARAH Of course.

MERRITT [*Rises*] Want to dine with me?

SARAH No. ...

MERRITT What's the matter? Feeling bad because your boyfriend spilled the beans?

SARAH Yes, I wanted to speak to you about that.

MERRITT Don't worry, I don't hold it against *you*.

SARAH If you're really as clever as I think you are, you wouldn't hold it against *him*.

MERRITT What!

SARAH Of course he had no right to fly off the handle the way he did, but what does that matter if he's got brains?

MERRITT I don't want lunatics around this office, Miss Glassman... I want sane people that work hard and keep their mouths shut.

SARAH He's worked like a dog over those statistics— he's been here every night, that's why he's in such a nervous state.

MERRITT Oh... On your account, Miss Glassman, I'll take him round to my club for dinner.

SARAH Not quite that—

MERRITT Maybe it would be enough if I petted him and gave him a lollipop.

SARAH If you should take him back now, he'd be tied to you for life.

MERRITT Thanks, I'd rather have him tied some other place. ...

SARAH He's got imagination and he knows a lot about business— he's studied everything about it.

MERRITT Is it an affair, you and him?

SARAH Not how you mean. It's something quite different.

MERRITT Spiritual? Well, let's have another look at this very spiritual young man. [*Picks up phone on desk.*] Hello, Beulah, has Ginsberg left yet? Oh, send him to my office.

SARAH You're quite nice, Mr. Merritt.

MERRITT I'll give him a chance to apologize.

SARAH If you let him go you're missing a chance to get a first rate man and get him cheap. Besides it would amuse you!

MERRITT I don't want to play God, Miss Glassman, especially to a kid from the Ghetto, who seems to hate me poisonously. [*A knock is heard on door right.*] That sounds humble, at any rate. [SARAH *hurries to the door and opens it;* SOL *enters sullen and worried.*]

MERRITT Come in, Ginsberg, have you anything to say for yourself? [*He sits at his desk.*]

SOL Yes, I have ...

MERRITT Out with it.

SOL What I said was true, but I was a fool to say it.

MERRITT That's not an apology.

SOL I was dead wrong to lose my temper; I... well, in a way I'm sorry; what I think is nobody's business but my own and I was a fool to say what I did. [*He turns to go.*]

MERRITT Wait a minute. That's all, Miss Glassman. Sit down, Ginsberg. [SOL *sits uneasily;* SARAH *takes a nervous look from the door right and exits.*] To admit one's a fool is the beginning of success.

SOL If you wanna give me a success talk, I suppose I've gotta listen.

MERRITT Hold on to yourself, kid... the reason you're so ready to blow up is that you're absolutely lacking in self-confidence. You have guts enough to give me a good drubbing down, but you haven't got guts enough to sit here and talk it over ...

SOL What do you expect me to do, put my feet on the desk an' take a fistful of cigars?

MERRITT [*Shoving the silver cigar container towards him.*] I beg your pardon, have a cigar.

SOL [*Taking one, gingerly*] Say, what are you trying to do?

MERRITT Conducting a little experiment in human values!

SOL You're a great josher, Mr. Merritt.

MERRITT Yes, that's one of my many faults... now keep your shirt on and tell me what's wrong?

SOL It's just that we're all so afraid of you here— an' you sit there kidding us along. I'm as good as you are an' it makes me sore bein' scared green.

MERRITT I've received a very high recommendation of you.

SOL From who? I don't know anybody.

MERRITT Miss Glassman. She says you're a square peg in a round hole.

SOL If that's a dirty crack, it's way over my head.

MERRITT I like your independence— I think you and I might reach some sort of understanding.

SOL Huh... [*He indicates the cigar in his hand.*] Have one yourself, this hasheesh is elegant.

MERRITT Let's get down to cases, what's your objection to your present work?

SOL It's dry— I ain't cut out for drawing up figures an' makin' lines on a chart— the first month I liked it, 'cause it gives me a picture a' the way the wheels go round ...

MERRITT You think you know it all now?

SOL Maybe!

MERRITT Have you read any of our copy?

SOL All of it; I went over all the stuff for the last two years in the files.

MERRITT What do you think of it?

SOL Rotten.

MERRITT Could you do better?

SOL If I couldn't I'd hop out of this window.

MERRITT Any other suggestions?

SOL Yeh... you're wastin' dough by the ton... you could save money in every department by usin' a little common sense.

MERRITT If you have any concrete suggestions, make a memorandum of them; make it detailed and concise; have it on my desk in the morning.

SOL I don't know whether I'll be here in the morning.

MERRITT Suppose you found yourself in a congenial job, with a private office, and a secretary, and an assured future.

SOL I'd take it.

MERRITT That's nice of you. There's something about you that puzzles me, Ginsberg— you're not frank— you're bitter as gall—
SOL You think so?

MERRITT What's in the back of your head, Ginsberg?

SOL I got brains both in the back an' the front, Mr. Merritt.

MERRITT That's not an answer.

SOL I'll give you an answer— since I was fifteen I been readin' an' studyin'... I'm a radical.

MERRITT Good, so am I.

SOL You don't know the meanin' of the word.

MERRITT Think the times are out of joint, do you?

SOL I know it.

MERRITT Go on.

SOL The way I figure it out, all this Capitalist graft is gonna bust up sooner or later.

MERRITT No doubt... what are you going to do in the meantime?

SOL That's what worries me.

MERRITT All right, my boy, I don't care whether you're a radical or a democrat— but I advise you to be alive; don't worry about dead issues.

SOL The bunch I know don't think it's a dead issue.

MERRITT Your opinions are of no consequence to me— in fact I think they're a joke.

SOL You would, it's all a joke to you.

MERRITT Go ahead, get looking higher, you'll think it's a joke too— then maybe you'll get almost rich and you'll think everything's a joke.

SOL If you wanna make me rich, Mr. Merritt, hop to it, see if I care.

MERRITT I'll give you a trial at fifty a week. Do you appreciate that?

SOL No, I think you're gettin' the best of it.

MERRITT Oh, you're doing *me* a favor?

SOL [*Nods*] When do I begin?

MERRITT Right now. [*He picks up the Glamour Cream copy.*] Just give me your reaction to this copy! [*He reads.*] Glamour Cream, the medical skin food, put it on at night, it penetrates the cells of the skin, works while you sleep.

SOL Sounds like somethin' for bedbugs.

MERRITT I agree with you, that's the wrong sales approach. I suppose you're familiar with the product— the latest and most expensive skin rejuvenator.

SOL Sure I know about it.

MERRITT It contains the glandular fluid of genuine alligators!

SOL I wouldn't lay that on too thick in the copy— no dame wants to look like an alligator!

MERRITT I believe in the stuff— I believe it can be a knockout in the luxury trade—

SOL It's a tough thing to put over at that price.

MERRITT Twenty-eight dollars a jar.

SOL You gotta put this stuff in a class with platinum and radium—

MERRITT Can you do it?

SOL God, I'll try—

MERRITT Sit down at my desk, make a rough set-up of your ideas— I'll be back in an hour or two.

SOL O.K. [*He sits at* MERRITT'S *desk.* SARAH *enters right.*]

SARAH Mr. Dennis is on the wire— they reached him where he was dining.

MERRITT Tell him to keep in touch with the office. You better get a bite to eat, Miss Glassman. I'll be back at nine. [SARAH *exits right.*] I can see you got a great gift for words, Ginsberg, you fool yourself with 'em— for the first time in your life, you're using words to fool other people. [*He exits left front.* SARAH *has returned right. She looks at* SOL *excitedly.*]

SARAH I'm glad, Sol; I knew it would happen.

SOL Fifty a week... to start...

SARAH You see, you were wrong about him—

SOL Don't be a fool, I haven't changed my mind about him— but I see my way— I can see dollar bills bein' thrown around like confetti—

SARAH I'll go over to the automat and bring you back some sandwiches.

SOL Bring back a pint a' coffee, too. [*She starts to go, turns back and looks at* SOL, *hesitatingly.*]

SARAH Sol... I want you to kiss me before I go—

SOL Cut it out, there's a time for everything—

SARAH Sol ...

SOL Get away— just 'cause I'm sittin' at his desk you don't have to treat me like you do him.

SARAH If you believe that, I'm going to quit tonight.

SOL No, you're not; why should you quit when everything's breaking so pretty? Sell your personality... me too! Don't think you're putting anything over on me— I'm here 'cause he's nuts about you... I don't care... nuthin' matters but get your hands on the cash... personalities for sale cheap!

SARAH Do you love me, Sol?

SOL Go on, I'll write you a letter about it.

SARAH Stop talking like you were possessed with the Devil, and listen to me a minute.

SOL I'm busy; I'm sold to the devil; I'm writin' copy—

SARAH I'm scared, that's all... where it may lead if you fall for it like this.

SOL Stuffed pockets an' a white shirt with a diamond stickpin... God, that's a long way off, there's no need for you to look mushy about it.

SARAH We must hold onto each other, Sol, I need you... now more'n ever... you need me... we're in danger ...

SOL Go way, you're makin' it up.

SARAH Then you don't love me?

SOL I dunno... love's not bread and butter, it's champagne, fine for them that can afford it.

SARAH Two people can't go on the way we are, wantin' each other an' stayin' apart ...

SOL We've done it so far—

SARAH What keeps us apart, huh? What makes us hurt each other all the time?

SOL I do... me. Oh, I'm sick a' the gab, gab about love, gab about social injustice— maybe this here job is a way a' gettin' down to brass tacks.

SARAH And I? Where do I fit in?

SOL Maybe you do an' maybe you don't—

SARAH But you told me I was the only girl—

SOL You're the only girl I seen; there's a lot of men in the world an' I only seen a few.

SARAH Your pride is something terrible, Sol.

SOL You don't know the half of it, so don't come crawlin' to me sayin' love... I take what I want, I make up my mind— when I want you I tell you, see ...

SARAH [*Turns sadly to door right*] All right... I'll bring you coffee and sandwiches. [*She exits quickly.*]

SOL [*Shouts after her violently*] You got me in such a state I can't work, damn you! [SARAH *has gone.* SOL *walks around the room excitedly, mutters to himself.*] Just when I need a clear head she goes crazy on me— [*He is trembling with feeling. He stops short center and mutters with a grim smile as if he were addressing an invisible audience.*] Workers of the world, Unite, you got nothin' to lose but your chains— an' all you got to gain is baloney! [*He laughs shortly, strides back to desk and sits down. He takes a fresh cigar, lights it, and immerses himself in the copy on the desk, starting to make notes, etc.* AGNES *enters quietly right. He doesn't see her. She hesitates right, looking at the boy sitting earnestly at the desk in the lamp-light. She approaches the desk, stands looking down at him, attracted and interested.* SOL *raises his head, stares at her. For a second they look at one another speechless.*] Oh... I thought I smelled perfume? [AGNES *laughs.*]

AGNES Sorry to interrupt anybody that looks so busy.

SOL [*Still staring at her, taps with a pencil on the top of the desk, making a rhythmic ticking*] That's all right.

AGNES Thank you... do you know where Mr. Merritt is?

SOL No, he might be in any one of forty thousand speakeasies.

AGNES First time I ever heard anyone tell the truth in this office. How long ago did he leave?

SOL Ten minutes.

AGNES [*Glances at her watch*] Just as I thought— he stood me up— I was waiting in one place and he went somewhere else.

SOL He knows a lot a' places.

AGNES Can I wait?

SOL Can I stop you?

AGNES Would you mind telling me who you are?

SOL I don't know—

AGNES You don't know?

SOL No, sometimes I'm me an' other times I'm a couple of other fellers.

AGNES You say such odd things—

SOL I ain't much of a social light, Miss Carter.

AGNES Oh, you know who I am?

SOL Did you think anybody around this office didn't know who you are, Miss Carter?

AGNES Oh, I never thought of that; I suppose they do talk.

SOL Talk! If you'd hear some of it, it would burn your ears off.

AGNES My ears don't burn easily... I've never seen you; what's your job around here?

SOL Well, I been a kind a' combination office boy, statistician an' boot-black— maybe you'd care for a shine?

AGNES What are you doing in Mr. Merritt's office?

SOL Writin' a revolutionary manifesto.

AGNES What?

SOL Sure! Calling on the Russian peasants to smear their tractors with Glamour Cream at twenty-eight bucks an ounce.

AGNES If that's the case, I'll wait outside.

SOL If it's all the same to you, stick around a minute.

AGNES Why?

SOL I was standin' within a foot of you when Merritt showed you out this afternoon—

AGNES I didn't notice.

SOL I did— I mean, the perfume.

AGNES [Sitting on the desk carelessly] Oh... the perfume went to your head?

SOL I'm glad a' the chance to get a whiff a' that stuff.

AGNES So you liked me?

SOL I dunno, I ain't had time to dislike you, but that lavender water sure gets my nanny.

AGNES [Handing him her handkerchief] Have a good whiff!

SOL [*Smells the handkerchief rather suspiciously*] What do you call it?

AGNES Fievre d'Amour.

SOL How much does it cost?

AGNES I haven't the remotest idea.

SOL Do you use it all over you?

AGNES Not exactly... I use other things.

SOL I can just see you in a hot bath of this amour stuff—

AGNES That's indecent.

SOL [*Nods*] I heard worse. [*They stare at each other. A very definite feeling of contact between them. AGNES gets down from the desk. This is a little more than she bargained for. She turns to him, looking across the desk, rather defensively.*]

AGNES Tell me worse! Well...?

SOL [*As if speaking to himself instead of to her*] I got you now... I see you ...

AGNES In that bath? [*He nods.*] You don't waste any time, do you?

SOL I'm not wastin' time— I was sittin' here tryin' to think up catch-words for the luxury trade— tryin' to tell dolls about some magic grease they rub on themselves to turn 'em to gold— an' suddenly I look up an' you're standin' there.

AGNES In all my glory.

SOL Yeh... shinin' like a light... rubbed with magic grease to make you shine.

AGNES I'm not shiny.

SOL I mean glamour. See, this is beauty they get for twenty-eight dollars a pot; you're a pot a' that, see! You ain't much, but I never seen another girl like you that was rich just standin' in her skin like you... it's the thing that makes poets cuckoo!

AGNES Go on, you're cuckoo yourself!

SOL If I could get you on paper I'd have the luxury trade in a nut-shell.

AGNES What are you up to? What's the big idea?

SOL I'm writin' copy; you're doin' it for me, 'cause you're it, see!

AGNES No, I don't; is this a new gag?

SOL You should worry about what it means... any words will do: shine, sheen, sheer, shock a' your body, you stepped out of a little pot of gold, out of a genuine Grecian urn that contains the vitality that made the Greeks famous, any woman can help herself to Greek Vitality for twenty-eight dollars, make herself like Venus standin' before me, Venus risen out of a sea of Amour, which means love in French.

AGNES I guess you're a poet, but you got me in a fog.

SOL When I seen you I seen the whole game... the game a' women an' the things they buy... oh, you're too dumb to get the idea.

AGNES What's your name?

SOL Sol Ginsberg.

AGNES You're writing that for him?

SOL For Merritt, yes.

AGNES It doesn't matter whether it's good or bad, I'll make him push you along. He'll do anything I say. I'll tell him you're clever. God knows you're crazy enough to be terribly clever.

SOL Suppose I tell you what I think a' you?

AGNES You have, you told me I was Venus.

SOL Sure. D'you know what I think a' Venus? Beauty? Bah, what's beauty? Don't I know you're a rotter? Sure I do... You're a piece a' pink fluff for the luxury trade— what's more... you're a parasite, a slave, a white slave an' blood sister to a street walker.

AGNES You're out of luck from now on, Ginsberg—

SOL You're sore, 'cause I tell you what's what.

AGNES No... I kind of want you ...

SOL For a lover, you mean... is that what you mean, huh?

AGNES No, just to crack the whip over you, any man that's so mad must be easy to get. [*He still holds her handkerchief, crushing it and tearing it in his hands.*] Give me my handkerchief.

SOL No, I want it.

AGNES I need it.

SOL If I had a million dollars I'd buy you, 'cause your skin's all gold—

AGNES You wouldn't get me, so that's that.

SOL Wanna bet?

AGNES Get the million first, then I'll bet.

SOL I will ...

AGNES Wild, aren't you... crazy? You'd take me now and smash me... wouldn't you, with one hand? You'll be sorry you ever called me names... I'll crack the whip...

[CURTAIN]

ACT TWO

[*The same scene. A morning in the Fall, 1930. The office is unchanged in all essentials. Bright sunlight shines outside the big windows rear, mellowing the room. It is one of those lucid Autumn days, the sky as clear as crystal. The objects on the table are somewhat different, a jar of Glamour Cream among them. SARAH, wearing the same type of simple office dress as in Act I, sits at the desk, left center, telephone in hand.*]

SARAH [*At telephone, taking notes on pad in front of her*] Atlas Motors opened at ten and three-quarters, last sale nine and seven-eighths... a block of ten thousand shares... What about Warner Drug Products?... Yes... Universal Motors, thirty-eight and one-half; Colby Manufacturing seven— I'll tell him.
[*While SARAH has been talking , SOL has entered right, and listens to what she says. He is an altogether different person from the uncouth boy of the previous act. He is a brisk, self-possessed young business man, wearing a conservatively snappy blue suit.*]

SOL [*As SARAH rings off*] Not so good!

SARAH What?

SOL The market... a lot of jackasses thought we hit the bottom last summer— I knew better...

SARAH You know everything, don't you?

SOL Not quite— where's R-M?

SARAH Mr. Merritt hasn't come down yet.

SOL [*Picks up slip of paper which SARAH has placed in center of desk*] What a headache he'll have when he sees these figures— only ten-thirty and Atlas Motors is down a point— [*SARAH is silent.*] Lost quite heavily these last two months, hasn't he? [*SARAH nods.*] How much do you figure he's dropped?

SARAH Well, he's had to put up more collateral every day and it's been quite a drain on him— but he's able to hold on--

SOL I wonder how long...

SARAH What?

SOL How about Turner?

SARAH I think he's borrowed from Mr. Merritt—

SOL Huh! They must be in a stew— is that right?

SARAH Sol... I'm clever enough to know when I'm being pumped—

SOL Sure, I like to get the low-down, Sarah; it helps me to figure things out—

SARAH Figure out what?

SOL Oh, just what they're doing and how they do it.

SARAH Have you been losing in the market?

SOL Not me— I don't take their dumb tips— I been selling short and making money—
[DINAH *enters right with papers.*]

DINAH [*As she crosses*] From Mr. Fisher— he says this is urgent, Miss Glassman—

SARAH Thank you.

SOL [*Facing DINAH as she turns back toward right*] Tell me, Dinah, how do you like working on the statistics with Fisher?

DINAH I like it, Mr. Ginsberg. Mr. Fisher's just lovely to me.

SOL Sure, Fisher's a good old scout— I had your job once myself.

DINAH Yes, sir... [DINAH *exits.*]

SOL When do you expect R-M?

SARAH Any minute, he has an appointment with Mr. Sonnenberg at eleven-thirty.

SOL Sonnenberg? He's coming here? [SARAH *nods.*] Is that so? Got any idea what it's about?

SARAH Oh, the usual things I suppose, plans for the business! [*As* SOL *bangs the little bronze statue of a naked woman down on the desk hard*] — what are you so nervous about?

SOL I got lots on my mind... [*He sits on desk.*] What if I was your boss instead of Merritt? How would you like that?

SARAH What?

SOL Things move fast in this world— but I guess you wouldn't care... one man is just like another to you... you'd take my dictation, huh? With love and kisses?

SARAH I wish you wouldn't say things like that.

SOL Don't kid me, baby, I got eyes in my head; when a guy looks at a woman like he does at you, it's a cinch he knows every curve of her body—

SARAH My God, what a mind you've got.

SOL Yes, I'm smart—

SARAH Just because a man looks at a woman, you think they must be having an affair— is that your theory

SOL Certainly— that's how men and women are. I don't blame you, Sarah— enjoy yourself— have a dozen men at once— so long as I am not one of the lucky fellers, I don't care—

SARAH Then why do you keep asking me questions?

SOL I'm just joshing you— we're still friends, Sarah— am I right?

SARAH I don't know— you've changed—

SOL Both of us! We're getting along— from rags to riches, huh?

SARAH I don't know about the riches—

SOL Oh, the salary I get is nothing— it's the market that counts, the sweet words I read on the tape— you're a careful girl, Sarah, you must have quite a pile put away yourself...[*She nods her head.*]
Maybe I'd do you a favor, Sarah— how would you like to triple your money? Get four times, five times what you put in?

SARAH I'd like that.

SOL Wait 'till I get something I'm working on now straightened out— I'll be in a position to do something for you in a big way.

SARAH What are you planning?

SOL Never mind ...

SARAH Sol, I'm afraid for you, afraid you're riding for a fall.

SOL What are you always criticizing me for? Anybody would think it was a crime for a guy to make good—

SARAH No, it's fine if that's what you want.

SOL What do you think I want?

SARAH I wish I knew and I wish I could give it to you.

SOL I'll get what I want without you—

SARAH So it seems—

SOL Watch my dust— say, it gives me a kick to look back at the radical type we used to fall for— that stuff's a religion for misfits— Huh! I'm no misfit, I know where I belong—

SARAH That sounds like a Rotary club speech—

SOL That's bunk too— most everything's bunk when you know your way round— the trick is, to use the bunk without being taken in—

SARAH Why are you so bitter about it?

SOL Me bitter! I'm laughing— looking back at a raw kid that got drunk on words he found in books— God! it seems like a million miles away— [SARAH *nods.*] I haven't been near the East Side in a year, not since I went to my brother's funeral— there's the whole thing in a nut-shell— two boys come out of the Ghetto, one gets killed in a gang fight, and the other ...

SARAH What about the other? I can't see him very clearly, Sol—

SOL You're looking back— you should look ahead like me—

SARAH Sol... now and then, the way you smile or something, I see you like you used to be! Where's the boy I used to know, named Sol Gins-berg—

SOL That kid is dead... Bury the past, put it in the ground and throw dirt on it—
[*He stops short as* TURNER *enters right.*]

TURNER Good morning, Miss Glassman... hello, Sol... where's the boss?

SARAH He's sure to be here soon, Mr. Turner; will you wait?

TURNER [*Nods*] Yes, I have some information for him.

SOL Got some information, have you? You don't look very happy about it.

TURNER Don't I? [SARAH *exits right* — TURNER *stops and stares at model of Atlas factory left.*]

SOL You're worried about Atlas Motors?

TURNER What makes you think so?

SOL The way you look at that model of the factory... [*Joining him at the model*] It's a monument to bad business judgment— not a wheel in that dump will ever turn again.

TURNER Got any Atlas stock yourself?

SOL I'm on the short side and I intend to stay there.

TURNER You'll be squeezed till you scream one of these days.
SOL It takes a lot of squeezing to make me scream. [*A key has turned in door front left.* MERRITT *enters wearing overcoat, carrying hat and stick.*]

MERRITT Good morning.

SOL We were just discussing the market, Mr. Merritt.

MERRITT [*Glances at papers on desk*] What about it?

TURNER Sol's very pessimistic about it.

MERRITT Nonsense, a rise is overdue—

SOL Don't you believe it— I studied the charts— when those little black lines start going down, it takes more than optimism to stop 'em—

TURNER As usual, he's sure that he's right and everyone else in the world is wrong—

SOL Your head's made of marble, Mark; you should have it polished—

TURNER I resent that—

MERRITT Don't mind him, Mark— [*He rings buzzer under desk.*] You're clever, Sol, but if you were as smart as you think you are, you should be taken around the country in a tent and exhibited. [SARAH *enters right, notebook in hand.*]

SOL I hope I'd rate something better than a tent.

MERRITT [*To* SARAH] Good morning, Miss Glassman— what's on deck?

SARAH Golden and Company want you to call them immediately. [*Indicating papers on desk*] Mr. Fisher said these reports were urgent... Mr. Sonnenberg will be here at 11.30.

MERRITT [*Nods, comparing his watch with clock on table*] Get me Golden and Company, I want to speak to Mr. Fletcher.

SARAH [*Picks up phone*] A line, please. [*She proceeds to dial.*]

MERRITT Something you wanted to see me about, Sol?

SOL Yes, I got inside dope that the Starkeley agency is going bankrupt— I want your permission to line up some of their accounts.

MERRITT Starkeley going on the rocks? In these days you don't know whose turn is going to be next!

SARAH [*On phone*] Mr. Fletcher, please... [*She hands phone to* MERRITT.]

MERRITT Hello, Nick, what's the latest on Atlas? Nine and one-eighth— what's the big idea? Rumors— ? Sure, I heard rumors myself... Warner Drug Products— acutely weak, huh! Yes, I'll send you a check by messenger— sure, I understand, don't mention it, Nick— [*He rings off, turns to* SARAH.] Make out a check to Golden and Company— twenty thousand— no, make it twenty-five thousand— better be on the safe side—

SARAH Yes, sir... and Mr. Halliburton is waiting to see you.

MERRITT I'll get rid of Halliburton right now. [SARAH *nods and exits right.*]

SOL How about it, R-M? Can I start negotiating for the accounts of the Starkeley agency?

MERRITT No, I'm sorry they're in trouble, but it wouldn't be square to go after their people until they actually quit.

SOL You're missing a chance to make some money—

MERRITT I don't do business that way—

TURNER Can I see you for a minute, Raymond?

MERRITT Sure you can, Mark; wait a minute in Miss Glassman's office. [JEFFERY HALLIBURTON *appears right.* TURNER *and* SOL *meet him as they start to exit right.*]

TURNER Hello, Jeff, I hear you're going to have a bang-up society wedding.

SOL Going to invite the whole staff, Jeff?

JEFFERY Why not? [SOL *and* TURNER *exit.* JEFFERY *shuts the door right.*] Well, Mr. Merritt, have you thought it over?

MERRITT Yes, I have. [*He turns and sits at desk.*]

JEFFERY Don't keep me in suspense.

MERRITT You're through, Jeff... I'll give you a letter saying your connection with this firm has been uniformly satisfactory—

JEFFERY Thanks—

MERRITT For Christ's sake, don't look so broken up— you'll find another berth right away.

JEFFERY Sure, I've been looking around since you warned me last week.

MERRITT [*Coming around the desk*] I want you to realize, my hand is being forced— we've held up very well in a bad year, but the bankers don't approve of our overhead.

JEFFERY Sure... I don't want to sit around being charged to overhead.

MERRITT [*Offering his hand*] I'll instruct the cashier to give you two weeks' salary, and I'll send you that letter this afternoon. [*They shake hands.*] I wish you luck.

JEFFERY Thanks, same to you. [*He turns and exits right.* MERRITT *rings buzzer at desk.* SARAH *enters.*]

SARAH Here's the check.

MERRITT [*Signing it*] Send it down by special messenger, attention of Mr. Fletcher. [SARAH *nods, turns away.*] Wait a minute; come here. Miss Glassman. [*She turns back to desk.*] Just want to take a good look at you... you know the most unpleasant part of my job is firing people— Halliburton— I kicked him out... nice kid but no character.

SARAH That's a shame, but perhaps a few hard knocks will give him character.

MERRITT You're a sentimentalist, Miss Glassman; hard knocks don't give people character, just make 'em mushy; the town's full of boys like Halliburton... Yale men, Harvard men, they play good golf and their clothes are always pressed, but they bum drinks in every speak-easy in town!

SARAH It's a hard-boiled town, Mr. Merritt.

MERRITT You said it. Maybe you'd join me on a desert island sometime, Miss Glassman?

SARAH I hardly think so. [*She goes to door right. As she is about to exit, he calls briskly.*] Tell Turner I'm ready for him. [*She nods and exits.* TURNER *enters.*]

TURNER The market's giving me the heebie-jeebies, R-M; what am I going to do?

MERRITT The first thing you better do is calm down, Mark... are you sure your heebie-jeebies are due to the market or to a hangover? TURNER Both—

MERRITT What a party last night, huh!

TURNER I have trip hammers in my head ...

MERRITT Have a Bromo?

TURNER I've had four... For God's sake, R-M, come out of the trance— I'm up to my neck— I'd have been wiped out last week if you hadn't carried me—

MERRITT Let's not worry about it, Mark... you bought on my advice, and as long as I can protect myself, I'll protect you ...

TURNER Suppose it just goes on breaking, where's it going to end?

MERRITT Hell, Mark, that's a philosophic question! Where's the world going to end?

TURNER How can you be so damned flippant?

MERRITT Stop tearing your hair, Mark. Want some Rye to clear your head?

TURNER No, Felix downstairs will fix me up a morning glory. [*Dictaphone buzzes.* MERRITT *answers it.* SARAH'S *voice over dictaphone, "May Mr. Fisher see you for a moment?"*)

MERRITT Sure— [*He rings off, rises.*] I'll join you— [*Glancing at watch*] I just have time. [FISHER *enters right. A thin grey man of about fifty, a typical office drudge, a pallid face, spare hair around a high forehead, timid eyes looking out from bushy eyebrows. He holds a telegram in his hands.*]

FISHER Excuse me, Mr. Merritt.

MERRITT Well, Fisher?

FISHER I just got a wire from the Blodgett Company asking for those reports from psychologists about the relation of perfume and... er... sex—

MERRITT Send it if you've got it—

FISHER It's on your desk, sir, I didn't like to forward it without your approval—

MERRITT What the hell do I know about perfume and sex? Get it out special delivery and wire them it's on the way— [*He picks up his hat, about to exit with* TURNER.]

FISHER Yes, sir; anything else, sir?

MERRITT Not unless you feel a passionate desire for a morning glory—

FISHER I... I don't care much for flowers, sir— [SARAH *enters right.*]

MERRITT Back in fifteen minutes, Miss Glassman. [*She nods.* TURNER *and* MERRITT *exit left front.*]

SARAH [*Turning back to door*] All right, Dinah...

DINAH [*Entering right*] Excuse me, Mr. Fisher, the man is there about the new filing cabinets. [SARAH *picks up* MERRITT'S *coat and cane and exits with them left rear.*]

FISHER [*Starting for door right*] I'll tell him what I want—

DINAH If you put in many more files, I don't know how you'll have room for me.

FISHER I couldn't get along without you, Miss McCabe. [FISHER *exits right, leaving door open.* SARAH *returns from left.*]

DINAH I want to tell you something, Miss Glassman, guess what! He wants me to marry him!

SARAH Who does?
DINAH Mr. Fisher... he says he ain't been the same since his wife died!

SARAH That's awfully nice ...

DINAH I gave him the horse laugh, Miss Glassman; I told him there was other fish in the sea. You should 'a seen his face work when I made that crack.

SARAH I'll bet you do, just the same— [SOL *enters right.*]

DINAH [*With her back to* SOL, *not having seen him enter, continues to* SARAH] I ain't got an impulsive nature, Miss Glassman; I wouldn't marry him—

SOL Marry who?

DINAH Oh nobody, Mr. Ginsberg—

SOL You better take what you can get, girlie—

DINAH Oh, Mr. Ginsberg!

SOL [*To* SARAH] I'll bet she's in love with me—

DINAH Oh, Mr. Ginsberg, how can you say that, Mr. Ginsberg? [*She backs to door right, turns.*] I guess you can come in, Miss, it's only Mr. Ginsberg. [AGNES *enters right,* DINAH *exits.*]

AGNES Only Mr. Ginsberg... I didn't come to see you but I'll have to make the best of it.

SOL When is Mr. Sonnenberg expected, Miss Glassman?

SARAH Eleven-thirty.

SOL [*Consulting his watch*] Very well, Miss Glassman, I'll ring if I want you. [SARAH *nods and exits right.*]

AGNES I must say the way you order people around here— they don't think much of you, but you act like you thought you were God!
SOL You come at a very bad time, I got lots on my mind.

AGNES I didn't come to see you— I came to see Raymond.

SOL You got nothing to see him about.

AGNES Oh, haven't I?

SOL Why are you here— answer me?

AGNES If you're really so upset about it, I'll tell you why— I want to borrow money from him.

SOL Damn you, you're not fair—

AGNES What? I'm telling you exactly—

SOL You want to make trouble for me—

AGNES I should think the trouble would be for him!

SOL Are you a woman or some kind of devil? You stick me with a knife right in the pride.

AGNES I don't give a damn for your pride—

SOL You told me it was all off, him and you?

AGNES Of course it is— I don't lie to you—

SOL How much are you asking him for?

AGNES That depends on what mood he's in— one thousand, two thousand.

SOL You expect me to believe a man will give you that and get nothing in return—

AGNES You ought to know; you tried hard enough and what have you got?
SOL Nothing...

AGNES Then you better trust me at least— Raymond's an old friend. I go to him just the way I'd go to a bank—

SOL A night and day bank. I'm not a fool; if Merritt hands you cash he has a reason—

AGNES Friendship—   [SOL *hoots derisively*.] I don't see what you're so hot about— he happens to be a generous person.

SOL I'm generous, why don't you come to me?

AGNES That's silly. I couldn't ask you for anything on the money you're getting—

SOL You wait—

AGNES Besides, I don't want anything from you— you never give me things, and I never ask you—

SOL I don't, don't I? How about that damn little Pekinese?

AGNES Oh, that doesn't count—

SOL Don't be mad at me, Aggie... it just worries me the way you don't think of anything but getting things— crazy over things, little jewels, and step-ins and nicknacks and chiffons!

AGNES That's all there is, there isn't any more! And do I get 'em? Not much—

SOL So you go to other men and hold me off like some kind of insect buzzing around—

AGNES I've been pretty nice to you. I don't see why you're always howling for more—

SOL What's it got me? I get my arms around you once, I'd never let go.

AGNES Lay off, Sol, you make me feel like such a brute; you chase me like a pet dog asking for something, and I've got nothing to give you.

SOL You got yourself!

AGNES No, you want it too much— it's more fun to have you all in a fever wanting something that's just a joke to me— that's the kind of a cold potato I am. I told you the first time we crashed up against each other right in this office.

SOL Some crash that was.

AGNES And we've been going on crashing; every time I step out with you, it's a free for all. You scare me, honest; you're so romantic you get my nerves all raw.

SOL Got no feelings, have you? A mechanical doll, huh? Well, there's some way I'll wind you up and make you go.

AGNES If I'm only a doll, why are you ready to steal, crawl, lie... for me?

SOL You're not even a person, you're a thing, the thing I want. What goes on in your empty little head?

AGNES Nothing... less than you think. You think I got a plan about you? That's foolish. I'm just lazy, I don't want to be bothered—

SOL Did you ever fall for anybody?

AGNES Not since I was sixteen—

SOL How about Merritt?

AGNES I'm fond of him, always been fond of him— a good pal— but no more sex appeal than a Great Dane.

SOL What about me, Aggie?

AGNES Oh, lay off, can't you?

SOL Suppose I got a million dollars— then you'll give in?

AGNES You got the tenacity of a bulldog.

SOL I'll give you stuff, jewels the size of an egg, stones that'll make you sweat to carry 'em on a hot day—

AGNES It's not healthy the way you go on... you better cut it out.

SOL Right now you got a tear in your eye. [*She sinks wearily into a chair right front.*]

AGNES I know it... I need a handkerchief. [*From his pocket SOL carefully takes out a little, soiled, rumpled handkerchief.*]

SOL I got one, see... yours ...

AGNES Gee, you're a fool. I must say you don't keep it very nicely.

SOL No, but it's perfumed... I put that Fievre d'Amour stuff on it. [*He crushes the little handkerchief to his lips.*] God, Aggie, for two years I been true to you, my dream of you, and I had nothing— do you wonder I'm near crazy—

AGNES Don't... don't... [*He is on his knees beside her, head against her breast.*] Give me a handkerchief, you fool. [*He hands her his own hand- kerchief.*]

SOL Here, take this if you need it. See... you got a soft heart; why, you'd warm up to love... me telling you sweet things... would be like a fire warming you... sweet fire ...

AGNES It listens pretty, but it's all talk—

SOL I'll give you the world for a present... oh, maybe not the whole world at once, but in time ...

AGNES I know how you feel— anything you can't get makes you sick and sour. I know how it is looking in shop windows—

SOL I'll make it legal—

AGNES What?

SOL Suppose we get married right away—

AGNES You've come to that, have you?

SOL I'll make you wild with love... in time...[*Slowly as if he were just realizing it himself*] I got a capacity for love!

AGNES Why do you do this to me? I'm no good, why should you marry a girl that's a... a... honest, Sol, sex is not so important as all that—

SOL I am the judge— if you are as bad as you say yourself, money will buy you—

AGNES You're wrong, it won't... not this time. I'm just the sort of a nut all the kale in the world won't buy—

SOL Then there's another way to reach you, there's always a way.

AGNES There is a way— but you're too dumb and selfish to know it— [*A knock on door right. SOL and AGNES stand staring at each other as enemies. The knock is repeated and SARAH enters right, closing the door behind her.*]

SARAH [*To SOL*] Mr. Sonnenberg-

SOL [*To SARAH*] I'll see Mr. Sonnenberg, until Mr. Merritt gets back— [*To AGNES*] Wait in my office, Aggie— promise you'll wait. [*AGNES exits right. SARAH stands hesitating.*] Hurry up, don't keep him waiting— [*SARAH nods and opens door right.*]

SARAH Mr. Merritt will be back in a moment, Mr. Sonnenberg.

SONNENBERG [*Enters, consulting watch*] Yes, I'm five minutes early—

SOL Glad to see you, Mr. Sonnenberg. [*They shake hands. SARAH exits right.*] How have you been since the other day?

SONNENBERG Nicely, thanks—

SOL What's up, Mr. Sonnenberg? How do we stand? When I heard you were meeting Merritt here today I figured things were coming to a head—

SONNENBERG [*Sitting*] Precisely.

SOL I tried to reach you on the phone half an hour ago, but you were tied up—

SONNENBERG Yes... I saw no point in discussing the matter further with you—

SOL You gave me encouragement the other day—

SONNENBERG I in no way committed myself— I told you your proposition impressed me; in fact, the proposition is nothing short of formidable—

SOL If you let me carry out my policies here, I'll double the profits of the business—

SONNENBERG I admire your ego, Mr. Ginsberg, although I find you shockingly lacking in tact—

SOL What good is tact?

SONNENBERG [*Amused*] Tact has served me very well on occasions... look at it from my point of view: why should I trust you when you come to me with a scheme for betraying your own employer?

SOL I'm not! [*Desperately anxious to justify himself, to show his own angle on the situation*] I simply got ideas, I got ambition. I've told Mr. Merritt my plans and he won't listen to me; he don't realize that times are different and things have got to be done differently— I got a right to go straight to you and tell you my plans: if they're good, they ought to be acted on!

SONNENBERG Your plans are interesting.

SOL Interesting? If you don't follow those plans, you're just throwing away our money!

SONNENBERG [*Raising one eyebrow*] *Our* money?

SOL I mean the firm... in tough times like these we got to use our wits!

SONNENBERG And your wits led you to appeal to me behind your superior's back?

SOL Anything I'm saying to you I'm ready to say right to Merritt's face, but he won't listen! I went to you and laid my cards on the table because I thought you'd understand what I was driving at. Only this morning I got a chance to get control of the accounts of a rival firm that's going bankrupt, I wangled it so we can get those accounts sewed up in a bag; Merritt wouldn't hear of it—

SONNENBERG I dislike the word wangle!

SOL I can't pick my words, business is business.

SONNENBERG There are limits; one must look at the ethical side.

SOL I don't get this stuff about ethics; you're the real power here, if I got money-making ideas, you ought to be glad to hear about 'em. All I want is for you to step in and enforce my views!

SONNENBERG That's simple enough!

SOL Then we're set?

SONNENBERG You mean I'm set... you, if I may say so without offense, are sitting on some very sharp pins and needles.

SOL What are you going to do? Don't keep me guessing?

SONNENBERG We shall see!

SOL If you just gimme a chance, I can make a showing, I can prove... [MERRITT *enters front left.*]

MERRITT I hope I haven't kept you waiting, Mr. Sonnenberg—

SONNENBERG Not at all. Mr. Ginsberg has been entertaining me admirably.

MERRITT No doubt— Come in the library where we can be comfortable. [*Indicates door rear left*]

SOL Call me if you want me--

MERRITT What?

SOL Oh, nothing—

MERRITT What is it, Sol? Anything you want to say?

SOL Me? Not a thing... not at present ...

SONNENBERG [*As he and* MERRITT *exit left*] I won't keep you long, Mr. Merritt—
[SARAH *enters right.*]

SARAH Where's Mr. Merritt?

SOL In there.

SARAH What's the trouble?

SOL [*To himself, deeply disturbed*] You'll know quick enough— Goddamn it, they don't even give me a chance to come in and speak my piece—

SARAH What are you mumbling about?

SOL They're deciding it in there right now— what I worked for for two years—

SARAH Do you mean you're trying to make trouble for Mr. Merritt?

SOL If he's looking for trouble, he'll get plenty of it.

SARAH It's too big for you—

SOL Nothing's too big for me, nothing ...

SARAH *You* say so!

SOL Oh you think I'm kidding, do you? I got Merritt right where I want him.

SARAH Have you?

SOL He's used this company's money to cover his margin in the market. [SARAH *reacts to this with definite fear. She knows the charge is true, but is on the defensive— she must protect* MERRITT.]

SARAH You can't prove anything like that—

SOL [*Taking a paper from his pocket*] Do you think I'd be fool enough to say it if I couldn't prove it? I got it down here in black and white— that's enough to satisfy a judge and jury—

SARAH What is it?

SOL That's a digest of the accounts— I been here every night studying the books, tracing every entry, checking every penny... it took work to get to the bottom of these accounts, but I did it— I got him! The money he sends down to his brokers comes out of this company's funds—

SARAH If he's done that, he had a very good reason for it.

SOL He had the same reason I got, to save his own skin—

SARAH No one would believe—

SOL If I sprung this on Sonnenberg—

SARAH You can't, as a matter of loyalty—

SOL You're full of pretty words— I haven't shown it, I never said a word about it to Sonnenberg—

SARAH I'm glad, the only decent thing—

SOL I wasn't being decent, I had a better use for it—

SARAH I'll tell Mr. Merritt about it—

SOL What do you suppose I'm telling you now for, except to have it get back to him as quick as possible— I know you—

SARAH I know you; you wouldn't do a mean action—

SOL If I get my back to the wall, I'll show 'em—

SARAH It's not worth it; it's not a question of what Mr. Merritt has done—

SOL All you're thinking about is him—

SARAH I want you to be careful, for your own sake—

SOL I won't lose everything I sweated for—

SARAH You're all wrong— you don't see—

SOL I'm going some place; anyone stands in my way I'll smash 'em—

SARAH You mustn't—

SOL I know what I'm after—

SARAH No you don't— this isn't what you've worked for—

SOL Go on—

SARAH It's not you; it's horrible— stop and think; promise me—

SOL How can I promise? I don't know how it's going to break!
[MERRITT *enters left rear.*]

MERRITT [*Turning back in the doorway, evidently addressing* SONNEN-BERG] No, I insist on settling this right now— [*He shuts the door.*]

SOL Want to see me?

MERRITT [*Icily*] That's exactly what I want— [SARAH *looks from one to the other, exits right.*]

SOL I suppose he told you—

MERRITT I hate to see a man I trusted plotting behind my back.

SOL That's what you call it— I went to Sonnenberg with a gilt-edge plan for reorganizing here— I told you my ideas and you stepped all over them— I thought he'd have sense enough to see it.

MERRITT I've believed in you and trusted you—

SOL That's tripe— I've given you what I was paid for—

MERRITT If you can't see what you're guilty of—

SOL Go on, tell me—

MERRITT Unethical conduct—

SOL Shut up about ethics, I got no time for 'em—

MERRITT I bear you no real grudge, but I can't employ a man I don't trust.

SOL Just a minute— that's up to Sonnenberg—

MERRITT He told me to use my own judgment—

SOL [*Bitterly*] The double-crossing fool— to turn on one of his own race— [*Leaning across the desk*] That ain't all: I haven't told Sonnenberg all I know about this business and the way it's run—

MERRITT [*Wearily*] If you want to have this out with him and me, that's your privilege—

SOL You're not afraid of anything I might say?

MERRITT [*Who is much moved and unhappy, flares up angrily*] I've had enough of this— [*Shouting*] You're out. You're through—

SOL All right, if you want to make it a fight—

MERRITT You can't fight me—

SOL I'll lick you yet— if I don't do it with my brains I'll do it with my hands—

MERRITT You're showing yourself up—

SOL I'll show you up.

MERRITT Don't try that gangster stuff on me—

SOL Gangster, huh!

MERRITT Nothing else—

SOL [*Stops short, then speaks with deep feeling*] Your talk about gangsters don't mean anything. My brother was a square guy and he was One-eyed Izzy that got his on Second Avenue—

MERRITT [*Looks at SOL with interest and amazement*] Have you gone looney? What are you talking about?

SOL This is a gangster's world and I'm out to beat it. The first bullet got Izzy's good eye and he staggered blind around the street; nobody on the East Side will forget that blind gunman for the two minutes before he fell. They buried him in a solid silver coffin with gold cupids, twenty grand, with twelve thousand worth of flowers—

MERRITT Why do you tell me this?

SOL I swore at the funeral— to get what he was after and to get it respectable. The gold and silver I'm after won't be on my coffin—

MERRITT [*Thinks a minute, then speaks coldly, with a certain thoughtful mockery in his voice*] Tell that to Rufus Sonnenberg, if it will give you any pleasure— [SARAH *enters right. She is quite distraught, nervous.*]

SARAH Mr. Merritt, I feel I must tell you something— it may be important—

MERRITT Go in the library, Ginsberg, and if you know what's good for you, you better keep your temper!

SOL Don't worry, I don't insult people with that much money! [*He exits.*]

SARAH Mr. Merritt, I must warn you.

MERRITT What about?

SARAH He's been telling me things, threats against you... he says he knows about your stock transactions, he says you've used the company's money—

MERRITT How much does he know?

SARAH He knows a great deal; he's been here at night studying the accounts, he has written proof— I tried to stop him and he wouldn't listen—

MERRITT Oh, I begin to see, that's what he meant.

SARAH It's my fault!

MERRITT Oh, no... after all, the mistake is mine! [*Very gently, putting his hand on her arm*] Funny, Miss Glassman, the way circumstances push us into doing things we don't want to do, you and me both!

SARAH How can he do it? How can he be so blind?

MERRITT You're still worrying about him? [*She is silent.*] For God's sa- ke, forget him! [*He turns vigorously to the library*.] We'll have a show- down if that's what he wants!
[*He exits into the library. AGNES enters right.*]

AGNES I'm awfully sick of waiting, Miss Glassman.

SARAH He's tied up; I think it will be some time, Miss Carter.

AGNES Well, there's nobody here, so why shouldn't I stick around?

SARAH I think it would be better if you waited in my office.

AGNES Do you? [*She sits idly on the desk.*] You know this business stuff doesn't impress me, Miss Glassman— [AGNES *picks up papers on the desk, tearing them nervously, crumples a sheet in her hand.*
SARAH *comes over, straightens out the crumpled paper, makes a neat pile of the sheets.*]

SARAH Excuse me, these might be valuable.

AGNES I was just reading about this Glamour Cream that they adver- tise so much. Do you think it's any good?

SARAH I guess it's all right, but it's a failure. They've lowered the price but they can't sell it.

AGNES Did you ever try it?

SARAH Yes, I tried a jar. It smells lovely.

AGNES I think they're all fakes— it's so easy to fool women, because they're so anxious.

SARAH That's what advertising goes on.

AGNES I've tried all of 'em— [*Pause*] Guess I'm afraid of getting old—

SARAH [*Obviously not meaning it*] You, Miss Carter, how could anybody think of *you* being old?

AGNES [*Smiling*] You mean where there's no thoughts, there's no wrinkles— Don't kid me, Miss Glassman, I know your opinion of me. Now take that mud they recommend— I smeared that on my face for weeks, but it's so messy and it makes you feel like such a fool— just think how embarrassed you'd be if a burglar should come in— [SARAH *laughs.*] Well, I believe you've got to be prepared for everything.

SARAH That's right.

AGNES You never know— that's what I always say.

SARAH [*Has been standing looking down at her. She suddenly bursts out, almost screaming with feeling*] How can he? God, how can he?— You're such a fool, that's all you are, how can he love you— how can he— [*Puts her hand over her mouth*]

AGNES [*A little breathless, her lips quivering a little as she smiles, but maintaining her poise*] Well, I'm glad you said what you thought at last.

SARAH I didn't mean to— [*She turns and exits right in helpless distress.*]

AGNES [*Alone*] Goddam it, I want to be a nun! [DINAH *enters right with some papers in a basket.*]

DINAH [*Over her shoulder, evidently addressing SARAH as she comes in*] Yeh— I'll put 'em on his desk. [*As DINAH crosses to Merritt's desk, the dictaphone buzzes — *] Guess I'd better take that call.

AGNES Go ahead.

DINAH [*At phone*] Oh, yes, Mr. Fisher— you know my voice— yes, Mr. Fisher—

FISHER'S VOICE [*At other end*] Is Mr. Merritt there?

DINAH No, Mr. Fisher. [FISHER'S *voice mumbles something indistinct.*] Oh, *Mr.* Fisher—

FISHER'S VOICE Tell him I sent the memorandum.

DINAH Yes, I'll leave a note. Good-bye, Mr. Fisher. [*She rings off, scribbles on pad.*] Do you know Mr. Fisher? [AGNES *shakes her head.* DINAH *looks triumphant and is about to exit right when* MERRITT *enters left rear.*]

MERRITT What the devil are you doing here?

DINAH [*Turning at door*] Me, Mr. Merritt?

MERRITT Not you, Miss McCabe—

DINAH I just left those papers from Mr. Fisher.

MERRITT [*Glances at the papers, and shouts angrily*] Miss McCabe— why do you bring these here? They're clearly marked for the accounting department.

DINAH [*Coming back to the desk*] Gee, I must have got the baskets mixed—

MERRITT Can't you read?

DINAH Don't fire me, Mr. Merritt, I just love it here—

MERRITT [*Shouts fiercely*] Don't be an imbecile, Miss McCabe— [*More gently*] You're not being fired— now get out—

DINAH Yes, sir. [*She exits.*]

AGNES Thank God I'm not in her shoes.

MERRITT What are you doing here, Aggie?

AGNES Oh, weeping and gnashing my teeth.

MERRITT If it's just the same to you, do it some other place.

AGNES You look all shot, Raymond—

MERRITT I just had a run-in with Ginsberg— right at each other's throats—

AGNES [*Interested*] Is that so? I guess that's the end of Ginsberg!

MERRITT Certainly, but he don't know it! He's in there talking his head off. I expected a showdown. I thought he was going to pull something big, but he's just juggling crazy schemes in his imagination— I couldn't stand it.

AGNES He gets my goat, too.

MERRITT I was really fond of Ginsberg— still am in a way!

AGNES Tell me, Ray, what's the matter with him?

MERRITT Pipe dreams— swelled head— [*Looking at her sharply*] What about it?

AGNES [*Trying to avoid showing the tension she feels*] I think he's the saddest man in the world.

MERRITT [*Amazed*] Why?

AGNES He's all twisted and funny, and he wants to be a great man— and he wants to be sweet—

MERRITT That's a funny word.

AGNES Yes, he wants to— but he can't— Gee, I like Jews, they're all poets or sugar daddies— or both!

MERRITT You can't generalize, there's all kinds. As for him, he's emotional and greedy, got no control.

AGNES No, but he's big at least, goes after things in a big way, smash-es after things like a madman!

MERRITT [*Thoughtfully*] Dangerous!

AGNES [*Nods understandingly*] Don't I know it? From where I'm looking he's got a danger sign on him as big as your hat. [MERRITT l*aughs.*] You're so nice and simple, Raymond. Thank God you're simple.

MERRITT That sounds as if you came to borrow money?

AGNES I did, but I don't want it now—

MERRITT Really?

AGNES I'm a mess; I've got no future and my past is unpleasant to look at—

MERRITT There are always men—

AGNES Always— too many! I don't like men, I don't like work, and I'm not the kind who can get comfort out of a really good book—

MERRITT [*Kindly*] I'm glad you're through with Ginsberg.

AGNES He's just the comic relief— [*Irrelevantly*] He wants to marry me— [MERRITT *laughs.*] Don't laugh, it's kinda wonderful the way he said it— but I'd much rather jump in the river.

MERRITT Don't do it, Aggie—

AGNES God, I want to be a white woman, Ray, but I'm just naturally rotten.

MERRITT Why don't you pray to God to make you a good girl?

AGNES But there's one rotten thing I won't do— I won't marry him, I won't—

MERRITT Why should you? He's probably dead broke. He's being fired and he won't find it easy to find another job—

AGNES Damn you, I wasn't thinking of that—

MERRITT Just making a practical observation— [SONNENBERG

enters left rear, followed by SOL.]

SONNENBERG [*To* MERRITT] I think there's no need to go into this further— Mr. Ginsberg has stated his case with great emphasis— since
you feel that his suggestions are not practical, I feel that I have no
course—

MERRITT [*Glancing at* SOL, *turns away*] Quite— may I present Miss
Carter, Mr. Sonnenberg?

SONNENBERG Charmed ...

MERRITT [*To* SOL] You've had your say—

SONNENBERG I think there's no question of your entire fairness in
meeting the issue, Mr. Merritt... Good day. [*He bows to* AGNES.] My
regrets, Mr. Ginsberg.

SOL O.K. Mr. Sonnenberg— I'm not a bum loser!

MERRITT [*Seeing* SONNENBERG *to the door*] What's your general impression of the market?

SONNENBERG Did you ever read the works of Confucius, Mr.
Merritt?

MERRITT Can't say I have— didn't know he was an export on stocks?

SONNENBERG That's my point— he knew just as much about them as I
do— [*He exits.*]

MERRITT That's that—

AGNES I'm going—

SOL [*To* AGNES] Wait a minute— [*Turning to* MERRITT] I'm going myself but I want to say a word first— a matter of business—

AGNES I can't stay—

SOL You'll hear me— and you too. I couldn't talk to that Wall Street mummy in there— [*He approaches* MERRITT.] Let's get down to brass tacks— [*He takes slip of paper, crumpled, from his pocket.*] I don't know all the legal terms, but I know what this means: an officer of a corporation that makes private use of the firm's money is in a hot spot—

MERRITT If you wanted to make any charges against me, why didn't you say so in there?

SOL That wasn't the chance I was looking for— I'm just showing you this to warn you— don't be so careless again—

MERRITT If you want to take me to a court of law, go ahead—

SOL Let's not talk about the law, it's so nasty— Aren't we friends? Would I do anything that would hurt the firm?

MERRITT You're no longer connected with the firm—

SOL O.K.

MERRITT What do you propose to do?

SOL I want to talk turkey—
[SARAH *enters right.*]

SARAH I beg your pardon, Mr. Merritt—

MERRITT Hold on a minute, Miss Glassman— [*Turns to* SOL] What are you going to do with that paper—

SOL What makes you so nervous? There's lots I might do with it if I wasn't so much of a gentleman—

MERRITT I don't get you—

SOL Whenever a guy is a gentleman, he wants to get something—

MERRITT What do you want?

SOL Well, I want to be General Manager of the department of Promotion and New Accounts.

MERRITT What?

SOL With a three-year contract permitting me to carry out my policies in my way!

MERRITT You've got your crust—

SOL A crust like I got— a man that can fight you tooth and nail like I have and will go on doing it— that's worth cash to you!

AGNES They've got no pride, his kind, I mean.

SOL Too much... I got too much to take a licking.

MERRITT You were ready to fight me with your hands a minute ago.

SOL Forget it and do business.

MERRITT You forget easily.

SOL I got to, that's my secret!

MERRITT I don't want you here on any terms— get out—

SOL Is that final?

MERRITT Take your proof with you, do what you like with it— but get out—

SOL You'll regret it—

MERRITT I won't deal with a crook—

SOL The Hell I am— [*He starts to tear up the paper, violently excited.*] I'm smart enough to get ahead, I don't need this— Here's your Goddam proof— [*He throws the bits of paper in* MERRITT'S *face.*]

MERRITT Go to the devil—

SOL All right! I bide my time, I handle the materials... it's you that's afraid, 'cause I beat you at this game or die! I go to the devil, yes, 'cause that's what I choose; he'll help me, too, 'cause I give my heart's blood for money, much money to win with— I'll get as much money as those Wall Street bankers, two years, five years, ten years maybe, this little dump of yours will be a drop in the ocean— I'll just spit in the ocean and you won't be here any more—

MERRITT Go on, you're dreaming—

SOL Sure... Can you turn down a man with a dream like that?

AGNES If you're ready now, I'll tag along with you, Sol—

MERRITT What?

AGNES If you're out of a job and licked, Sol, it's O.K. with me— just 'cause you're so romantic and impossible, I'll tag along!

SOL How far?

AGNES Any place; I'm going to marry you this afternoon.

SOL That's nice... sure, that's nice. [SARAH *watches speechless, broken.*]

MERRITT You talked yourself into something.

AGNES [*Puzzled by* SOL'S *apparent preoccupation with his own thoughts*] Glad?

SOL Nothing can stop me now— [*He turns to* MERRITT.] Sorry you can't see my proposition, but I'm not as sorry as you'll be. You'll be on the rocks in a year—

MERRITT Will I?

SOL You better get onto yourself, Merritt— you're a hand-shaker and a good fellow— you spend your time in speakeasies while I sweat my head off working— are you going to kill yourself just because you're sore at me?

MERRITT Your Goddamn conceit!

SOL You're cutting your throat right here in front of my eyes and you haven't got the sense to know it— you owe this firm money and the market's draining you dry— I can pull you out— Give me a free hand and I'll show a profit here that will knock your eye out—
MERRITT I have no authority to entertain such a proposition— You know as well as I do it's up to Sonnenberg.

SOL [Looks at MERRITT with quick comprehension] Oh, you been thinking? [MERRITT doesn't answer.] You better think fast— Don't give me that gaff about Sonnenberg— he was half sold on my ideas before he got to you—

MERRITT [Still thoughtful] No, I'll see you in hell first—

SOL That's a date, but you don't mean it— [Pursuing his advantage] You can fix it with Sonnenberg— Give him a line about ethics— we got enough ethics between us to fix anything—

MERRITT In a way I hand it to you—

SOL What, the job?

MERRITT Give me time to think—

SOL One minute is plenty of time— you already decided—

MERRITT [Nervously, exhausted by SOL'S pounding energy] Nothing else you want?

SOL Sure, there's the matter of salary— I want twenty thousand a year—

MERRITT Make it fifteen.

SOL All right, the main thing is to build up the firm's profit. I can wait for mine—

MERRITT Get this straight, it's not a matter of these threats... I see your side of it— your ambition— no reason why we shouldn't make a go of it— as enemies—

SOL Sure, stay sore, it keeps the mind active.

MERRITT I suppose you'll take my word—

SOL Sure. [MERRITT *turns to door left rear.*] Going to make the arrangements now?

MERRITT No, I'm going to get a drink— [MERRITT *exits left rear. SOL sits at the desk, drawing lines on the blotter moodily with a pencil, completely disregarding the two women.*]

SARAH [*Comes forward hesitantly*] I wish you both happiness.

SOL Oh, you mean her! [*He looks at AGNES thoughtfully, turns back to SARAH.*] Did I pull it off or didn't I? Who's the worm now? [*He is surprised at the expression of SARAH'S face.*] Why do you look so strange? I think you're cursing me in your heart!

SARAH No, there's a curse on you; it's not my fault. [*She turns abruptly and exits right.*]

SOL [*Looking at desk in front of him*] I like this desk. I'm going to have one like it in my office!

AGNES All right, but you might at least admit I'm here.

SOL Yes, I see you. What time does the license bureau close?

AGNES Don't know, I never went there.

SOL Four o'clock, I guess— lots of time— [*Softly speaking to himself*] I fit it together like a picture puzzle— money or love, you win if you wait and watch—

AGNES [*Quietly*] Now you got me, what are you going to do with me?

SOL We shall see— I'll give you things— houses, jewels— that stuff you're wearing is nothing— just wait— [*His eyes seem to be looking right through her. She shivers a little.*]

AGNES I'm scared.

SOL You don't have to be scared, you belong to me now!

CURTAIN

ACT THREE
Scene I

An afternoon in January, 1932.

The scene is the same. It is late on a winter afternoon. Outside the big windows, the grey of the sky is dismal and menacing.

Center, standing against the grey of the windows, stands SONNENBERG, rocking back and forth on the balls of his feet. At the desk left sits SOL. He is immaculately dressed. He has gained in weight and solidity. He looks older than he is. He is talking suavely as the curtain rises.

SOL But there's one point on which I insist... you can call it a matter of sentiment if you like, but it means a great deal to me— the name of this firm shall be Ginsberg and Company— it's a matter of pride with me. [*A pause. SONNENBERG looks at him smilingly.*]

SONNENBERG [*Chuckles, nodding*] Have you informed Merritt of the impending changes?

SOL [*Easily*] Of course not— I felt it was only right to get your O.K. before I proceed— any other course wouldn't be... [*With a sarcastic grin*] Well, it wouldn't be ethical, would it? [SONNENBERG *returns the grin.*]

SONNENBERG You're in a position to write your own ticket.

SOL I'm playing fair, Mr. Sonnenberg— [SONNENBERG *continues to smile and rock back and forth on his feet.*] I got control because every time the market dropped, Merritt needed money and he came to me. I did him a favor in helping him out: I consider I'm making a very generous settlement.

SONNENBERG There's no question that the arrangement you outline is more than generous.

SOL And a good thing for the business; it means we can push ahead!

SONNENBERG [*Walking over to the desk, scanning* SOL *thoughtfully*] I admire you, Ginsberg; you're a dynamo, an electric fountain of energy—

SOL I work like a dog, my brain buzzes so I can't sleep at night—

SONNENBERG Never satisfied, are you?

SOL [*Shakes his head gloomily*] No... [*Looking up at Sonnenberg suddenly*] Are you?

SONNENBERG I?...Of course; I know how to relax: take my advice and learn to relax--

SOL You can afford to take it easy. You're so rich you can sit back and laugh at everybody else—

SONNENBERG My dear friend, I've lost two-thirds of my fortune in the last three months—

SOL [*In amazement*] Is that a fact? You don't look worried--

SONNENBERG On the contrary, I'm accustomed to very expensive pleasures: I should rather die than curtail my pleasures.

SOL I got enough money right now to buy any pleasure there is—

SONNENBERG Then look around and choose—

SOL [*Gloomily*] Nothing to it—

SONNENBERG For my part, I have certain cultural interests: art, beauty, sensuality in moderation—

SOL I don't get a kick out of that stuff, I want something bigger—

SONNENBERG For instance?

SOL Power: money is power—

SONNENBERG I'm not so sure—

SOL What?

SONNENBERG You aim too high; I've studied your character, Ginsberg. [*Pointing his finger at him vigorously*] You're a revolutionist—

SOL The hell I am—

SONNENBERG Never content, pursuing a vision, you want to change the whole world in the image of your own ego— you want to stand on a platform among millions of faces— alone! Telling them what to do and how to do it... Am I right?

SOL You're kidding me, Mr. Sonnenberg.

SONNENBERG Not at all, I'm warning you. [*Gravely*] Take my advice— get some cultural hobby, it's a great comfort to the inner man.

SOL Thanks for the tip— [*He rises and they shake hands. Opening door, front, left.*] You're a great joker, Mr. Sonnenberg—

SONNENBERG I'm not joking. Good-bye— [*He exits left front. SOL closes the door, returns to the desk, sits, and rings buzzer under desk. MISS FARLEY enters right; she is a very trim college girl, attractive, with a rather cultured voice, an ideal secretary, efficient and unassuming.*]

MISS FARLEY Yes, sir.

SOL Mr. Merritt hasn't returned yet, has he?

MISS FARLEY No, sir. Your wife called a few moments ago— I told her you couldn't be disturbed and to call back—

SOL Anything else?

MISS FARLEY Mr. Fisher wants to see you.

SOL Tell Fisher I'll see him shortly— [*He moves a key on dictaphone.*] Hello— you got those papers ready? [*A voice answers on dictaphone— "I've drawn them up, but I'd like to see you about this"— Meanwhile telephone rings, and* MISS FARLEY *answers it.*]

MISS FARLEY [*At phone*] In a moment, Mrs. Ginsberg—

SOL [*On dictaphone*] Bring 'em in right now— [*He turns off the dictaphone.* MISS FARLEY *hands him the telephone.*]

SOL [*On phone*] Hello, dear— [*Looking up at* MISS FARLEY.] All right, Miss Farley, send Turner in. [MISS FARLEY *nods and exits right.* SOL *continues on phone.*] How was the auction? I don't know where we'll put all that antique furniture, but if you want it it's all right with me... Sure, come in and get it— will a couple of hundred be all right? Sure... [*He rings off. Meanwhile* TURNER *has entered right with a contract in his hand. He waits for* SOL *to finish.* SOL *looks up.*] Sit down, Mark, have a cigar—

TURNER Thanks— [*He takes one from the silver box.*]

SOL Let's have a look at that contract— [*He takes it.*] You're lucky you're not married, Mark— my wife's just bought a set of old French furniture. She's got the house so full of truck you can't move around without falling over something that used to belong to Louis the Fifteenth—

TURNER [*Laughs*] You can afford it—

SOL I work like a horse making it and she works like a horse spending it— she buys everything she sees, and never so much as asks the price— can you picture it?

TURNER All in the game—

SOL Money to buy stuff to fill the house to get a bigger house to hold more stuff— it's a Goddam treadmill—

TURNER That's America—

SOL [*Who has been studying the contract while he has been talking*] You're sure he'll never have any come-back if he signs this?

TURNER It lets him out— if he's fool enough to sign it.

SOL I'll force him to sign it.

TURNER Is there anything human left in you at all?

SOL You better watch your own step, Turner— you're not up to scratch— a man that has a hangover three hundred and sixty-five days out of the year—

TURNER If that's the way you feel about it, I'll walk right out--

SOL No, you won't, because you're useful to me, and you haven't got the guts to leave a soft berth and start law practice all over again—

TURNER Yes, I'm weak enough to stay!

SOL [*Feeling quite master of the situation, he speaks with suave good nature*] I apologize for being so crude just now— forgive me, will you?

TURNER Forget it.

SOL [*Looks up at him with a thoughtful smile*] I'll tell you something, Mark, if it'll make you feel any better... I envy you!

TURNER [*Astonished*] Why?

SOL Sure... you enjoy life... am I right?

TURNER [*Amused*] In my own simple way—

SOL You drink like a fish and you have a different woman every night—

TURNER [*Shrugs*] It's a habit—

SOL An expensive habit—

TURNER Yes, I pay my way—

SOL You think it's a pleasure to go to bed with something you've bought?

TURNER They're all bought— some of them work on a long term basis, but I prefer the cash and carry girls— they're less trouble—

SOL You're a lucky man, Mark.

TURNER Not so lucky.

SOL Sure... you don't want much, but you get it. [TURNER *exits right.* SOL *rings buzzer at his desk.* MISS FARLEY *enters right.*] Get me three hundred dollars from the cashier, in tens and twenties—

MISS FARLEY Yes, sir... will you see Mr. Fisher now?

SOL [*As if he were thinking of something else*] Sure— [MISS FARLEY *goes to door right, motions* FISHER *to come in and exits.* FISHER *appears, looking greyer and soberer than ever. He stands hesitantly, evidently in real fear of* SOL.] What's on your mind, Fisher?

FISHER It's something personal— I... the fact is—

SOL [*Interrupting*] Don't dodder, Fisher, you make me nervous—

FISHER Sorry... I'd really prefer my wife to tell you: may I bring her in?

SOL Drag her in— what's it all about? [FISHER *goes to door right, and* DINAH *enters bashfully.* FISHER *takes her hand and pulls her toward* SOL'S *desk.*] Are you having a fight and want me to fix it up for you? This isn't a court of domestic relations, you know—

DINAH Oh, we don't fight—

SOL Then you belong in a museum—

FISHER Tell him, Dinah—

DINAH I'm quitting work, Mr. Ginsberg—

SOL Is that so? Has old Fisher struck oil?

DINAH You tell him, Harry—

FISHER She's expectant, Mr. Ginsberg—

SOL Oh—

DINAH What I expect is a baby—

SOL That's probably what you'll get! Name him after me and I'll start him off with a savings account--

DINAH I thought I'd name him Harry—

FISHER That's natural, isn't it, Mr. Ginsberg?

SOL The whole thing is so natural it don't need any comment—

DINAH I want to come back afterwards, Mr. Ginsberg. I been here nine years and I just love this place—

SOL Nine years... and in all that time you've never learned how to spell! Well, I'm surprised and pleased that the two of you can create a child between you— it's something to be proud of.

DINAH [*Quite transfigured*] It does seem wonderful—

SOL [*Looking at her keenly*] Does it? As wonderful as that, huh! This once you can have your job back, Dinah, but don't make a habit of it—

DINAH Thanks, Mr. Ginsberg.

SOL [*Pushing them both toward the door*] And take up spelling while you've got the leisure— You can quit this week, Dinah, you'll get a month's pay—

FISHER She's been scared to tell you, Mr. Ginsberg— but I told her you'd be a Prince about it. [FISHER *and* DINAH *exit.*]

SOL [*Alone, with a grim smile*] A prince, huh... [SARAH *enters right. She is well-dressed, businesslike, suggesting a woman who holds a responsible position.*]

SARAH Can I see you?

SOL Why not, Sarah?

MISS FARLEY [*Entering right*] Here's the money, Mr. Ginsberg.

SOL Thank you. [*He stuffs the bills in his trouser pocket without counting them.* MISS FARLEY *exits.*]

SARAH It's a personal matter.

SOL Sure. Don't be so formal, Sarah... just because I'm your employer doesn't change an old friendship, does it? [*She says nothing.*] Every time I look at you, I envy you... you're a lucky girl and you deserve it— handling some of our biggest accounts and drawing down a classy salary: you're young... handsome you are too! Me, I feel like an old man, I've got too many worries and not enough money! [*Looking at her with a sly smile, consciously kidding her*] You look to me like you didn't have a worry in the world... radiant, that's what you are! That's the word for you, radiant!

SARAH Thank you... I'm only worried about one thing right now: I wondered if you'd mind giving me an accounting, the money, you know?

SOL [*His brow clouding, shrugs before he replies*] Oh, why bring that up? Didn't I explain it all to you last week?

SARAH You told me a lot of complicated things about the stock market, I couldn't understand what it really meant— but for two years now I've been giving you half my salary each week to invest for me; you promised you'd double it and triple it for me—

SOL Well, have I, or haven't I?

SARAH I don't know, you act so queer about it.

SOL Call me a thief next.

SARAH [*In the same simple straightforward manner*] I don't want to leave it in your hands any more. I want you to give it back to me.

SOL Maybe right now I haven't got it.

SARAH [*Frightened, reacting to this as he knew she would*] What do you mean?

SOL [*Watching her sharply*] What are you so frightened about? Is money so important?

SARAH It's all I've got, it's my life savings—

SOL Glad to hear you say so, that's a healthy attitude: In the old days we didn't know money was so important. [*He chuckles.*]

SARAH What are you laughing at?

SOL Thinking of old times— remember how we talked about changing the world?

SARAH It still needs changing!

SOL Good! A brave little idealist, but just the same you want money in a sock— tell me, are they still at it? Do they still sweat at those crowded meetings? And we here, high up where the air is clear, we never hear a whisper!

SARAH I see what it is: I'm the old times to you, so you want to kill me because I haunt you like a memory... something you can't escape—

SOL What do you mean? I'm not escaping from anything—

SARAH Aren't you?

SOL My better self, is that the idea? Don't get excited about the money, Sarah; before you lose a cent I would give my heart's blood, I'd give blood if it would do you good, Sarah.

SARAH I don't want your sloppy sentiment, I can't stand it! I want what you owe me, I want it today.

SOL Just today you must trust me— maybe tomorrow—

SARAH It's always tomorrow with you.

SOL No, no, a happy tomorrow will come.

SARAH [*Bursts into wild tears*] Not for me, never for me!

SOL [*Touched, with genuine kindness*] There... you shouldn't worry so much.
[MISS FARLEY *enters right, with a card.*]

MISS FARLEY This man says he knows you, Mr. Ginsberg.

SOL [*Takes the card*] I'll settle up with you today, Sarah. [*Glancing at the card, surprised*] I'll say he does— send him in, Miss Farley— MISS FARLEY Yes, sir. [*She turns to door right.* SOL *passes the card to* SARAH.]

SOL Can you beat that, Sarah?

SARAH That *is* funny—

SOL Stay here and see him— you remember the boy— [JEFFERY HAL-LIBURTON *enters right. He is well-dressed, but he looks a little seedy— he has none of the cockiness of his earlier days. He is afraid, but forcing himself to appear sure and confident. There is a certain plodding sincer-*

ity about him. He carries a leather brief case which is rather worn.]

JEFFERY How are you, Mr. Ginsberg?

SOL Glad to see you, Halliburton— [*They shake hands.*]

JEFFERY Hello, Miss Glassman, this is like old times—

SARAH Indeed—

SOL [*Interrupts*] No it isn't, it's very different--

JEFFERY Yes, you're right, Mr. Ginsberg—

SOL Oh, I'm right, am I? Once upon a time you weren't so quick to agree with me—

JEFFERY I hesitated a long time about coming to see you, Mr. Ginsberg—

SOL [*Interrupts him, sizing him up, looking at the worn brief case, with brutal directness*] Then you're selling something! Is it the Encyclopedia Britannica, or a novelty cigarette case?

JEFFERY [*With an uneasy laugh*] Not quite that! I'm handling bonds, for McIntyre and Jones ...

SOL [*Wearily*] Don't make the rest of the speech— I've heard other fellows make it, but I don't want to hear it from you—

JEFFERY [*Crestfallen*] If you feel that way about it—

SOL [*Still sizing him up*] You ought to get a new brief-case! How long have you been in the bond business?

JEFFERY About two months— I've tried my hand at a lot of things—

SOL Married, aren't you? [JEFFERY *nods.*] How big a family have you got?

JEFFERY Two kids— we're out in Forest Hills.

SOL [*Brutally*] And all you can do for your family is pound the pavement with a brief-case full of lousy securities— [JEFFERY *gives* SOL *an angry look and turns away.*]

JEFFERY I'll be going...

SARAH [*Angrily*] Why do you want to make it harder for him?

SOL Why should I pity him? He started with all the cards stacked on his side— a college education and a lot of rich friends—

JEFFERY [*Turns vigorously*] Don't worry about pitying me, Ginsberg, I'm getting along— I'm a happy man—

SOL [*Startled*] What do you mean, happy?

JEFFERY Thanks for giving me two minutes of your time—

SOL [*Stopping him*] What's your hurry? I'll make you a proposition— [JEFFERY turns to him.] How would you like a job?... [*He hesitates.*] As Fisher's assistant, in the statistical department— at fifty a week?

JEFFERY Are you being funny?

SOL Not me.

JEFFERY [*His voice actually trembling*] When can I begin?

SOL Come along, I'll bring you to Fisher right now—

JEFFERY Thanks— [*As they start for door right , MERRITT enters left rear.*]

MERRITT I just got back this minute, Sol—

SOL Here's a fraternity brother of yours, R.-M.

MERRITT Hello, Jeff.

JEFFERY Hello, Mr. Merritt—

SOL [*Patting* JEFFERY *good-naturedly*] He's going to be with us from now on. Come with me, Jeff— I'll be back in two minutes, Raymond. [SOL *and* JEFFERY *exit right.* MERRITT *is astonished.*]

MERRITT Well I'll be damned! [*Thoughtfully*] I didn't know Sol would do anything as kind as that.

SARAH I did! Every now and then Sol comes out of his shell and you see how fine he really is.

MERRITT [*Understandingly*] That means a lot to you, doesn't it? [*She is silent.*]

MERRITT You're a fool, Sarah; you waste your life on a single-track emotion— you can't go on like this.

SARAH [*Quietly*] I can go on—

MERRITT I've been watching you, you're unhappy... I love you—

SARAH Love... You don't know what it means!

MERRITT Don't I? That depends on how you look at it! But it's done me a lot of good: loving you, even at a distance, has made me see something I never believed in— the soul, I think—

SARAH Mine's all twisted and dark.

MERRITT I've caught glimpses once or twice.

SARAH Awful, isn't it? Like looking down a deep well... you look at me now like you thought I was crazy—

MERRITT Why don't you marry me?

SARAH [*Laughs hysterically*] I suppose I should be grateful to you for asking, but I think it's funny—

MERRITT What's to prevent it? It's a sensible plan!

SARAH I don't want sensible plans— oh, any psychologist would size me up for you in about five minutes— I'm a highly emotional woman, so high-strung that it almost crosses the borderline of common sense—

MERRITT [*Gravely*] If you'd give me a chance—

SARAH To make a normal woman of me— a cozy love-life for two! [*She laughs harshly.*] Thanks, no... Love for me is something that burns you up, kills you... you die of it... For all you know, I may be dying of it right now—

MERRITT [*Tenderly, holding her arm*] My dear—

SARAH [*Breaking away violently*] Don't touch me, I'll scream—

MERRITT Sorry—

SARAH It's not your fault— you're sweet to me, and I'm so wrought up I bawl you out like a mad woman— [SOL *enters right.*]

SOL [*To* MERRITT *briskly as he enters*] Did you get the Excelsior Paint people sewed up?

MERRITT Yes, we're to start a hundred thousand dollar campaign immediately for the household varnishes—

SOL [*Briskly*] Miss Glassman will take care of that—

MERRITT All right... [*To* SARAH] It's a rush job; I'll explain it to you to-night if you're not too tired—

SARAH I'd like to start right away—

MERRITT You'll find a memorandum on my desk— look it over— I'll be in shortly— [SARAH *nods and exits left rear.* SOL *sits at his desk.*]

SOL Sit down, Raymond; have a cigar.

MERRITT No thanks— [MERRITT *lights a cigarette.*]

SOL [*Thoughtfully fingering the contract brought by* TURNER, *which lies on his desk*] I'm thinking of making some changes around here.

MERRITT [*Sarcastically*] It's nice of you to consult me.

SOL In this case, it's necessary to consult you: are you satisfied with our present association, Raymond?

MERRITT [*Uneasily*] It's all right, I'm not as ambitious as I once was.

SOL Is that so? I am—

MERRITT [*Drily*] So I've noticed: what are you getting at?

SOL I worry a lot, Raymond.

MERRITT [*Amused*] About the poor and needy, I suppose?

SOL Yeh... sometimes... when you see those breadlines on Broadway, it shows you how insecure everything is... why we know men that were millionaires a year ago that haven't got the price of a beer—

MERRITT You're pretty safe.

SOL Not enough, never enough! I wouldn't be safe if I had money to control the world.

MERRITT What's the good of all your money, if you're not satisfied?

SOL Are you? Don't you ever look at the moon and think, "I want to own it?" Don't you ever look at women, the glittering shiny kind you see sometimes in shows, and say "I'd like to show that Jane where to get off!"

MERRITT [*Looks at* SOL *sharply*] What's this for, Sol? What are you getting at behind this smoke screen?

SOL It's no smoke screen... I'm just trying to tell you I'm not satisfied— I got to think of myself... my own future... I could make three times the money if I ran this business alone.

MERRITT What do you expect me to do?

SOL What do you suppose? [*Leaning across desk*] You're quitting—

MERRITT This is my business—

SOL Don't be dizzy, Raymond! It's not yours any more, it's out of your reach, just like the moon is—

MERRITT Been planning this, have you? Nursing a grievance.

SOL What would I have a grievance about? We are friends.

MERRITT Yes, there's really a very strong bond between us.

SOL Sure. Let's not get soft about it.

MERRITT A bond which makes us fight to the death, is that it?

SOL It's got to be, Raymond! You and I are different people, we have different ideas, different methods. There's no room for both of us in one concern; it's not fair to either of us.

MERRITT You can't buy me out of here with a million.

SOL [*Suavely*] Well a million is a lot of money... what would you say your interest here was worth right now?

MERRITT I haven't thought.

SOL I have! I figured it out to a penny: a hundred thousand cash and five percent of the yearly net from now on: that would cover your rights, wouldn't it?

MERRITT I don't know.

SOL Well, what I'm offering you is two hundred thousand and eight percent of the yearly net: that's almost double what your share is worth, but it's not a question of money with me, Raymond, it's a question of pride. [*Tossing the contract to* MERRITT] Look it over.

MERRITT Did you ever consider that I have a little pride myself? [SOL *shrugs.*] Is Sonnenberg in on this?

SOL Certainly—

MERRITT You can't run this business alone, you're too unbalanced— I'm the ballast—

SOL That's funny from a man that's lost his shirt in the market, while I've been piling up a fortune—

MERRITT You've been lucky— crazy man's luck—

SOL Sure, personally I'm crazy— even should I lie down on a piece of toast and tell you I'm a poached egg, my money mind keeps right on working— when I get violent put me in a straitjacket, but I'll still be able to guess the market!

MERRITT Of course I'm in a position where I need ready money; I suppose you figured on that?

SOL I'm being fair, Raymond, but I want my own way and I'm going to have it!

MERRITT This is the rottenest thing you ever pulled.

SOL Sure it's rotten, don't I know it? If a man's in business, he's got to use the methods that fit: I got no choice, business is rotten from the ground up!

MERRITT You're actually talking like a radical—

SOL Not me! To Hell with that— I turned my back on it, and I got to go on— I was a radical once, a boy... a fool of a boy— I murdered him, and he's waiting round every corner to murder me now—

SOL Probably be another brawl— don't wake me up when you come home.

AGGIE All right— why so gloomy?

SOL I just had a fuss with Raymond—

AGGIE Haven't you done enough to him, kicking him out of his own office?

SOL I didn't kick him out: he preferred the library because it's more comfortable and it's got a shower— but that don't matter now, he's through.

AGGIE Through? I suppose you'll say he'll be more comfortable out of the business entirely.

SOL What's it to you?

AGGIE The more I see of you, the sorer you make me—

SOL Same here— why argue? [*He pulls the roll of bills out of his pocket and tosses it across the desk.*] Here's what you came for—

AGGIE [*Stuffing it in her purse*] Thanks—

SOL You still come around for your pay, Aggie, just like with him—

AGGIE My God, can't you forget?

SOL No.

AGGIE You hold against me things that happened years ago, drag 'em up on every occasion— for what?

SOL For what?

AGGIE It's a mess—

MERRITT What the devil do you mean?

SOL Nothing... I mean you got to sign that, no help for it.

MERRITT Turner drew this?

SOL Sure.

MERRITT I'll consult another lawyer in the morning and let you know—

SOL Then it's as good as settled—

MERRITT I don't know—

SOL All friendly, huh, Raymond? [MISS FARLEY *enters, right.*]

MISS FARLEY Excuse me, Mr. Ginsberg, Mrs. Ginsberg.

SOL Send her in... wait a minute, Raymond; say hello to Aggie— [AGNES *enters right, expensively dressed, her manner nervous and artificially gay.*]

AGNES Hello, people.

MERRITT How are you, Mrs. Ginsberg?

SOL Why so formal? [*They laugh.*]

AGNES [*To* MERRITT] You must come to dinner soon; we'll get a fourth and play bridge—

MERRITT I should be delighted. See you later, Sol. [*He exits left rear;* SOL *turns to his desk, and sits gloomily.*]

SOL Are you in a hurry, Aggie?

AGNES No, I'm meeting these people at eight— plenty of time to go home and dress.

SOL What's so bad about it? Everything you want I give you— have I ever refused you anything?

AGNES You hang jewels on me like a faithful slave; but I don't happen to be a slave and I don't like it.

SOL You're no slave, you don't wear a ball and chain— you go out to parties with your own friends, you jazz around without so much as asking me—

AGNES Nerves—

SOL Sure nerves make you buy everything you lay your eyes on— a painting by Cézanne or a Marie Antoinette bed or a new electric vibrator— pile up things... rosewood and teakwood and mahogany... diamonds, rubies, gold— for them, you make an ape of me—

AGNES Do you know what I'm going to do! I'm going out to Reno and get it over with—

SOL No you don't—

AGNES Why not?

SOL I won't let you go— never—

AGNES What do you want me for? We're at each other's throats all the time.

SOL If the whole facts about us were spoken, I mean all of it, it's fit to make anyone kill themselves, jump from that window... [*She walks over and stares out the window.* SOL *repeats bitterly*] Yes sir, jump from that window.

AGNES You know it, why don't you jump?

SOL Money keeps me here, tied down with bags of it.

AGNES You just worry about that to keep your mind off other things— just to cover up your own lack— bah... you're not a man!

SOL Why not?

AGNES Because all you've got is sensuality and greed and imagination.

SOL I thought that was enough to make one of God's creatures—

AGNES No, there's courage... courage to throw one thing away to get the other.

SOL Would you mind explaining that... in words of one syllable?

AGNES You won't give up anything— you won't give me up, though you hate me. Look at it fairly, Sol: when you put the ring on my finger I was crazy happy. Love, honor and obey is gonna mean something in this case, I said to myself— then I found out you just wanted to torture me all the time.

SOL I won't let you go, Aggie... I know you're no good... but I go hot and cold when you're near me!

AGNES Then, Sol, why don't you have the courage to try— make it real—

SOL Get away from me— you can't trap me with that stuff; it's not you at all— the lust and splendor I've known are in my won mind— there's pure beauty burning in my mind—

AGNES Damn your imagination!

SOL It's like the places in the ads— Deauville, Riviera, Lido— they're heaven in your mind, but they're a lot of noise and a dollar for a twenty -cent cigar when you get there. Hell, it's all dust!

AGNES Then what in the name of common sense do you want?

SOL Me! I lust after strange women and strange gods—

AGNES Oh, nonsense—

SOL To you it's nonsense, 'cause you got no heart—

AGNES Oh, haven't I?

SOL A woman that cheats her marriage bed with practical strangers 'cause it's a habit she contracted in youth—

AGNES That's a lie, you're the one that cheats—

SOL I'd like to tear your skin to make you feel— but it's no use! I know your heart— what there is of it— the dirty little reality of it.

AGNES You don't know me at all— you make up things about me— you got every part of me in a card index, haven't you? The wax face— the jewels— the hot kisses— [*She beats her fists against him violently.*] That's not me— You're too selfish to see the real me that's standing here screaming, "Look at me!... look at me!"

SOL [*Seizing her roughly*] I'm looking right through you—

AGNES You're hurting me—

SOL Am I?

AGNES You got fingers like claws—

SOL I'd like to kill you just to see you squirm— [*Agnes screams. The room has become quite grey— suddenly the door left rear opens, casting a bright beam of light on the two struggling figures. MERRITT enters , SARAH following him, remaining at edge of lighted doorway. SOL quickly releases AGNES.*]

MERRITT What's up?

SOL Nothing much— for a minute I felt like killing my wife— I guess that's old-fashioned stuff, isn't it, Raymond?

AGNES I was scared green—

SOL She says she's through with me, Raymond— why don't you take her?

MERRITT Calm down, Sol—

SOL It's a fair proposition, I take the business and you take my wife in exchange... We four have been tangled up together long enough— I'm through with the bunch of you— I'll go on alone— you're out, Raymond— [*Turning to* AGNES] Get a divorce— [*Turning to* SARAH] And you, Sarah, meet me here tonight. I'll give you an accounting and hand you a check— Let's make an end of it, bury our loves and hates in the ashcan— and start over! I'm going out and cool off— [*He exits left front. The three people stare at one another.*]

AGNES He doesn't mean a word of it— He's just letting off steam—

MERRITT I'm going out of here and get a stiff drink.

AGNES Several, I'd say— may I come, Raymond?

MERRITT You?

AGNES Don't look so dumb about it! An old-fashioned riot would do us both a lot of good.

MERRITT Not a bad idea— one moment. ... [*He exits through open door left.*]

AGNES Want to come, Miss Glassman?

SARAH No, I'll wait here for him... [MERRITT *reappears carrying hat, coat and cane.*]

AGNES Nothing like drowning your sorrows... [MERRITT *looks at* SARAH *for a minute. There is nothing he can say. He exits left front with* AGNES. AGNES' *musical laugh echoes for a moment as the door shuts.* SARAH *sits at* SOL'S *desk, her face in shadow, the light from open door left rear falling on her hands that twist on the desk in front of her.*]

SARAH [*Mutters in agonized voice*] Drown your sorrows... drown your sorrows ... [*Her voice becomes almost a scream as she repeats the words and the stage goes black.*] Drown your sorrows...

[*Black out.*]

[*Curtain.*]

Scene 2

The same scene. Early the next morning.

The icy winter dawn is brightening outside the windows left. The lamp on SOL'S desk is lighted, and SARAH sits beside the desk, waiting quietly. After a moment , SOL enters right, looks at her with a pleased grunt. He is distraught and tired, evidently under a considerable strain.

SOL Um... you? What you doing here?

SARAH I've been here all night.

SOL You? Just sitting there? That's foolish. What time is it?

SARAH Nearly six, getting light.

SOL So you've been here all night?

SARAH Yes, you heard me. You told me to wait here. I didn't mind, I had to think about such a lot.

SOL Me too! [*He takes a small pearl-handled revolver from the pocket of his overcoat, tosses it on the desk, takes off the coat, throws the coat in a corner and sits.*]

SARAH What's that?

SOL Oh, that? Pretty, isn't it? I gave it to her for her birthday; said she wanted it beside her bed, scared having so much jewelry and things... maybe she wanted it for something else, maybe she was scared of me.

SARAH But you're really a gentle person, Sol.

SOL No, I've treated her pretty rough all along, couldn't help it. She's had that power over me, just to look at her would often give me the heebie-jeebies.

SARAH You seen her since last night?

SOL No— I waited home for her till four o'clock this morning— then I went out—

SARAH [*Picks up revolver*] With this in your pocket? Why?

SOL What did she say when she left here?

SARAH She and Merritt went out together.

SOL There you are— the cheap tart! But it don't matter—

SARAH You'd use this?

SOL [*Taking the revolver from her and looking at it*] Was I looking for her or looking for myself?... Been walking through empty streets for hours— zowie, it was cold... too cold to think— too cold to breathe— Can you help me?

SARAH If I could, Sol—

SOL How about it, Sarah? Why don't you shoot me yourself? You'd save me such a lot of trouble.

SARAH One of your jokes—

SOL Never more serious in my life!

SARAH On account of her, your wife? You love her so much?

SOL Love's got nothing to do with it— it's black magic!

SARAH Don't you ever look at anything simply, Sol—

SOL No, I prefer to make it complicated: I'm always contriving things; I got a demon in me makes me twist and turn people... I live in a series of contrivances, like a picture in the funny papers—

SARAH It's not worth it—

SOL What in Hell is worth anything?

SARAH Ask yourself—

SOL I'm not on speaking terms with myself. Help me, Sarah— there's so much between us!

SARAH For God's sake, Sol, why do you lie so much? What does it get you?

SOL My life has got me plenty.

SARAH Has it?

SOL Well, I'm young yet... maybe when I get a billion I'll support a theatre or an art gallery— these fellers that paint and write has got the goods on us— they create— I'd give my heart and liver to be able to create—

SARAH There are other ways of creating— you're a failure and you're just making excuses!

SOL Can a man be a failure with so much money in the bank?

SARAH You've given yourself to the wrong things.

SOL I have given nothing, I have taken, but not enough: I want to be a king and I'm a little business man. I used to dream about estates and yachts.

SARAH Well, you've got them.

SOL I got a lawn stretching all the way to the sea, blocks of it out on Long Island, but I can't go there, I hate it... no children... Now I'll never have those brats, I'll never have anything, I'll just want and make it up, nothing to it— I wanted too much.

SARAH Then stop wanting and be yourself.

SOL I can't... that's the curse on me, the desire eating me, to be a great man, leading armies, plotting for the earth... this feller Christ took me up to a high mountain and showed me the earth, you know the story?

SARAH You've got the story mixed.

SOL No, this is my story... this Christ was a Jew dressed in a rainbow, and He said, "Do you want the earth, Solomon Ginsberg, or do you want to join me in a cellar, sweating and plotting with a few close friends?" Well, I made my choice and somewhere Christ is in a cellar laughing at me right now— don't I know it?

SARAH You mean the people in cellars are stronger than you are?

SOL Stronger than all Hell because they know what they want. Maybe I'll have the laugh on them yet— maybe when I get a billion I'll hand it to the Communist party—

SARAH You're joking—

SOL But a good joke, huh? Sol Ginsberg has built, now he tears down!

SARAH I see one thing... sometimes I've thought you had ice water in you instead of blood... But the blood's boiling in you—

SOL The blood of a race. There's that, too—

SARAH I don't mean that—

SOL It goes back a long way— but how far ahead? I've broken the chain with the past... then what am I? A missing link—

SARAH Of course, if you're afraid to look back or look ahead... Why won't you be faithful to yourself! To your own strength? There's greatness in you!

SOL For what? To make me smash my head against stone walls?

SARAH You smash your head if you try to be what you're not.

SOL I suppose I should be a sappy poet, an idealist?

SARAH No, that's the whole trouble with you— you put two and two together and make six, and when you find it don't work you're so frightened you can't stand it— you think you're good 'cause you get money and spend money, you're just a cog in a wheel; you're so dumb you're surprised that you can't run the machinery— That's like putting your head on a railroad track and being surprised at what the train does to you: that's being soft— but you have brains enough to see what's going on and take sides... One minute you brag about millions and the next minute you want to destroy! One's as crazy as the other— Go ahead and destroy, it just shows how weak you are! bring things, smash things— smash yourself too!

SOL You're a big help: you knock the props right out from under me.

SARAH You won't see; you'd rather die than see!

SOL All this time, for several years, there's been a feeling between us, a little spark. I've kept it alive by this little fuss over money; that's why I did it, holding onto you, making you hate me! Foolish, wasn't it? [*He takes a check from his pocket, glancing at it thoughtfully.*] Now that's clear, I might as well give you the check... Tell me, Sarah, what are you going to do with all this money?

SARAH I have plans.

SOL Huh? [*He offers her the check.*] Seventy-two thousand dollars.

SARAH [*Astonished, frightened*] I only gave you a little over four thousand!

SOL I used it. I told you you'd get plenty of interest.

SARAH But I couldn't—

SOL You're not going to argue about money, after what we said about the filthy stuff? I wasn't unfaithful about the money, Sarah... I been unfaithful in other ways.

SARAH I'm going away, that's why I was so anxious.

SOL Going away? Where to?

SARAH I don't know— anywhere. ...

SOL You leave me? You leave the business? Just when I need you?

SARAH You don't suppose I'm so fond of it here, do you?

SOL I don't want you to go away. ...

SARAH I'm thinking of myself— I want to go somewhere where it's different—

SOL There's no such place—

SARAH I'm not sure—

SOL That's just a way of escape... then you're just as mixed up as I am!

SARAH Of course I am— I don't believe in anything— I've got to find some way of going ahead— I must—

SOL I don't know which way to turn.

SARAH Sol. ...

SOL I can't lose you— you! You and me are one; there's part of you locked in my heart—

SARAH Why do you do this to me? What do you want of me?

SOL Something to believe in, something to hold onto!

SARAH You're so romantic, you won't see anything as it really is: for years you've hardly spoken a word to me, and all of a sudden you want me to believe you're dying of grief about me! It's ridiculous; people aren't like that; you don't know anything about people—

SOL You're right there. Look at us in this office! Two men with a poisonous loving hatred, Merritt and me, both in love with a woman's soul, which is you— and in turn we possessed a woman's body— a cheap thing— a rotten thing to buy with money—

SARAH You've got no right to say that—

SOL You want the truth— there it is! That woman is nothing, a bone to be squabbled over! Bah!

SARAH But you said—

SOL Do you think I was upset about her today? Nonsense; I didn't give her a thought— it was other things... *you!* I turn to you now, a blind man turning to the light.

SARAH I can't listen to you—

SOL [*Seizing her.*] Answer from your heart— Look at me, answer me! Has it ever changed?

SARAH If you have any pity, don't—

SOL I have no pity, I am trying to save myself. Do you know what it means to give in like this, after the years I've battled against it?... to turn to you like a man that's had every shred of pride torn from him?

SARAH I don't give a damn for your pride—

SOL Neither do I! Do you see what that means? Neither do I! I'm begging you!

SARAH It's too late... a year ago maybe, if you'd told me this then... but now it's too late.

SOL Why?

SARAH What?

SOL You heard me, I said *why?* You hold love in the hollow of your hand, maybe that's enough! All along it would have been enough, something as simple as that!

SARAH You can't kill a person and then bring them back to life, Sol. If I gave in now, you'd make me more miserable—

SOL [*His arms about her*] We're tired... both of us so tired. ...

SARAH You've turned a knife in my heart... and I haven't minded, because it was you turning the knife, turning. ...

SOL I hold you against me, gently... gently... [SARAH'S *arms go about him, she presses his head to her bosom.*]

SARAH It's no good, it hurts too much... bitter... it cuts into you, makes your flesh sore... Hold me tighter, tighter! Crown me with thorns, burn me with kisses, tear me down, limb from limb... tear my body, trample me, make me a wilderness— we been walking in a wilderness, walking in the dark— show me the light—

SOL We been blind; we haven't seen each other. [*The telephone rings.*]

SARAH Answer that.

SOL [*At phone*] Hello... oh, it's you, Aggie; where are you? Who's with you? Merritt? The others went home? Oh you're dancing? Sure I can hear the music... you ought to have more sense... no, there's nothing unusual; I couldn't sleep so I came down to the office... is that so? You *must* be squiffy to feel so sentimental... Sure I do... I was upset last night but it's nothing serious... No, don't come down to the office... you'd better go home and get some rest... Alright darling... [*He rings off.*] Jazzing around with Merritt, damn her! [SARAH *looks at him with bitter understanding.*]

SARAH [*Slowly*] You said— nothing serious— nothing unusual— you and your black magic!

SOL What?

SARAH You want everything to go on as it is— you won't give up anything— and me! You think you can fit me in?

SOL It's complicated, we must arrange—

SARAH You insist on cheapening everything, you dirty everything...

SOL Life is just like the market: you can't beat the game.

SARAH For a minute you really loved me— for one awful minute—

SOL I love you now—

SARAH Don't spoil it with lies— I won't be mixed up in your black magic— I've seen you squeeze the blood out of everyone near you—

SOL You think you're so far above me, you sit in judgment—

SARAH No, I just want to get away.

SOL Listen Sarah, I've been lucky; everything I've touched has turned to gold and it's no good—

SARAH You won't turn me into gold.

SOL [*His arms tight about her*] The money don't matter to you, I know that—

SARAH Then let me go! Let me go— I'll kill you!

SOL Because you love me?

SARAH Yes, if that's the only way—

SOL That's comic— that's funny—

SARAH I see you now— loving nothing— lost— Let me go—

SOL No, you're mine—

SARAH It's my whole life, you'd break it for a moment's excitement, to show your strength— it's not fair—

SOL I don't care what's fair.

SARAH Don't do this, Sol, don't— I love you—

SOL Say it again, say it with that crazy voice!

SARAH Let me go! I love you, Sol, get away from me; don't touch me— you're horrible— it's not you— I love you, Sol, I— [*Her hand, fighting for freedom, has touched the pistol on the desk. Suddenly she raises it to his side and fires. He crumples against the desk. She stands away from him. The revolver clatters to the floor. They stand there looking at each other.*]

SARAH Sol, I didn't mean—

SOL Yes you did, don't spoil it by apologizing. You did right, I deserve this, I like it... You... you got a fine sense of comedy, Sarah. I hand it to you.

SARAH You're not hurt, you can't be—

SOL I been dead a long time! Where the Hell is that revolver? I want it in my hand. Give me that gun, we got to make it look right— Give it here— and then get out— [AGNES *enters right. She is in a lovely evening dress, low-cut, gorgeous. She shows the effects of a night out. She comes gaily into the room, stops short, facing* SARAH *who still holds the revolver in her hand.*]

AGNES Sol... [MERRITT *follows* AGNES *into the room, in a dress suit, also rather exhausted by a big evening.*]

SOL My God! This business of dying is the bunk like everything else... Let me look at you, Aggie... you'll be a snappy widow and rich too... change your name from Ginsberg to Grinnel, like we talked about, and don't... don't spend money too fast.

AGNES Don't talk like that.

SOL Can't I kid a little, even at the end?

MERRITT I'll get a doctor—

SOL Forget about doctors, Raymond.

SARAH Sol—

SOL [*To* SARAH] One time there was a Jew named Christ dressed up in a rainbow, he told the world plenty, maybe there'll be some more like him... Me, I don't care! I'm only thinking of myself. Put me in a solid silver coffin with gold cupids— don't matter what it costs... [*Starts to laugh, stiffens in* SARAH'S *arms*]

MERRITT There's a doctor in the building; he's coming—

SARAH I don't think a doctor will do much good.

MERRITT Better give me that gun--

SARAH I did it! I don't want any lies about it—

AGNES Don't be a fool, nobody will say anything.

SARAH I will. I want everyone to know—

AGNES Shut up; pull yourself together; don't you suppose this hits me as bad as you? You don't know... He was locked in here and he killed himself. We came down— we three together, and round the door locked. Get that straight, somebody's got to use their head— take that telephone and call up somebody— Take the telephone, Raymond—
[MERRITT *helplessly picks up telephone.*] Get the police; tell 'em exactly what I say; take hold of that phone and call them— Tell the police it's a suicide, tell 'em he had a nervous breakdown... too much work... too ambitious...

      [*Her voice goes on as* THE CURTAIN FALLS.]

GENTLEWOMAN

GENTLEWOMAN

THE GROUP THEATRE
IN ASSOCIATION WITH D. A. DORAN, JR.
presented
GENTLEWOMAN
by JOHN HOWARD LAWSON
Opening at the Cort Theatre, March 22, 1934
Directed by Lee Strasberg
Settings by Mordecai Gorelik
Lighting by Feder

CAST

CONNIE BLANE	Claudia Morgan
ELLIOTT SNOWDEN	Lewis Leverett
HAVENS	Russell Collins
DR LEWIS GOLDEN	Morris Carnovsky
MRS. STONELEIGH	Zamah Cunningham
GWYN BALLANTINE	Stella Adler
COL. RICHARD FOWLER	Roman Bohnen
RUDY FLANNIGAN	Lloyd Nolan
VAUGHN	Neill O'Malley
HATTIE	Frances Williams

THE RE:GROUP THEATRE COMPANY
presented
GENTLEWOMAN
as a staged reading
February 28, 2011
The Barrow Group Mainstage Theatre
New York, NY

ACT ONE

SCENE: *Library of the Ballantine house. Evening. The room is paneled in
fine polished wood, with a large number of bookshelves built into the
walls in an irregular design. Center, facing the audience, a large comfortable couch. Left rear, an arched doorway, across which hang shim-
mering curtains. Through these curtains, when they are later drawn
aside, can be seen the brightly lighted drawing room of the house. The
entire wall space right is occupied by windows with leaded panes, under
which runs a cushioned window seat. Outside the
windows is the white glow of summer moonlight. At right end of the
couch is a table. There are two doors in rear wall, center and at right.
Between these a fine old Colonial mirror. Under the mirror a long heavy
table of Colonial design. Left, on an extending shelf, is an
intricate model of a clipper ship.*

*The architectural lines of the room are gracious, and the whole
atmosphere radiates wealth and good taste. The design is early
American, and every item of decoration has been chosen to fulfill the
Colonial pattern perfectly. Each piece of furniture is correct,
unobtrusive, priceless. The light comes from lamps and brass wall
brackets.*

*The room is empty. A subdued chatter of polite conversation can be
heard from the drawing room through the curtains. A girl enters through
the curtains. This is* CONNIE BLANE, *a graceful young thing, a débutante
who has been out of finishing school just long enough to know her way
about: she is not a clever or unusual person, but she has freshness and
beauty; rather sensual mouth, and big pleading eyes. She stands at the
curtains for a moment and beckons.* ELLIOTT
SNOWDEN *follows her into the room, tiptoeing guiltily; he is a blond
man of thirty, who has enjoyed all the social advantages of wealth and
education, but he is not the athletic type. In the seven years since his
graduation from Harvard, he has become a famous novelist and has be-
gun to show a tendency to stoutness. He is still a little surprised that his
books are being translated into twelve languages, and is trying to live up
to his literary reputation. But he is much too nice a person to be conceit-
ed. He has the face of an attractive spoiled child. He is genteel, good-
tempered, negatively likable, with the rather imbecile air that frequently
characterizes the successful literatus. Both are in evening dress.*

The buzz of subdued conversation continues from the farther room.

CONNIE [*Pulling him along*] They didn't even notice our leaving, did they?

ELLIOTT Aunt Kate noticed, she winked at me in a very malicious way—

CONNIE [*Turning to him, behind couch center*] How do they stand it, Elliott?

ELLIOTT How do they stand what?

CONNIE All this heavy talk about Russia and social planning and the unemployed!

ELLIOTT [*With mock solemnity*] My dear child, haven't you heard that civilization is all in a dither and Spengler says we're all doomed?

CONNIE [*Giggling*] Oh, shut up... [*Looking into his eyes encouragingly, one hand on his shoulder*] You and I are not doomed, are we, Elliott? [*Kiss*] I really don't understand you, Elliott. I'm not sure you're crazy about me at all.

ELLIOTT [*Just a bit vaguely*] Mad as a hatter about you!

CONNIE [*Lying back on the couch with a yawn*] Thanks... that's consoling! [*She looks off toward drawing room.*] Are they always like this? Do they always sit around and chatter about Russian education and trouble in China?

ELLIOTT Why not? There's a lot in it—

CONNIE As long as they stuck to Freud, I listened because I thought it might get dirty—

ELLIOTT You'll get used to Gwyn's parties—

CONNIE Let's have a drink!

ELLIOTT Good idea. [*He rings bell by door right rear.*]

CONNIE I'm a little tight now...

ELLIOTT I noticed you kept filling up your glass with straight whiskey.

CONNIE [Who *can't keep her mind off the annoying subject of* GWYN BALLANTINE] What's her husband like?

ELLIOTT Jack's a brilliant man. They're a perfect match.

CONNIE When a woman whom one hardly knows invites one to dinner and her husband isn't there—

ELLIOTT She explained that he was called to Wilmington to a directors' meeting.

CONNIE [With a *little smile*] I don't believe everything I hear. [HAVENS, *the butler, enters right rear. He is a thin, elderly man in black, very correct and noncommittal.*]

HAVENS You rang, sir?

ELLIOTT Scotch and soda, Havens.

CONNIE If you don't mind, Havens, I'll have some of that Napoleon brandy we had after dinner.

HAVENS Very good, miss. [He *exits.*]

CONNIE [Beckoning *to* ELLIOTT] Come here, Elliott... [He *sits beside her.*] I might as well tell you my guilty secret and take the consequences... [She *whispers dramatically.*] I don't *like* Gwyn Ballantine!

ELLIOTT [Palpably *shocked*] What?

CONNIE [Rises, *annoyed*] There! You act as if I'd spat on your patron saint!

ELLIOTT You're being absurd, Connie.

CONNIE Am I? [She *crosses to window right.*]

ELLIOTT Gwyn's Aunt Kate is my mother's dearest friend... I'm practically a member of the family— Gwyn and I have grown up together.

CONNIE And you're so much under their influence, that I have to be brought here for approval.

ELLIOTT [Laughs, *joins her at the window right*] You've stood the test beautifully.

CONNIE [Trying *to open one of the windows right*] Open this window, will you, Elliott? I'm suffocating.

ELLIOTT [*Opening the window*] That's the result of six highballs.

CONNIE [*Correcting him*] Four! [*At the moonlit window, looking out*] What a lovely garden!

ELLIOTT Yes... she's crazy about it, she works out there a few hours every day.

CONNIE [*Triumphantly*] She *would!* I'll bet she does it with rubber gloves like a surgeon.

ELLIOTT As a matter of fact she does.

CONNIE And she knows all about flowers and calls them by their Latin names.

ELLIOTT Well, isn't that rather nice?

CONNIE She's much too nice. And what's more, she doesn't like me, she thinks I'm a little fool who's trying to catch you in a steel trap—

ELLIOTT You're absolutely wrong, she says it's an ideal match.

CONNIE You didn't tell her, did you, that we hadn't decided yet whether it should be a match or an affair?

ELLIOTT No, she wouldn't understand that!

[HAVENS *enters right rear with drinks on a tray.* ELLIOTT *turns to him.*]
Thank you, Havens, we'll pour them.

HAVENS Very good, sir—

CONNIE [*Hotly*] Oh, she wouldn't understand— she's far above such earthly problems as sex—

ELLIOTT [*Discreetly nudging her to wait until* HAVENS *has left the room*]
Please, darling, one moment—

[HAVENS *walks to the door with measured steps, and exits.* ELLIOTT *rises and starts to pour the drinks.* CONNIE *stands beside him; she is very upset, nervous and angry.*]

CONNIE You know you're a fool, Elliott— you write books that make millions of women cry—

ELLIOTT [*Easily*] Not millions!

CONNIE [*Disregarding the interruption*] But you don't know a thing about how people feel!

ELLIOTT I know how *I* feel, Connie, and I hope you feel the same way.

CONNIE [*As he pours brandy into a big liqueur glass*] Fill it up to the top.

ELLIOTT It's not supposed to be full; you're supposed to wiggle it around and get the aroma.

CONNIE To hell with the aroma! [*He obediently fills her glass to the brim. She sits on the couch again, thoughtful and troubled.*] You're right... Since we feel as we do, the sensible thing is to go ahead and try it out. I don't know what's the matter with me, but nature just didn't design me for a tart!

ELLIOTT [*Pouring seltzer into his glass*] My temperament is hardly that of a roué either—

CONNIE Elliott— we're both so hopelessly old-fashioned. Imagine two people nowadays arguing for weeks and weeks about whether they should live together— as if it mattered—

ELLIOTT It matters to us.

CONNIE It's really your fault. You're much more moral about it than I am. Whenever I'm ready to fall into your arms, you start warning me about what a young girl ought to know—

ELLIOTT Darling— [*He is interrupted by the entrance of* DR. MORRIS GOLDEN.]

DR. GOLDEN I hope I don't intrude. [*He goes to a ladder at the side of the room and begins to look for a book.*]

ELLIOTT Not at all.

CONNIE We were having a little scientific discussion, Dr. Golden, about the sex life of the clam.

DR. GOLDEN Really? I'm not very familiar with their habits.

CONNIE They palpitate and stay in their shells.
[DR. GOLDEN *has now reached the ceiling and is scanning the top shelf earnestly.*]

ELLIOTT [*Looking up at him, innocently*] Are you looking for something, Dr. Golden?

DR. GOLDEN Yes, for a book.

ELLIOTT I thought you were chasing butterflies.

DR. GOLDEN [*Laughs good-naturedly*] I'm trying to find a volume for Colonel Fowler.
[MRS. STONELEIGH *draws aside the curtains leading to the drawing room, and stands in the opening. She is a vigorous, metallic, hard-boiled old lady, brusque and opinionated in spite of her sixty years. She wears a lot of valuable jewelry and dresses in a rather old-*

fashioned manner.]

MRS. STONELEIGH [*Surveying the room*] As I suspected: While we talk of weighty matters, the younger generation is in here drinking boisterously.

CONNIE We haven't reached the boisterous stage yet, Mrs. Stoneleigh.

ELLIOTT I don't know why you always refer to me as the younger generation, Aunt Kate.

MRS. STONELEIGH After a careful reading of your latest novels, Elliott, I'm surprised that you don't still wear diapers.

ELLIOTT You just don't like modern writing.

MRS. STONELEIGH [*Dismissing the matter*] Fiddlesticks! [*She looks up at* DR. GOLDEN *with twinkling eyes.*] You look like a flagpole sitter, Dr. Golden.

DR. GOLDEN I can't seem to locate the book.

MRS. STONELEIGH [Calling *into further room*] Come and rescue Dr. Golden, Gwyn—
[GWYN *enters from the drawing room. She is thirty, a queenly woman wearing a simple evening gown which sets off her calm beauty to perfection. Her charm is not at all saccharine. She has poise and brains; she is disarmingly direct in her attitude toward people and things. It would be rather difficult to shock or disturb her, not because she is vapid, but because she is well-balanced and knows herself. She wears a lovely necklace of matched pearls. She is followed by* COLONEL FOWLER, *a tall, big-boned, athletic man of forty-five. He is handsome in a florid way; his hair is beginning to turn gray. He is a matter-of-fact, hearty man of affairs, a distinct contrast to the dry scientific personality of* DR. GOLDEN]

COLONEL FOWLER I'm sorry I'm causing all this trouble— I can get the book from Jack some other time.

GWYN It wouldn't be up there, Dr. Golden— [*She indicates shelves front left.*] All the books about Russia are on these two shelves.

DR. GOLDEN [*Descending from the ladder*] Ah, so they are... then it must be here.
[DR. GOLDEN *has come down to earth and is studying the titles in the section indicated by* GWYN]

CONNIE [*Sarcastically*] Are you arguing about Russia? Why don't you ask me? Perhaps I can settle it for you.

COLONEL FOWLER [*Gallantly*] My dear Miss Blane, I'm sure you could settle anything, simply with a smile.

DR. GOLDEN [*Pulling book out of shelves*] Here we are, Colonel. [*He holds out the book to Colonel Fowler*] You'll find that the fairest account of collective farming that's appeared.

COLONEL FOWLER Thanks, I'll take this with me and read it tonight. I want to compare it with my own impressions.

CONNIE Did you like Russia, Colonel Fowler?

COLONEL FOWLER I was so busy with engineering problems that I hardly had time to like or dislike it... you can't help admiring their energy... there's a great deal to be said for their political philosophy... of course one can't swallow it whole.

MRS. STONELEIGH Are we to swallow pieces of it?

DR. GOLDEN As a matter of fact the next few years are likely to bring... [*He coughs.*] stupendous changes!

ELLIOTT [*Holding up his highball glass*] Ladies and gentlemen, I drink to the next world war!

DR. GOLDEN You're young enough to jest about it.

ELLIOTT I'm not jesting, Doctor. I think Spengler's got it all in a nutshell: read him and weep!

COLONEL FOWLER Well, you can't do away with wars. If I had my way, this country would be preparing for war right now.

GWYN [*Smiles at* COLONEL FOWLER *affectionately*] You are bloodthirsty! I'm glad I have no children.

MRS. STONELEIGH It would be a good thing for you if you had a dozen brats, it would keep you from worrying about these silly abstractions.

GWYN I don't know why you should call war an abstraction, it won't be an abstraction when it happens.

ELLIOTT I shouldn't wonder if the whole show busted up in a big way!

CONNIE What show?

ELLIOTT Civilization... all that sort of thing... Spengler.

MRS. STONELEIGH [*Harshly*] Elliott, if you make any more of these calflike references to Spengler I shall scream... [*She laughs.*] I only ask for ten years more; then I don't care whether I'm taken over by the worms or the Bolsheviki.

DR. GOLDEN [*In a mood for making a speech*] The real question is whether our culture is equal to the tasks which face it: I mean the culture of educated people, the ideals and standards which we represent in this room. Can *we* remake the world? Can we create a decent standard of living? Can we preserve peace?

MRS. STONELEIGH If we can't, who can?

DR. GOLDEN I don't know: in my day-to-day work I notice an alarming increase in hysterical cases... an ethical sterility—

MRS. STONELEIGH [*Who has been fidgeting during this, breaks in sharply*] Stuff and nonsense!

DR. GOLDEN [*Peers at her as if he was sure he had misunderstood*] I beg your pardon?

MRS. STONELEIGH You can't crush me by heaping big words on my head, Dr. Golden. You psychoanalysts have a lot of queer ideas, because you never come in contact with sane people; people like myself never go to a doctor unless we have a broken leg or a stomach-ache!

DR. GOLDEN You're fortunate! [*He turns away coldly.* GWYN *joins him, left rear.*]

GWYN You mustn't mind my aunt, Dr. Golden, she doesn't mean half of it.

MRS. STONELEIGH [*Overhearing this, belligerently*] Oh, don't I?

ELLIOTT [*Interrupting, standing in front of* MRS. STONELEIGH, *looks down at her smilingly*] Do talk some more, Aunt Kate, I'm putting you in my next book.

MRS. STONELEIGH I'll thank you to do nothing of the sort: the first rule of decent conversation is that everyone forgets it immediately.

COLONEL FOWLER [*Turning to* DR. GOLDEN] I wonder if I may have a word with you, Doctor: I want your advice on a certain matter. [*He and* DR. GOLDEN *walk through arch to drawing room.*]

ELLIOTT [*Turns to* GWYN, *consulting his watch*] I don't know what can have happened to my friend Flannigan; he promised to come at ten; I suppose he's asleep somewhere in a gutter.

MRS. STONELEIGH [*Overhearing this, breaks in vigorously*] What are you talking about? Who's asleep in a gutter?

ELLIOTT A friend of mine.

MRS. STONELEIGH What's he doing in a gutter?

ELLIOTT He's a genius.

MRS. STONELEIGH [*Sarcastically*] And what is your idea of a genius?

ELLIOTT [*Vaguely*] Oh... someone with a vision.

MRS. STONELEIGH Pink elephants?

ELLIOTT [*Nods*] That's the trouble, I can't get him sober long enough to write, and I'm responsible because I discovered him.

MRS. STONELEIGH And this paragon, what was he doing when you discovered him?

ELLIOTT Nothing... everything... he's been a coal miner, reporter, tramp, mixed up in strikes... just a wandering red!

MRS. STONELEIGH [*Snorts*] Did you ask him here to organize us?

GWYN I suggested it.

MRS. STONELEIGH Why is it that wanting to break up things is considered so enormously diverting?

ELLIOTT Don't be a prig, Aunt Kate.

MRS. STONELEIGH I am *not* a prig. Gwyn, did I or did I not give one hundred dollars for the Scottsboro boys?

GWYN [*Smiles*] You did.

ELLIOTT That's not the point. My interest in Flannigan is literary—
[*With real feeling, chiefly addressing* GWYN, *who, he feels, understands him*] This man can put words on paper that jump at you like a blow of a fist—
[CONNIE *has been standing by the open window, looking out.*]

CONNIE The odor from your flowers is simply delicious, Mrs. Ballantine.

GWYN [*Crossing to her*] You must come to tea soon, and let me show you the garden in the daytime.

CONNIE I like it by moonlight. [*To* ELLIOTT] Shall we go out and look at the flowers?

GWYN [*Smiling at both of them*] Please do— and be sure to notice the peonies.

MRS. STONELEIGH I wondered how long it would be before you two would make your escape again.

ELLIOTT [*Grinning at her across the room*] The younger generation, Aunt Kate...
[ELLIOTT *and* CONNIE *exit right rear. As soon as the door shuts* MRS. STONELEIGH *speaks up like a judge rendering a decision*]

MRS. STONELEIGH A charming couple, Gwyn.

GWYN Yes, I'm so glad you like her.

MRS. STONELEIGH Her family is not brilliant socially but quite decently connected. [GWYN *nods absently.*] On the whole, I think he'd better do the right thing by her as soon as possible.

GWYN [*Amused*] Are you inferring that he's doing the wrong thing by her?

MRS. STONELEIGH Certainly. [*She sighs.*] It smells clandestine to me.

GWYN Does that really matter? [DR. GOLDEN *and* COLONEL FOWLER *reenter.*] They're nice people and whatever they do is their own affair.

DR. GOLDEN [*As they come*] I think it's an excellent plan. [*To* GWYN] Colonel Fowler has given me some very exciting news, Mrs. Ballantine; he tells me your husband is going into politics.

GWYN They want him to run for governor on a reform ticket, but he's quite undecided about it.

DR. GOLDEN A great idea. If we get men of Ballantine's caliber into the government there's some hope for us.

COLONEL FOWLER [*Rubbing his hands*] Right you are.

GWYN [*Quietly*] I don't agree with you, I've begged him not to do it.
DR. GOLDEN Why?

GWYN [*Hesitantly, evidently having given a great deal of thought to this*]
I can't convince myself that politics is important... it's all sound and
fury. [*Putting her hand on* COLONEL FOWLER'S *arm*] You're Jack's best
friend, Richard, you know he has a real capacity for living and thinking.

COLONEL FOWLER Why not apply that capacity?

MRS. STONELEIGH [*Stifling an evident yawn*] Your little dinner for six,
Gwyn, seems to have turned into a dull debate for four.

GWYN I'm sorry you're bored, Aunt Kate... but Jack and I are both very
serious about this, and we want to accomplish something.

MRS. STONELEIGH And what on earth do you want to accomplish, besides living decently and dying gracefully?

GWYN [*Uncertainly, trying to express her troubled thoughts*] One ought
to have some sort of ideal, that's worth fighting for.

DR. GOLDEN [*Gently*] That's what we all lack, Mrs. Ballantine.

COLONEL FOWLER [*Good-naturedly*] You're looking for a prophet,
Gwyn!

MRS. STONELEIGH [*Briskly*] How about Mahatma Gandhi? You could
wear a white robe and weave and make salt!
[HAVENS *walks through the drawing room and enters left rear*]

HAVENS Pardon me, madam.

GWYN Yes, Havens?

HAVENS [*Imperturbably*] A gentleman who won't give his name
insists that he's expected— the gentleman insisted—
[RUDY FLANNIGAN, *not waiting to be announced, walks through the
drawing room, and into the library. He is in extremely disorderly*

condition. He has a bloody mark on his cheek, his trousers are baggy and muddy, the coat of his old suit is slightly torn, he carries a soiled soft hat crumpled in his hand and his hair is in wild disorder. He is a handsome young Irish tough, clever, ill-mannered, irresistible to women, ambitious to be a success and too disorganized to work for the fulfillment of his ambition. He has a penetrating mind, has read and thought a good deal, but has never coordinated his ideas clearly. He is a heavy drinker, and sufficiently hard-headed not to show it when he makes a real effort to get himself in hand. He is really embarrassed as he walks into the room, but he covers it by being a little more bumptious than necessary.]

RUDY [*Interrupting HAVENS carelessly. Looking around at the group of strange faces*] I don't know whether I'm in the right dump or not, I lost the address— is Elliott Snowden any place around here?

GWYN [*Approaching him graciously*] You're Mr. Flannigan, are you not? I'm Mrs. Ballantine.

RUDY [*Looks at her fixedly, then remarks with undisguised and childlike awe*] Christ, you're perfect.

GWYN [*Smiling*] Thank you.

RUDY [*With his broad Irish smile*] Shouldn't I have said that?

GWYN Of course you should— [*To the butler*] That's all, Havens. You might bring some more glasses and some ice.

HAVENS [*Bows, turns to RUDY*] Your hat, sir.

RUDY [*Handing the hat to the butler*] Sure. Thanks ...

GWYN May I present Mrs. Stoneleigh, my aunt.

MRS. STONELEIGH How do you do?

RUDY [*Shaking himself as if he were trying to putt himself out of the drunken haze which surrounds him*] I'm pretty groggy, taking it by and large.

GWYN This is Colonel Fowler... and Dr. Golden... Mr. Flannigan.
[*The men shake hands.*]

RUDY I don't like to be personal, Doctor, but that's a great beard you have with you this evening.

DR. GOLDEN [*Politely in his cold, dry voice*] Thank you, I take very good care of it.

RUDY Yes, they say they're more trouble than a dog.

MRS. STONELEIGH [*Feeling that the subject should be changed*] You're not very punctual, Mr. Flannigan: Mr. Snowden expected you to drop in at about ten.

RUDY [*Genially*] You know how it is, one thing leads to another.

MRS. STONELEIGH Does it really?

RUDY I got in a fight about something; it seemed important at the time but I can't remember what it was about. [*He sees whiskey bottle on table right of couch. To* GWYN] May I take a shot of this? It's just what I need.

GWYN Of course, there'll be some ice in a moment.

RUDY [*Pouring a straight drink*] I'm used to it without ice. [*He drinks it down.*]

GWYN Do you feel better? [MRS. STONELEIGH *continues to stare at* RUDY *fixedly.*]

RUDY [*Turns to* GWYN *and inquires uncomfortably*] Do I look funny?

MRS. STONELEIGH Don't worry about your appearance, Mr. Flannigan, you're a perfect picture of an inspired Bohemian.

DR. GOLDEN [*With cold politeness*] If I might make a suggestion, Mr. Flannigan, I think putting your head under a cold faucet for about a minute would do you a world of good.

RUDY [*Who is feeling better and at the same time more conscious of his own shortcomings*] Very sound advice, Doctor; are you a specialist in deliriums and hangovers?

DR. GOLDEN [*Smiling*] Not exactly... my field is psychology.

RUDY Oh, one of them? Which do you prefer, extroverts or introverts?

DR. GOLDEN I see you're familiar with the terminology.

RUDY Yes, I've run across it. [*He feels his cheek, looks at his hand which has blood on it.*] Lucky I caught it there instead of in the eye!

GWYN If you'd like to wash up, Dr. Golden will show you the way.

DR. GOLDEN With pleasure.

RUDY [*To* GWYN] You're a good sport, I apologize for living. [*He and* DR. GOLDEN *exit right rear, leaving the door open.*]

COLONEL FOWLER [*Helpfully*] Refreshing, to say the least.

MRS. STONELEIGH I am not refreshed, I'm wilted!

GWYN He's rather nice. [DR. GOLDEN *returns right rear, closing the door.*]

MRS. STONELEIGH If you think boorishness is nice, why not ask a group of truckmen to dinner?

GWYN But he's not at all like a truckman; he talks about extroverts and introverts.

MRS. STONELEIGH He has the manners of a truckman.

GWYN So have you, Aunt Kate, and they're very becoming.

MRS. STONELEIGH [*Crosses to window right*] I hope those young people haven't been overcome by the moonlight and the flowers. [*At open window, she calls out into the night*] Oh, Elliott, are you there?

ELLIOTT'S VOICE [*From below in the garden*] Hello ...

MRS. STONELEIGH [At *open window*] Come up and control your wild man of Borneo- [GWYN *laughs.*]

ELLIOTT'S VOICE [*Below*] We're coming up.

DR. GOLDEN You're giving the young man more than his due, Mrs. Stoneleigh— he seemed a rather ordinary type to me.

MRS. STONELEIGH The idea of such a person writing what is mistakenly termed literature. [*With a sigh*]
[ELLIOTT *and* CONNIE *enter right rear.* CONNIE *is flushed and excited.*]

CONNIE [*To* GWYN] I'm crazy about your garden, Mrs. Ballantine.

MRS. STONELEIGH I don't believe you even noticed it.

ELLIOTT [*To* MRS. STONELEIGH] From your remark at the window, I gathered that Flannigan had put in a belated appearance.

MRS. STONELEIGH Belated, but sensational!

GWYN Aunt Kate was simply fascinated by him!
[MRS. STONELEIGH *snorts.* HAVENS *enters right rear, with a tray of glasses, ice, white rock, etc. At the same time , RUDY returns left. His face is washed, his hair is carefully combed, and he looks fairly spruce in spite of his seedy clothes. He has also succeeded in pulling himself to-gether and is tolerably sober.*]

ELLIOTT Greetings, Rudy, glad to see you.

RUDY Hello, Elliott.

CONNIE [*To* RUDY] How are you this evening?

RUDY I'm O.K. [*Turning to* GWYN *politely*] You certainly go in for fancy plumbing, Mrs. Ballantine.

MRS. STONELEIGH Flatterer!

CONNIE [*To* RUDY] I'm glad you got home safely the other night, we were worried about you.

MRS. STONELEIGH [*To* RUDY] I wasn't aware that you and Miss Blane had already met?

CONNIE Yes, indeed, Elliott took us up to Harlem last week.

HAVENS [*Offering a glass of sherry to* MRS. STONELEIGH] I thought you might care for a glass of sherry, madam?

MRS. STONELEIGH That's exactly what I want, thank you, Havens.

CONNIE [*Glances at* MRS. STONELEIGH *mischievously*] But we didn't see much of you, did we, Mr. Flannigan? You spent all your time dancing with negresses.

MRS. STONELEIGH [*Greatly impressed*] Indeed?

RUDY [*Quite unconscious of criticism*] You can't beat those high yellows when it comes to dancing.

MRS. STONELEIGH Very interesting!

CONNIE [*To the butler*] Will you pour me some brandy, Havens?

HAVENS Very good, miss.

COLONEL FOWLER Nothing for me.

DR. GOLDEN [*Taking highball offered him by* HAVENS] Thanks, I will have a nightcap. [HAVENS *offers a drink to* RUDY.]

RUDY [*Waving him away*] Not for me, I won't have any more...
[*To* GWYN] I've been going it pretty strong ever since noon.

GWYN [*With a smile*] One wouldn't guess it... I don't suppose you even stopped long enough to eat dinner?

RUDY You're a mind reader; all I had was some olives and pretzels at a bar.

GWYN Will you fix a plate of cold cuts and salad, Havens?

HAVENS Very good, madam: for one?

GWYN Is anyone else hungry?

MRS. STONELEIGH Couldn't think of it—

ELLIOTT Not for me.

GWYN How about you, Colonel?

COLONEL FOWLER No, thanks.

GWYN For one, Havens. [HAVENS *bows and exits.*]

RUDY [*To* GWYN, *looking after* HAVENS] What a job for a grown man!

COLONEL FOWLER [*Being social and good-natured, to* RUDY] Havens? Havens is all right— he's a good servant, and a good servant never thinks.

RUDY Neither does a good colonel.

COLONEL FOWLER [*Laughs*] You're not far wrong, but I haven't been in the active service for several years, so I'm free to think what I please.

RUDY I see... what racket are you in now, Colonel?

COLONEL FOWLER I'm an electrical engineer... I recently spent a year in Russia—

RUDY What were you doing in Russia?

COLONEL FOWLER Dnieperstroy.

RUDY Like it?

COLONEL FOWLER I always like big projects... that's my business... but I don't think the system could be applied in this country.

RUDY Well, something's *got* to be applied. What's your idea, government by engineers?

COLONEL FOWLER [*Coughs sadly*] I'm afraid I still believe in government by the people.

RUDY [*Who always likes an argument, pokes his finger into* COLONEL FOWLER'S *chest energetically*] Which is just about as sensible as saying you believe fifty angels can stand on the point of a needle. Democracy can't swallow capitalism any more than a goat can swallow a five-ton truck— what happens? The truck runs over the goat. What's the result? Fascism!

GWYN [*Amused*] You make it perfectly simple.

RUDY We're heading straight for a military dictatorship, blue shirts, silver shirts, some kind of shirts. People like me that want to pick our own shirts will be stood up against a wall and shot.

MRS. STONELEIGH I hope you're right.

RUDY [*Quickly good-natured, with a pleasant nod to* MRS. STONELEIGH] O.K., Madam Chairman, I've said enough, five minutes for rebuttal.

COLONEL FOWLER [*Graciously*] I'm afraid I couldn't answer you in five minutes; it's a familiar argument. Are you really a serious Communist?

RUDY [*With a laugh*] Do I look like I'd be a serious anything? I'm the lunatic fringe.

MRS. STONELEIGH [*Feelingly*] I'm glad to hear it.

DR. GOLDEN [*Thoughtfully, to* MRS. STONELEIGH] After all, it's all psychological--

RUDY [*Swinging to* DR. GOLDEN *sharply*] What in hell are you talking about?

DR. GOLDEN [*Smiles at him kindly and addresses* MRS. STONELEIGH] The safety of America lies in its sense of humor— as long as we can laugh at revolutions, we're safe.

RUDY You're a card, Doc, you look like Lenin and talk like Arthur Brisbane.

DR. GOLDEN [*Dryly*] Thank you.

GWYN Tell us some more of these dangerous ideas!

MRS. STONELEIGH Not for me, if you don't mind!
[RUDY *looks at* GWYN *fixedly. He has forced himself to become sober. He is now alert, increasingly interested in* GWYN, *puzzled about her, wondering expertly what sort of woman she is, watching his opportunities to make an impression.*]

RUDY Do you go in for dangerous ideas?

GWYN [*Hesitantly returning his look*] I'm curious.

RUDY [*With cool mockery*] What's the matter? Down to your last few million?

GWYN [*Laughing*] No, it's not that!

MRS. STONELEIGH [*Rises, addresses* COLONEL FOWLER] Shall I drop you at your club, Richard?

COLONEL FOWLER Please.

MRS. STONELEIGH [*To* GWYN, *indicating* RUDY] For a moment, my dear, I was afraid to leave you at the mercies of this dangerous radical, but I suspect his bark is worse than his bite.

DR. GOLDEN I shall run along too, I have a busy day tomorrow, Mrs. Ballantine.
[MRS. STONELEIGH *nods to* RUDY]

COLONEL FOWLER [*Shaking hands with* ELLIOTT] Good night, Snowden, come downtown and lunch with me some day next week.

ELLIOTT Glad to.

COLONEL FOWLER [*Bows to* CONNIE] Good night, Miss Blane.
[DR. GOLDEN *shakes hands with* ELLIOTT. COLONEL FOWLER *bows swiftly to* RUDY.] Good night, sir. [COLONEL FOWLER *turns to* GWYN] Don't be too hasty, Gwyn, in influencing Jack about the political matter.

GWYN Jack makes his own decisions, Richard.

COLONEL FOWLER I'm not so sure of that.

DR. GOLDEN [*Examining* RUDY *with scientific thoughtfulness*] Good night, you're very amusing.
[RUDY *starts to answer, but* DR. GOLDEN *exits hastily*]

GWYN [*Handing* COLONEL FOWLER *the book which he had selected from the library*] Don't forget your book.

COLONEL FOWLER Thanks... [*As he and* GWYN *walk through curtains left*] The governorship is a big thing for any man. There's a powerful group behind this plan, and I should strongly advise—
[*They have disappeared, and* COLONEL FOWLER'S *voice can no longer be heard.* MRS. STONELEIGH *gives* CONNIE *a friendly pat on the arm.*]

MRS. STONELEIGH You're a sweet child, come and see me.
[*She turns at the archway left, surveys the room, looks from* RUDY *to* ELLIOTT *with derision.*] Good night, Elliott. [*To* RUDY] I presume you'll put my name in your secret list of persons to be guillotined.

RUDY You belong right at the head of the list. [*She follows the others.* ELLIOTT, RUDY *and* CONNIE *are left in the room.* RUDY *sits down with evident relief, sprawls his legs out comfortably.*] What a gang! Now that they've cleared out, I suppose we can quit being social—

CONNIE Isn't he cute, Elliott? He thinks he's been social!

ELLIOTT You behaved very nicely, Rudy— Gwyn was amused.

CONNIE [*Sarcastically*] Isn't that *lovely?*

RUDY [*With assumed carelessness*] She's got the looks all right, but she doesn't mean anything to me, I don't like 'em highbrow.

CONNIE [*Gives RUDY a shrewd glance*] Liar! Any woman who can make a man sober up the way you did... why, it's nothing short of a miracle!

RUDY I did that on account of the old dreadnought.

CONNIE [*To ELLIOTT*] Let's go, Elliott, and leave him to his fate.

ELLIOTT [*Frowning, annoyed*] His fate?

CONNIE [*Mischievously*] Don't you see, he's filled with a burning desire to find out whether your goddess has clay feet!

ELLIOTT He wouldn't be such a fool.

RUDY Don't worry, I've got sense enough to know what's good for me!

ELLIOTT [*Uneasily*] We three had better all trot along pretty soon- polish off the evening at Luigi's!

RUDY [Carelessly] I'm in no hurry. [CONNIE *is thoroughly angry, there is a touch of hysteria in her voice.*]

CONNIE [*To ELLIOTT*] Remember what I told you in the garden—

ELLIOTT My dear— of course I—

CONNIE [*Quite hysterically*] Well, you act as if you'd forgotten— or as if it didn't matter.

ELLIOTT Please, Connie...[GWYN *returns through the drawing room left.*]

CONNIE [*Sweetly, to* GWYN] I'm dreadfully tired, Mrs. Ballantine, I'm afraid Elliott and I will have to run along very shortly.

GWYN Oh, please don't— we can have a real talk now that the others have gone... I want Mr. Flannigan to make some more speeches.

ELLIOTT Don't start him.

CONNIE He's been very uncomplimentary about your other guests, Mrs. Ballantine.
[HAVENS *enters with a plate of salad and half a chicken on a small tray.*]

HAVENS [*Setting the tray on table for* RUDY] I thought half a chicken would be just the thing, sir.

GWYN Don't bother with the drinks, Havens, we'll pour our own.

HAVENS [*Arranging the tray and a chair for* RUDY] Yes, madam.

GWYN [*To* RUDY] You didn't like my guests?

RUDY Not much. What did you think of 'em, Havens?

HAVENS Sir!

GWYN [*Quite unruffled*] By the way, what do you think of those people, Havens?— I've never asked you.

HAVENS [*Gravely*] I find them quite congenial, madam.

GWYN I agree with you, Havens.

HAVENS [*Turning gravely at the door*] Thank you, madam. [*He exits*]

CONNIE [*To* GWYN] What a nice man. Have you had him long?

GWYN He's been with my family for twenty years. [ELLIOTT *is pouring himself another drink.*]

CONNIE [*To* ELLIOTT] Don't forget me.

ELLIOTT [*To* CONNIE] You've had enough.

CONNIE [*Taking the brandy bottle*] Really?

RUDY [*To* GWYN] They've all got the same look— the butler and the doctor and the colonel and the old lady— the eye of a dead codfish. In another ten years, Elliott will have that look!

ELLIOTT [*Good-naturedly*] Oh, I'm going to be a dead codfish, am I?

RUDY Sure.

GWYN [*To* RUDY] And what about me?

RUDY [*Eating ravenously*] How should I know? You're out of my line.

GWYN There's a barrier between us, Mr. Flannigan, but I'm not sure it's a barricade.

RUDY You'd look dandy on a barricade with the machine guns going pitter-pat—

GWYN [*Seriously*] You see, I don't think those machine guns are as far away as we pretend— and I don't *want* to face them—

RUDY Don't worry, you won't— you'll be doing your knitting in a cellar, and... I'll probably be right there with you. [*He laughs unhappily.*]

GWYN How nice. But that hardly settles the problem, does it?

CONNIE Please let's go, Elliott.

RUDY [*Who has risen, confronts* GWYN *suddenly*] Have you a husband hidden away in some corner of this dump?

GWYN He's not here.

RUDY Oh, I thought maybe he was the kind of husband that goes to bed at ten.

GWYN You must come again soon and meet him; he went to Wilmington this afternoon for a directors' meeting.

RUDY Any children?

GWYN No... any more questions?

RUDY Sure... are you a faithful wife?

ELLIOTT [*Laughing*] Have you any doubts, Rudy?

GWYN Why shouldn't he ask? That's one of the more important aspects of a wife.

CONNIE [*Giggling foolishly*] This is getting funnier and funnier.

GWYN [*Sadly to* RUDY] I'm shockingly, immorally faithful.

RUDY What a waste.

ELLIOTT I told you he'd amuse you, GWYN

GWYN He does.

CONNIE We must run along, Mrs. Ballantine. I'm getting rather a headache.

ELLIOTT [*To* CONNIE] Just as you wish... are you ready, Rudy? [RUDY *looks at* ELLIOTT, *rises, deliberately starts to pour a drink at table right of couch*]

RUDY [*To* GWYN] May I stay for one more drink?

GWYN [*Looking at him levelly*] Of course you may!

ELLIOTT [*Disturbed and yet feeling ridiculous, because he is intensely aware that any suspicions he may entertain of* GWYN *are completely unwarranted*] Suppose we all stay.

CONNIE [*Smiling graciously*] Oh, I can't. [*She holds out her hand to* GWYN] Good night, Mrs. Ballantine, I've had a lovely time— I wonder if it would be too much trouble to call a taxi for me. [GWYN *rings a bell.*]

ELLIOTT I can't permit you to go alone.

CONNIE [*Bravely to* ELLIOTT] It's not very gallant— but that's a little thing to forgive— I can forgive bigger things than that—
[HAVENS *appears right rear.* RUDY *is carelessly siphoning water into his highball.*]

GWYN A taxi, Havens. [HAVENS *bows and exits.*]

CONNIE [*To* ELLIOTT] Call me up in a few weeks, won't you?

ELLIOTT [*Confused and angry*] Connie, please!— What are you thinking of?

CONNIE You'd never even guess— good night. [*She holds out her hand to* ELLIOTT.]

ELLIOTT [*Helplessly, forced to act*] No, indeed, I'll cancel the taxi, Gwyn, I have my car at the door.

GWYN I'll tell Havens. [*She exits left rear.*]

ELLIOTT [*Following her*] I'll attend to it, Gwyn, permit me.

RUDY [*To* CONNIE, *with a friendly grin*] You did that very nicely.

CONNIE [*With an understanding look*] You're doing very well yourself— you're almost smart enough and brutal enough to get around any woman.

RUDY [*Good-naturedly*] Want to try me out some time?

CONNIE [*Giggling*] Cad!

ELLIOTT [*Reentering left rear*] Good night, Rudy— I've told Gwyn to give you a lecture on sobriety and hard work.

GWYN [*Reenters smiling*] He seems more disposed to lecture *me*.

CONNIE [*To* RUDY] Let's all go to Harlem again soon.

RUDY Why not— the four of us?

GWYN I've never been to Harlem, I should love it. [ELLIOTT, GWYN and CONNIE *exit through drawing room left. RUDY stands thoughtfully, he looks at the drink in his hand, starts to drink, shades his head and puts the drink down. He waits tensely. The front door is heard slamming.* GWYN *reenters through curtains left. Smiling, friendly, and self-contained*] It was nice of you to stay!

RUDY [*Returning her smile*] Alone at last!
[HAVENS *enters through the curtains left, goes to table, putting glasses on tray, etc.* RUDY *lights a cigarette, looking at* HAVENS *with amusement.*] Almost, but not quite!

HAVENS Some more ice, madam?

RUDY Not for me— I don't want another drop.

GWYN Nor do I! You might leave the bottle in case Mr. Flannigan changes his mind— and that will be all, Havens, you needn't wait.

HAVENS Thank you, madam. [*He exits right rear.*]

RUDY [*With a grin*] What a look he gave me! I guess he'll wait in the hall to defend you.

GWYN [*With frank gaiety*] That's a morbid thought, Mr. Flannigan! I don't need a bodyguard!

RUDY You ought to, with that body!

GWYN [*Charmingly*] Your technique is awful; you should at least let a decent interval elapse before talking about my body.

RUDY [*Undaunted*] Why? There isn't much doubt about my intentions.

GWYN You made your intentions so comically obvious that I could hardly help laughing: hurry away, you seemed to say, I shall stay here and have a brief, flashy and successful affair with a woman whom I've never seen before and shall never see again.
[*She turns electric switch, turning off wall brackets, leaving room in the soft glow of the three lamps*]
That's better, isn't it? But we can't be friends unless we know a little about each other, can we? I don't mind being regarded as a potential love-object, but let's talk sense.

RUDY All right, shoot.

GWYN Are you a revolutionist or a faker?

RUDY If you really want to know, I'm about one-tenth radical and about nine-tenths faker.

GWYN Sorry, I thought you were honest about ideas.

RUDY I've read a lot, figured out a lot of things, now and then I get all choked up with zeal... but when you come right down to it, isn't everything a lot of hooey?

GWYN I don't know ...

RUDY I used to think I was a Communist, I messed around with that but I didn't get anywhere. You got to hand it to those babies, they know where they're going and they're on their way. If I had the nerve maybe I'd join up with them and stick to it— [*Laughs*] Maybe I'm just a bourgeois slob...

GWYN So am I, that's one thing we have in common. [*Hesitates*] There are so many people like yourself, who know that a change is coming. Can't they get together to prevent violence?

RUDY Sure, the capitalist class is just going to shake hands all around and hand over the works— can you see your own husband doing it?

GWYN Yes.

RUDY When the fight comes, you'll stick right with your own people— what's the use of kidding ourselves— you're a rich dabbler, and I'm a philosophical tramp—

GWYN Then what do you want to do?

RUDY [*Violently, the words come like a pistol shot*] Make love to you!

GWYN [*Unabashed*] How unfortunate!

RUDY All right— but that's all I'm thinking about.

GWYN My dear sir, if you'll just stop fidgeting and sit in that chair... [*She again indicates chair left of couch*] you may think anything you please.

RUDY [*Throws himself into the chair*] All right. [*Pause. She looks at him with kindly curiosity.*] May I tell you what I'm thinking?

GWYN If you must.

RUDY When I first saw you, it took my breath away. I sobered up like a shot.

GWYN Brilliantly; that shows a great deal of character.

RUDY From then on I couldn't take my eyes off you.

GWYN So you showed your emotion by calling me names?

RUDY You knew what I meant?

GWYN I'm a very simple person, Mr. Flannigan, I like admiration.

RUDY You like this sort of thing?

GWYN [*Simply*] Of course. If I didn't, I'd give you your hat and send you packing— I'm flattered— I'd be even more flattered if you'd control your... mad lust, shall we say?

RUDY Can't you see that I've fallen for you like a ton of bricks, and it's a damn' upsetting experience?

GWYN Really? A case of sin at first sight?

RUDY [*Rises, lights another cigarette*] You're a swell thing, nothing real about you— like you were made of gold foam!

GWYN Thank you; that's the result of some very expensive toilet preparations.

RUDY All you care about is balancing yourself on a pedestal.

GWYN [*Gaily*] But you're quite welcome to try to kick me off my pedestal.

RUDY I'd like to.

GWYN But even so, I don't think you could kick me into a bed.

RUDY Why did you turn off the lights a little while ago?

GWYN I look better in a soft light, and I'm extremely fussy about my looks, especially when a man is looking at me from under a ton of bricks... I'm pleased, and I think it's cute of you to be so... [*She hesitates.*] so physical about it.

RUDY [*Angrily*] Oh, I'm cute, am I?

GWYN [*Consolingly*] You're straightforward... most men make a polite fuss over one, and then all of a sudden one finds oneself kissed on the nape of the neck. You're much nicer, you want me tonight, and you say so... the fact that we met only half an hour ago adds piquancy to the jest.

RUDY Wouldn't the joke be even better if you gave in?

GWYN That would be the very cream of the jest.

RUDY [*Encouraged*] How about it, just for the laugh?

GWYN I haven't that kind of a sense of humor.

RUDY Nothing simple about you; you've got more stops and keys than the organ in a movie palace.

GWYN That's poetic, but it's not true.

RUDY [*Quietly, examining her*] I wonder— I wonder if you're good because you're too dumb to take chances— or the other thing.

GWYN [*Intrigued*] What's the other thing?

RUDY Women who keep their emotion bottled up— because it burns 'em up and frightens 'em— [*Looking at her more closely*] Your eyes are sort of icy, but you have something behind them— something dangerous ticking in your heart...

GWYN [*Gravely hesitant*] I hope that's true, but if it is, I'm not conscious of it.

RUDY Better get conscious of it— better use your body before it shrivels up on you! [*He laughs.*] Do you suppose I'm nuts about your beautiful soul— or your natty little brain? [*He suddenly stands over her, his voice trembling.*] Here I am, me and my five senses— I don't want to hand you any spiritual hokum: It's every curve of you, it's the way your dress folds around you now as you sit there, the way you'd be to touch— [*He stops short, changes his tone, with brutal abruptness.*] Don't worry: I'm not going to try it. [*Picks up a China vase left and toys with it threateningly*] The only way to stimulate you would be to break this vase on your dome!

GWYN [*Briskly*] Stuff and nonsense!

RUDY [*Triumphantly*] *Now* I know what you remind me of! The old lady, the war horse with the diamonds! In thirty years you'll be the spitting image of her.

GWYN Very likely! Now suppose I tell you about yourself: you're a bitterly unhappy person, you want things desperately, you follow your impulses relentlessly.

RUDY You're talking like a silly intellectual woman.

GWYN If I've put myself on a pedestal, I at least intend to speak from it; you pretend to be hard as nails... you're a sensitive young man with a troubled soul; you pretend to be casual and destructive... if I let you, you'd destroy me for a little excitement and never give it another thought.

RUDY Why should it destroy you?

GWYN Because I'm a person, my life is arranged in a certain balanced design.

RUDY Is your husband the center of the design?

GWYN [*Calmly*] No, the center of it is my own integrity—

RUDY [*Abruptly*] What's your husband do?

GWYN Corporations and models of sailing ships— [RUDY *is surprised. She indicates the ship on shelf left.*] That's his masterpiece— [RUDY *looks at the ship with mild curiosity.*] It took him over a year; it's a vessel called the *Gloria* and was owned by his great-grandfather— every detail is correct—

RUDY That's one way of bringing back the past—

GWYN He has a workshop upstairs— he works half the night—

RUDY Juggles millions all day, and whittles wood at night—

GWYN It's rather fun, I've tried it myself—

RUDY You live according to a design, do you? That's about like saying you don't live at all... you're lying in state right now! God, what a beautiful corpse!

GWYN [*Reasonably, looking up at him with a bright smile*] Why don't you save me?

RUDY [*With startling abruptness*] You know, you've been untrue to your husband tonight!

GWYN [*Genuinely startled*] What? What do you mean?

RUDY Sure... you admit you're unhappy— you want to escape.

GWYN [*Quietly*] Our friendship has moved very fast, but not as fast as that: I *can't* discuss my husband with you. [RUDY *nods, smiles*] Don't smile in that sinister way—

RUDY How you must hate the poor fellow.

GWYN You're being quite needlessly insulting—

RUDY Thank God! I've tried hard enough!

GWYN [*Quite herself again*] You've won a point in our little duel, you've made me angry. It's rather fantastic that I should be sitting here at this hour of the night, trying to justify my marriage to you! But I assure you that it's perfect.

RUDY A perfect design? [*She nods.*] And you call that love?

GWYN Love can mean almost anything—

RUDY It means something that knocks you down and rolls you over.

GWYN I don't want to be knocked down and rolled over. I prefer a perfect companionship which nothing could disturb or destroy.

RUDY *Nothing?*

GWYN Nothing but a major catastrophe! You insist on picturing me as a neurotic woman with a dull husband— you pretend that I'm swimming in a lot of funny inhibitions. It's not true: I'm an intelligent person married to a clever man: I'm devoted to him, and I'm entirely willing to sit here with you all night and give you breakfast in the morning.

RUDY All right... if you're as perverse as that. [*Sits in armchair right*]

GWYN I never saw anyone so obsessed with one idea; you seem to think promiscuity is a cure for all evils—

RUDY That's a very big word for such a little thing.

GWYN I'm not at all afraid of the idea— but I simply don't think it's becoming.

RUDY [*Laughs*] Maybe not, but it's awfully congenial. [The *telephone rings. As* GWYN *rises and crosses to telephone which is in little cabinet by window front right*] Husband? Long distance?

GWYN I hardly think so. [*At telephone*] Hello... Yes, Elliott... I had no idea it was so late! But how sweet of you to be thinking of me. [*Looking across at* RUDY] Oh, he's very much here... we're having a delightful talk... good night... pleasant dreams. [*She puts the telephone down.*]

RUDY [*Rising angrily*] Snowden's got his nerve, calling you at this hour to spy on you. ...

GWYN He couldn't spy very well over a telephone wire.

RUDY He's insane with jealousy— that was obvious when he left.

GWYN You distort everything: Elliott is a dear and trusted friend of mine, and he's very much in love with Miss Blane.

RUDY He's on the make for Miss Blane— I'll bet you dollars to doughnuts he took her home with him tonight and she was standing sobbing by the telephone when he called. Having used her as a substitute for you, he got to worrying about you so much he couldn't stand it!

GWYN That's a very vulgar story and I don't believe a word of it.

RUDY Sure, I'm vulgar, because I've seen things with my eyes. You've hidden yourself away behind your silver curtains— with a lot of antique furniture— [*Examining the furniture glumly*] What is this truck anyway?

GWYN Colonial!

RUDY A Colonial dame... a lady in waiting... but you haven't got the sense to know what you're waiting for.

GWYN You know, you're two entirely different people rolled into one... a little boy who likes to thumb his nose at people and a poet singing a brave song!

RUDY If I've got any poetry in me, it's because I've had a lot of raw experiences and spent a lot of time in the gutter.

GWYN [*Glances at him inquiringly*] Women I suppose... lots of women?

RUDY All kinds. ...

GWYN My kind?

RUDY [*Sincerely*] No... I've never been in a room like this in my life before... I've been in some pretty good hotels, but this is different. [*She laughs.*] Everything I know I've learned myself, from watching people and imitating.

GWYN You've learned a lot, almost too much!

RUDY [*Nods*] But there's a lot I don't know... I'm just one of the flotsam and jetsam boys.

GWYN But you must have a family?

RUDY Sure. My dad's been a coal miner out in Illinois for twenty years... got a raft of kids... hasn't been enough to eat out there since the war— that's why I beat it.

GWYN What did you do?

RUDY Moved around... a year in the stokehold of a tramp steamer, worked down in the Imperial Valley, got tarred and feathered in El Paso, Texas, had a job on the Chicago *News* , got fired pronto when they found I was a radical.

GWYN Go on; it's exciting.

RUDY Get a kick out of hearing things, don't you?

GWYN It's the only kick I do get.

RUDY You're a coward; you're safe and you want to stay safe.

GWYN [*Troubled*] I don't... I don't think I'd be afraid of anything, if it was good enough! [*She looks at him, turns away. She walks near the window, her face etched in pale moonlight.*]

RUDY Tell me, were you ever drunk?

GWYN Yes, mildly.

RUDY Oh, mildly is worse than nothing— I mean a Bacchic souse, when everything dissolves and turns itself into new shapes.

GWYN No, I've never had that pleasure.

RUDY Try it; it would do you a world of good.

GWYN [*Turns on him vigorously*] What you offer is no good! It isn't even amusing! You suggest a drinking bout and a Greenwich Village romance.

RUDY All right, I'll give you the truth if you want it! If you get down to brass tacks it's a question of money. You'd like to do lots of things but you're scared of being caught, because too much cash is involved. You're made out of money, got the clink of gold in your voice— a hundred years of specializing to make you a fine instrument of pleasure— and now you get the depression blues and you want something new. Go buy yourself some adventures— Monte Carlo and half a dozen Russian Counts is about your speed—

GWYN That's a lie. [*She sits helplessly, tearfully*] Why do you want to hurt me?

RUDY I don't want to— [*Moved by the misery in her voice*] I guess I don't get your kind of woman... maybe you're right and I'm wrong.

GWYN [*Slowly, with deep feeling, making a difficult admission*] No... You *are* a little bit right... that's what... frightens me.
[RUDY, *awed and touched by the tone of her voice, starts to put his hand out toward her. She sits very stiff, tense, lost in thought.*]

RUDY [*In a low voice, understanding her mood*] What?

GWYN [*After a pause, thoughtfully*] I can hardly tell you... people who want more than they've got are bitterly unhappy. ...

RUDY [*n the same low voice*] You?

GWYN [*Nods*] And you! That's rather a bond, isn't it? [*He looks at her gravely.*] Oh, I'm not being sentimental... I hardly know whether I like you or not... I'm sorry for you... and sorry for myself! We're both adrift on separate rafts, and we've suddenly collided ...

RUDY If you'd only see—

GWYN [*Quickly*] You don't even want me in that way— you want Beauty— you want to put your arms around the body of love— we're not pagans, we can't go back to ancient Greece.

RUDY I don't know much about ancient Greece, except it's full of broken statues.

GWYN [*Smiles*] And each statue is a broken dream— we can't put them together again— we can't raise Venus again from the sea—

RUDY Why... why go back to a lot of dead mythology?

GWYN It's easier... I'm afraid to look ahead.

RUDY No, you're not.

GWYN I am, I'm frightened. [*She laughs softly*.] I've told you so many lies this evening— I've pretended to be calm, but my head is crowded with strange thoughts... [*She stands before him, as calm as a statue, but a strange vibration in her voice.*] I can even imagine myself dropping this gown from my shoulders and standing before you!

RUDY [*Moved, quite a new note in his voice*] I don't want you to.

GWYN I know: That's why I dare suggest it—

RUDY Perhaps, if I wait...? [*She shakes her head. He adds quite simply*] You see I've fallen in love with you!

GWYN You don't understand your own feelings— one minute you want to gobble me up as if I were a bit of hors-d'oeuvre and the next minute you think you're in love... What about the five senses now?

RUDY They've played an awful trick on me.

GWYN Perhaps some day people will learn to understand themselves.

RUDY Meanwhile?

GWYN Meanwhile one can at least be careful!

RUDY You're right... and the most careful thing I can do is go home. Good night!

GWYN Not good night... good-bye.

RUDY [*Protestingly*] Well, I hope—

GWYN [*Interrupting, definitely*] You don't think I'd do this *again* , do you? My attempt to be friends with you has come an awful cropper. [*The doorbell is heard ringing off right.*]

RUDY [*Angrily*] There's that idiot Snowden.

GWYN [*Laughing*] If it is, we must give him credit— his suspicions weren't so far wrong— [*The bell rings again. GWYN exits.*]

VAUGHN'S VOICE [*Off-scene*] Sorry to disturb you at this hour, Mrs. Ballantine.

GWYN'S VOICE. Come in, Mr. Vaughn... you're not disturbing me.

VAUGHN'S VOICE. It's most essential that I see you alone.

GWYN [*As she appears at archway right*] Very well. [VAUGHN *appears reluctantly in archway. He is a stiff gray man, evidently suffering under a terrific strain, which has quite undermined his customary dry, businesslike manner. The black derby which he holds in his hand trembles violently*] But first, may I present Mr. Flannigan... Mr. Vaughn, my husband's secretary. [*They nod to each other. GWYN becomes a little frightened, seeing his confusion.*] What's the matter with you, Mr. Vaughn...? [VAUGHN *trembles, thoroughly distraught.*] You have a message from Mr. Ballantine?

VAUGHN [*Confusedly*] Not a message, you couldn't call it a message.

GWYN [*More frightened*] What is it? Tell me immediately—

VAUGHN. At least sit down, Mrs. Ballantine—

GWYN [*Almost hysterical*] Tell me this instant! [VAUGHN *tries to form the words and cannot.*] If you have a message, give it to me now—

VAUGHN [*Bursts out suddenly*] Dead, Mrs. Ballantine... [*He takes out his handkerchief and mops his face wildly. She stands perfectly still, as if she hadn't heard the words.*]

GWYN [*After a pause*] How?

VAUGHN. He cut his throat in his compartment on the train to Wilmington.

GWYN Oh... [*After a moment she speaks in a small voice, but with a very social and polite manner, addressing both men*] You'll forgive me, I should like to be alone—

[*She turns and starts to walk to door left rear. She walks very straight and with dignity, but she walks right into a chair that stands between her and the door without seeing it, stumbles and almost falls RUDY jumps to her side, supports her.*]

RUDY May I...?

GWYN No, no... please... [*He moves away from her.*]

VAUGHN. There's nothing to be done tonight, Mrs. Ballantine... I shall come in the morning.

GWYN Do. [*She bows and walks unsteadily with halting steps to the door and exits.*]

VAUGHN [*To RUDY*] Do you think it's safe to leave her?

RUDY [*Quietly*] What can anyone do?

VAUGHN. She has great self-control.
[*RUDY, shaken to his depths, walks to table left of couch, pours himself a stiff drink with trembling hands.*]

RUDY Any reason?

VAUGHN [*Wildly*] I know nothing about it... nothing... [*He mutters helplessly.*] Horrible...

RUDY [*Holding the drink in his hand, slowly*] Yes, you might call it a major catastrophe!

VAUGHN. Pardon me... are you a friend of the family?

RUDY [*Vaguely staring into his glass*] No... no, you'd hardly call me that.

CURTAIN

ACT TWO

SCENE: GWYN'S *sitting room. Six weeks later. An autumn afternoon. A charmingly feminine room, on the second floor of the Ballantine house. The room is clearly a reflection of* GWYN'S *personality. There are no saccharine frills and no ultra-modernistic touches. There are a few fine paintings by modern artists which blend with the color scheme. At rear, a big bay window, with a cushioned recess. It is cold outside, the sky is slate-gray, the windows frosted. Right rear, door to hall of house. Farther front right, a big open fireplace, in which logs are blazing. Door left to* GWYN'S *bedroom. Rear left a desk open, showing cubbyholes stuffed with papers. A chaise lounge left center, and several comfortable chairs scattered about. Beside chaise lounge is a magazine rack. Freshly cut flowers in profusion around the room. On the mantelpiece a smaller ship's model, not so elaborate as the one down-stairs.*

AT RISE: GWYN *sits before the fire, hands clasped on her knees, staring into the flickering flames. She is charming in black. Near her on a low broad stand is a tray with tea things— big silver pot, cups, little cakes, etc. Center on a small chair, sits* VAUGHN, *a black brief-case be-side him, thumbing nervously over papers in his hand. He is less tragic, but just as sour-looking as in the first act.* COLONEL FOWLER *is walking up and down, making what is evidently a long oration, as the curtain ris-es.*

COLONEL FOWLER [*As the curtain rises*] I was therefore forced to the conclusion that this was the only logical procedure— [*As he pauses , GWYN looks around, nods brightly to show she is listening, and returns to gazing into the fire*] I've had very little difficulty in getting the consent of the major stockholders, for the simple reason that the arrangement is to their advantage as well as yours!

GWYN [*Turning sharply*] How about the minor stockholders?

COLONEL FOWLER [*Shrugs*] They've formed a protective committee— but they can be managed.

GWYN [*Looking at the fire for advice*] Ah—

COLONEL FOWLER [*Annoyed by her tone*] It's done every day.

GWYN [*Nods and smiles*] I'm sure it is; one need only remember Kreuger and Insull and Harriman— [VAUGHN *looks woefully shocked*]

COLONEL FOWLER Do you suppose I'd do anything without the best legal advice available? The reorganization is entirely proper, and it means you save a reasonable part of the fortune which Jack spent his life building—

GWYN [*Rises, speaks with calm vigor*] I know what Jack spent his life doing— I've found out every detail by reading those wearying papers. He built a series of inflated holding corporations— the house that Jack built fell down when he died. You want me to save scraps of his estate by a piece of legal hocus-pocus that would shock a pick-pocket!

COLONEL FOWLER That's not fair. I entirely approved of your using the life insurance to pay Jack's personal debts— but we've struggled for six weeks to save part of the estate. This proposition must be acted on immediately— I warn you, if we don't act on this you won't have a dollar.

GWYN I know it.

COLONEL FOWLER You take it very lightly.

GWYN [*Her voice trembling*] I don't want to be poor, but I don't see any other decent course. [VAUGHN *rises and coughs uncomfortably.*]

VAUGHN. Ethics is one thing, Mrs. Ballantine, business is another.

GWYN [*Looks up at him with a bright smile*] I've never heard you come so close to an epigram, Mr. Vaughn.

VAUGHN. I've been loyal to Mr. Ballantine— and to you. This is a crisis, Mrs. Ballantine, and we ought to put your interest above everything.

COLONEL FOWLER Why throw money away on account of childish scruples?

GWYN Perhaps right and wrong are childish scruples— but I'm a dreadful Puritan, Richard. Being a pauper may strengthen my character— it needs it.

COLONEL FOWLER Poverty doesn't strengthen people.

GWYN Oh, doesn't it?— Cream or lemon?

COLONEL FOWLER [*Tragically*] Neither... one lump.

VAUGHN. None for me, Mrs. Ballantine, I have an appointment at the bank at five. [*He glances at* FOWLER *apprehensively.*] In regard to the notes, Colonel Fowler, what shall I tell them?

COLONEL FOWLER There's no chance of any further delay?

VAUGHN [*Shakes his head*] I talked to Sellers at the bank this morning; he's nervous, he insisted on definite action this afternoon. [*Both men look at* GWYN]

COLONEL FOWLER [*To* GWYN] I beg you, Gwyn, give us a chance—

GWYN [*Interrupts him angrily*] I'm sick and tired of this nonsense. How often do you want me to tell you— if we can't save anything that's the end of it.

COLONEL FOWLER [*To* VAUGHIN] That's all there is to it, Vaughn.

GWYN One moment, Mr. Vaughn... you've both been enormously kind, but— can't you clear up the details quickly? We all agree that nothing can be saved. [*She looks at them. They both nod.*] Then won't you finish it off as painlessly as possible?

COLONEL FOWLER Of course. We shan't bother you again. [*He turns to* VAUGHN.] Call me at the office at nine o'clock tomorrow, Vaughn. VAUGHN. Yes, sir. [*Turning to* GWYN *awkwardly, moved*] Mrs. Ballantine, I want you to believe me—

GWYN [*Quickly*] I do— thank you— good-bye.

VAUGHN. Good-bye. [*He exits.*]

COLONEL FOWLER [*As the door closes on* VAUGHN] He's an excellent man, I'm going to give him a job.

GWYN Shall I sell my jewels?

COLONEL FOWLER Perhaps you'd better.

GWYN This house?

COLONEL FOWLER It will take several months to dispose of the house... you might as well stay here in the meantime.

GWYN I can't tell you how oppressive this house is. I went into the library last night and I distinctly smelled the smoke from Jack's pipe... in fact, I saw the bowl of his pipe glowing in the dark ...

COLONEL FOWLER That's upsetting.

GWYN Rather jolly of a ghost to smoke a pipe.

COLONEL FOWLER [*Troubled by her manner*] I don't understand you.

GWYN I feel as if Jack were here in the house, I keep expecting to see him whenever I walk into a room— I depended on Jack so completely, I thought there was something so great and safe about him— I want to go on depending on him, I don't want to make decisions, I don't want to be lost in a new strange world. [*Her voice has been quite quiet and low, but there is a tension in her words that startles* FOWLER. *She is interrupted by the ringing of the telephone. As* FOWLER *starts to cross to the instrument,* HATTIE *enters left.* HATTIE *is a thin bony Scotchwoman of fifty, very grim. She is a privileged servant, rather more of a housekeeper than a maid, and rather more of a duenna than a housekeeper*] Don't bother, Hattie will take it. [HATTIE *picks up the phone*]

HATTIE Hello— [*Putting hand over mouthpiece*] Mr. Flannigan.

GWYN Tell him I'll call him later, Hattie.

HATTIE Mrs. Ballantine says to call her later, Mr. Flannigan— What? No, sir, *later*. [*She rings off.*]

GWYN What did he say?

HATTIE An oath, Mrs. Ballantine. [*She exits.*]

COLONEL FOWLER [*Mutters thoughtfully*] Flannigan ...

GWYN It's not very good taste to say "Flannigan" in that tone of voice.

COLONEL FOWLER [*Heavily*] Gwyn, I'm an old friend; will you permit me to give you a little advice?

GWYN I'm simply swamped in advice already.

COLONEL FOWLER [*Upset, apologetic*] Well, under the tragic circumstances—

GWYN One can't go on living in the past, can one?... after all, I was mistaken about Jack ...

COLONEL FOWLER Mistaken?

GWYN [*Slowly, gravely, trying to make herself clear*] I'm ashamed of him for having been pitifully weak when I thought he was strong; I'm ashamed of myself for having failed him—

COLONEL FOWLER You didn't.

GWYN Oh, yes; if there'd been anything real in our relation he would have come to me when he was in trouble— [*She shudders a little, the cup shakes in her hand, but she steadies herself and smiles.*] There was nothing real, nothing he could turn to— lies—

COLONEL FOWLER The best thing for you is not to think about it at all. I imagine this money question is weighing on you heavily— If I were able to step in and save Jack's estate on my own responsibility, I'd do it. I'm not wealthy enough to do that— but as far as your personal needs are concerned, you need have no worry.

GWYN [*Interrupting*] It's so foolish of you to say that, Richard; I couldn't possibly accept, and it makes us both uncomfortable.

COLONEL FOWLER It's difficult for a woman alone— you need someone whom you can trust and rely on absolutely—

GWYN [*Leaning against fireplace, she eyes him thoughtfully.*] I can read your thoughts, Richard— you think you should wait at least six months before asking me to marry you— [COLONEL FOWLER *chokes on his tea.*] Oh— perhaps it's not as serious as that: perhaps you want to hide me away in a love nest?

COLONEL FOWLER [*Upset*] Gwyn, I've got to talk to you like a Dutch uncle— I'm willing to admit that I have a very intense feeling about you—

GWYN That's more like a Viennese count than a Dutch uncle ...

COLONEL FOWLER [*At the end of his resources*] Don't be so inhuman. I've loved you for a long time ...

GWYN I can't believe you. You never suffered these passionate hallucinations while Jack was alive.

COLONEL FOWLER Yes, I did.

GWYN Why didn't you tell me?

COLONEL FOWLER Is that a fair question?

GWYN You mustn't be sentimental about me. I don't know what I want or where to look for it— but it's something quite different.

COLONEL FOWLER Perhaps I could help you find it.

GWYN You wouldn't like it... perilous seas and fairylands forlorn.

COLONEL FOWLER [*Bleakly*] In a leaky boat? Believe me, Gwyn, a house on dry land is far more comfortable ...

GWYN [*Laughs*] What you offer is a house on quicksand— exactly like this.

COLONEL FOWLER Don't underrate the value of security.

GWYN What do you believe in that makes you feel so safe, Richard? God, country and Yale?

COLONEL FOWLER I went to Harvard— [A *knock on door right and* HAVENS *enters.*]

HAVENS Dr. Golden, madam.

GWYN Ask him to come in. [HAVENS *bows and exits.*]

COLONEL FOWLER Are you using the doctor? What's he here for?

GWYN I don't know, I hope he doesn't want to marry me.

COLONEL FOWLER He has a wife and four children. [DR. GOLDEN *enters right.*]

DR. GOLDEN How do you do, Mrs. Ballantine— how are you, Colonel?

COLONEL FOWLER I'm just leaving, Doctor.— I'll phone in the morning, Gwyn.

GWYN [*Leading* FOWLER *to door*] Do.

COLONEL FOWLER I hope you'll give a little thought to what I've said—

GWYN I shall. [*She pushes him out the door and shuts it, turns to* DR. GOLDEN.] It's so nice to see you, Dr. Golden— [*Indicating tray*] Have some strong tepid tea?

DR. GOLDEN Thank you, I don't like strong tepid tea.

GWYN Highball?

DR. GOLDEN Not at this hour. You adapt yourself charmingly to black, Mrs. Ballantine.

GWYN Thank you. Do you believe in ghosts, Doctor?

DR. GOLDEN [*Smiles*] I have to, my patients insist on it.

GWYN What does one do about them?

DR. GOLDEN [*Dryly*] Visual or mental?

GWYN Mental. That makes it simpler, doesn't it?

DR. GOLDEN No, indeed, much more difficult! Your ghost, as you call it, is simply the guardian of your will— what people formerly called the voice of conscience—

GWYN You mean a feeling that one has done a terrible wrong and it's too late to make up for it? [*He nods. She thinks about it.*]

DR. GOLDEN I know very little about you, Mrs. Ballantine, but one can make certain general assumptions: you've received a shock, which produces an inner conflict... you want to settle the conflict quickly, but your ghost, as you call it, keeps warning you, "Settle with me first, we loved and hated each other, you must understand me clearly before you can forget me." [*He takes typewritten report from pocket.*]

GWYN In other words, one can't run away, one must go back and face things.

DR. GOLDEN I've come here in a semi-professional capacity, to make you aware of certain unhappy facts: I've waited so that you might be a little better prepared— I was in daily contact with your husband for months before the end—

GWYN [*Startled*] I had no idea—

DR. GOLDEN [*In dry crisp phrases*] It was understood that my treatments should be strictly confidential— the record is here. I have no desire to afflict you, the truth is painful, but it may help you to a quicker adjustment—

GWYN I want the whole truth— I've been puzzled. They said money was the only reason. But I couldn't believe it. Day and night I've thought about it, asking why, trying to remember things he'd said and done.

DR. GOLDEN The loss of money was a minor factor ...

GWYN But the other factors?

DR. GOLDEN Acute melancholia— bitter jealousy of you— accusations against himself— the sense that he was no longer adequate— psychic impotence—

GWYN If you'd let me know—

DR. GOLDEN He took every precaution to keep you from knowing— he lived in constant fear that you would leave him. I told him to discuss it with you but he couldn't... in my office I've seen him give away to an insane rage, break things and then cry like a baby... he believed you hated him and that you were in love with another man.

GWYN [*With deep simplicity*] I thought we loved each other.

DR. GOLDEN I've had many similar cases... in fact, it's very typical—

GWYN Typical?

DR. GOLDEN [*Nods*] Among men of Mr. Ballantine's class. Read the papers... the golden age of suicides— [*He hands it to her, neatly folded.*]

GWYN Isn't it a little ghoulish to talk like that?

DR. GOLDEN [*He hesitates apologetically*] I'm not unaware of feeling, Mrs. Ballantine. When I sat in your drawing room six weeks ago the shadow of this was before me... [*There is almost warmth in his cold voice— he stops abruptly, taps the paper.*] If you want to discuss it again you know where to reach me.

GWYN [*Abstractedly*] Oh... I've never had much faith in you, Doctor, I mean in your profession.

DR. GOLDEN [*Chuckles*] Sometimes we help and sometimes we don't.

GWYN [*Tapping pages in her hand*] You want to reduce me to a few typewritten sheets ...

DR. GOLDEN I might be of assistance to you; that would depend on you. Good afternoon. [*He bows and exits. The room has been growing gradually darker. Quiet twilight now pervades the scene. The firelight casts an uncertain glow. GWYN stands quite still for a minute after the door closes. HATTIE enters left, a light cast from the farther room.*]

HATTIE Excuse me, Mrs. Ballantine ...

GWYN [*As HATTIE turns to switch*] No light, Hattie— I like the twilight—

HATTIE Shall you dress for dinner, Mrs. Ballantine?

GWYN No. [*HATTIE starts to leave.*] Hattie... [*HATTIE turns.*] Oh, nothing... I want to get away: where do you suppose I could go?

HATTIE Anywhere... east, south, north or west.

GWYN That covers the ground. Unfortunately, all the points of the compass are equally expensive. Do you know how much money I have in the bank, Hattie? [*HATTIE shakes her head.*] Three hundred and fifty dollars.

HATTIE Well, that's something.

GWYN It's not enough. [*With sudden feeling*] It's not that, Hattie, it's not money, it's everything.

HATTIE Whatever it is, you'll get over it. One thing you can rely on, Mrs. Ballantine, I'll stay with you.

GWYN Thanks, Hattie, that's kind of you, but I don't want you, I'm sorry.

HATTIE You can't get rid of me, whether you want me or not.

GWYN I don't know where I shall go, but wherever it is I can't drag you about with me: I suppose you've saved some money.

HATTIE Yes, now and then I've thought I'd like to die in Scotland.

GWYN I'm not even as clear as that.

HATTIE You'd better decide where you're going and when you're going there.

GWYN I don't know— I'll tell you as soon as I can— and don't start to cry, or I'll choke you! [HATTIE *exits, troubled, unhappy. GWYN unfolds the paper she is holding, and tries to read it in the fading light. It is too dark. She turns to the twilit window rear, and stands beside window, trying to read the words. A whispered, agonized cry*]
No— No—
[*She crumples the paper and drops it to the floor. She turns to the window, looking out at the darkening winter twilight, pressing her face against the pane as if she were looking for something. The door right opens quietly and RUDY enters. GWYN turns. A moment's silence as they look at each other*]

RUDY Gwyn—

GWYN I don't want to see you. [*She turns away from him, turns to light switch, illuminating the room brightly.*]

RUDY Look at me, stone sober and dying of love.

GWYN You're neither one nor the other. I told you not to come here until I sent for you.

RUDY How long do you expect me to wait?

GWYN I hardly know—

RUDY I've come here for a show-down— you might as well face an issue and make up your mind.

GWYN About you? [*He nods. She laughs.*] Not this afternoon, I haven't the strength to make up my mind this afternoon.

RUDY Listen, Gwyn, I know you, I know exactly what you mean when you pretend to be detached and flippant... it means you're so unhappy you can't stand it. If you're unhappy I want to know it.

GWYN You *do* know it.

RUDY What's it about?

GWYN I'm. bankrupt— my heart's in shreds and my bank account is in tatters.

RUDY So you're broke?

GWYN [*Nods and smiles*] Think it's good for me?

RUDY It won't make much difference— you'll get along— [*His foot kicks the paper she dropped on the floor. He looks down at it, picks it up.*] What's this?

GWYN The inside of my husband's mind... An analysis... how he felt... what he thought ...

RUDY Why dig that up?

GWYN [*Looks at him coldly*] Because it's important. [*She shrugs, walks over to the fire, studying the flames for a moment. RUDY watches her with troubled eyes.*]

RUDY Oh... so that's what you're upset about? [*She is silent.*] It's not important, Gwyn... you're kidding yourself. What are you trying to do, make yourself think you're in love with him?

GWYN [*Turns to him gravely*] No.

RUDY [*Angrily*] You're not and you never were. If he were alive, we'd love each other ...

GWYN No.

RUDY He was nothing... a shadow of a man... [*He looks at the ship's model on mantelpiece, derisively.*] His ancestors sailed ships like this— and this little half-man made piddling models to put on mantelpieces. [*Turning on* GWYN *angrily*] Why don't you clean this place out? Throw out all the truck that reminds you...

GWYN I can't.

RUDY [*Explosively*] For God's sake, stop it— stop flirting with corpses—

GWYN [*Controlling herself with difficulty*] I don't want you here, I don't want to see you—

RUDY [*Facing her furiously*] O. K. with me. If I go, I won't come back. It's up to you... either you take me on my own terms or not at all.

GWYN You can't seriously think I'd walk out of this house with you, at this time?

RUDY You've got to do one thing or the other! You can't play along with me and have this stuff at the same time. You say you're broke— we'd be broke together—

GWYN For how long?

RUDY What do you want me to say? Forever? How do we know? Have a little courage— no guarantees are necessary ...

GWYN [*Seriously*] I think it's callow and romantic... [RUDY *laughs angrily.*] There was magic when we first met— but you've spoiled it.

RUDY When we first met, it was all soft soap and star dust— I was a fool to get into this, dizzy, dazzled by a jewel in a jewel box. There's a bread line just around the corner, hundreds of 'em with the wind whistling through their pants— and you sit in here smeared with perfume and emotion! To hell with it. [GWYN *takes all this without emotion. She stops him as he turns to the door.*]

GWYN Wait. [*In a low strained voice*] What you say is true— I admit I'm a coward— I want to hold you in my arms and I can't— [*Lightly*] I can't have an affair with you, it wouldn't work. When a woman's in love, she wants understanding and dignity and beauty... love is important, like having babies and being born— [*He takes her in his arms. She struggles, hysterical.*] Don't kiss me, Rudy, don't—

RUDY We love each other— you and I... don't be afraid— [MRS. STONELEIGH *bustles in right. She wears a plumed hat and elaborate furs. She stops short, taking in the scene at a glance.*]

MRS. STONELEIGH [*Cheerfully*] Hello, Gwyn, how lucky that I dropped in! [RUDY *is trying to collect himself and not succeeding very well; bows to her stiffly.*]

RUDY [*Mutters*] Mrs. Stoneleigh.

MRS. STONELEIGH A man of your experience should never be embarrassed, Mr. Flannigan.

RUDY I'm not.

MRS. STONELEIGH [*Looking at* RUDY *coldly*] What do you see in him, Gwyn? He looks hopelessly ordinary to me!

GWYN He's at his best in a tête-à-tête. [MRS. STONELEIGH *snorts.*]

MRS. STONELEIGH [*Turning to* GWYN] I brought Elliott and that Blane girl with me, Gwyn; luckily I left them downstairs.

GWYN I've been begging Elliott to bring her to see me— [GWYN *turns to door.* MRS. STONELEIGH *stops her.*]

MRS. STONELEIGH Don't rush, pet, I want to talk to you. [*To* RUDY, *pointedly*] Perhaps Mr. Flannigan will be kind enough to entertain them for a few minutes—

GWYN [*Gives* RUDY *a level glance*] Mr. Flannigan can't stay— he has an urgent appointment.

RUDY Oh, no, I'd rather stay a while, if you don't mind. I'll go downstairs and talk to Elliott.

MRS. STONELEIGH [*As the door shuts*] That young man is a nuisance—

GWYN I just said good-bye to him forever.

MRS. STONELEIGH So I noticed!— I've read about slaves of passion, but I didn't expect to find one in my own family.

GWYN [*Laughs, turns to ring bell*] Let's not talk about it— won't you have some hot tea?

MRS. STONELEIGH No, I had tea with Elliott and Miss Blane. [*She picks up a cake.*] I'll nibble a cake to steady my nerves— [*Plunging ahead recklessly*] Gwyn, I've kept quiet and respected your grief for six weeks, but when I walk in and find you being kissed, I don't think your grief deserves any more respect. Can't you be frank with me?

GWYN A heart-to-heart talk in the grand style?

MRS. STONELEIGH Now listen to me and be practical! I've always followed a very simple rule— when people get emotional, put them on a train or a steamer... suppose we go to Florida immediately.

GWYN I don't like Florida.

MRS. STONELEIGH Neither do I! I hate the place. What about the Riviera? I hate that too, but one must go somewhere.

GWYN I can't go anywhere, Aunt Kate— no money.

MRS. STONELEIGH I'll give you some bonds so that you can feel perfectly independent.

GWYN Thank you, I don't want your help.

MRS. STONELEIGH Of course you want my help. What do you
expect to do, take in washing? I'm an old woman, and money is of very
little value to me... don't refuse me, Gwyn, you're the only
living person I care about.

GWYN [*Gently, with feeling*] But you really don't understand.

MRS. STONELEIGH Tosh! You're afraid of shocking me. One expects a
widow to sow a few wild oats... most of them wait a few months, but
perhaps it's wise of you to get it over with—

GWYN What do you call getting it over with?

MRS. STONELEIGH Getting it over with is getting it over with— you've
been a little hasty in jumping into an affair with the young man, but—

GWYN An affair? You think I'm having an affair with him?

MRS. STONELEIGH [*Looking at* GWYN *with troubled surprise*] You
mean there's all this smoke and not a bit of fire? [GWYN *is silent.*] Then
I *am* shocked! What on earth do you do with yourselves?

GWYN [*Smiles*] Aunt Kate, I never thought you were such a ribald old
lady.

MRS. STONELEIGH The next thing we know, you'll be marrying him.

GWYN He has a wife in Chicago

MRS. STONELEIGH In Chicago? How amusing. Well, it's all very clear
to me... You'd better get the thing on a physical level immediately and
get away from all these vapors and fancies.

GWYN I've said good-bye to him.

MRS. STONELEIGH A likely story! You deceive yourself! I've seen
plenty of people do it... from the first day of our marriage, my
husband promised to give up fast women. [*She sighs.*] They were tele-

phoning him on his death-bed. [*With finality*] We'll leave for Europe immediately— take him with us. I'll pay all the bills.

GWYN [*Amused*] A dowager and a widow and a gigolo! Haven't you any morals?

MRS. STONELEIGH Certainly not, I'm much too interested in manners. Whatever you do, do it gracefully.

GWYN [*Bitterly*] Don't you see, I can't make a little social intrigue out of this... [ELLIOTT *enters right, rosy-cheeked and a little tight in a very nice way.*]

ELLIOTT Hello, Gwyn— there seems to be a small party in the making downstairs.

MRS. STONELEIGH In that case, I'd better go.

ELLIOTT What's the matter, Gwyn? You don't look well.

MRS. STONELEIGH Of course, she's not well! She's out of her mind.

ELLIOTT Aren't we all?

MRS. STONELEIGH You've been drinking, Elliott.

ELLIOTT Just enough! My head's as clear as a bell!

MRS. STONELEIGH It doesn't agree with you, it makes your face red. [*Turning to* GWYN] I despair of you, Gwyn—

ELLIOTT What has she done?

MRS. STONELEIGH Ask her.

ELLIOTT I wouldn't dream of asking her: the trouble with you, Aunt Kate, is that you love to meddle—

MRS. STONELEIGH [*Briskly*] Since I'm in a mood for meddling— are you engaged to that Blane girl or are you not?

ELLIOTT I'm not, don't expect to be.

MRS. STONELEIGH In my day, gentlemen never had mistresses of their own class.

ELLIOTT I protest—

MRS. STONELEIGH Don't try to be a gentleman, it's out of your reach. [*Turning abruptly to him*] Do you believe in God, Elliott?

ELLIOTT No.

MRS. STONELEIGH I thought not— I'm told nobody believes in Him any more. Good night. [*She exits.*]

ELLIOTT [*Mutters thoughtfully*] I've never seen her in such a state--

GWYN My fault.

ELLIOTT [*Sits beside her*] Stop worrying, Gwyn, it's foolish to worry.

GWYN You know there's something rather saintly about you, Elliott—

ELLIOTT What do you mean?

GWYN You never give advice and you never ask questions.

ELLIOTT Do you know why? [*She shakes her head.*] Because you're my standard of conduct! Anything you do is absolutely unquestionable because you do it.

GWYN Always?

ELLIOTT [*Looks at her with level eyes*] Always— [*Changing the subject to cover up his feeling*] Want any money?

GWYN No, everyone's been offering me money. If I could only get away from people.

ELLIOTT Oh, yes, that is what you must do, and I know just the place for you— my camp in the Adirondacks. I'll drive you up and leave you. There's a farmer and his wife that take care of everything and I guarantee nobody will bother you.

GWYN How soon could we leave?

ELLIOTT Right away. My car is at the door. [*A knock on door*]

GWYN [*Calls*] Come in. [HAVENS *enters.*]

HAVENS May I take the tea things, madam?

GWYN I'll go tonight... Elliott... you won't tell anyone in New York where I can be found?

ELLIOTT Of course not.

GWYN Please... Havens... [*He turns to her.*] I'm going away, Havens... this evening... I don't know when I shall come back.

HAVENS Yes, madam.

GWYN I shall explain to the servants... perhaps you'd be kind enough to prepare them for it.

HAVENS I shall.

GWYN Sit down a minute, won't you?

HAVENS Thank you, I prefer to stand.

GWYN The house will probably be sold as soon as possible... I doubt if I shall come back to it... for the present, I wondered if you would stay here to take charge of everything?

HAVENS Very gladly... I shall be alone, I suppose?

GWYN Yes.

HAVENS Very good, madam, anything else?

GWYN I'm sorry, Havens, I'm broken-hearted.

HAVENS [*Gravely*] So am I! [*He turns and busies himself with the tea tray, collecting cups, etc.*]

GWYN [*To* ELLIOTT] I'll tell Hattie to pack my things. [ELLIOTT *nods. As* GWYN *turns to door left* , RUDY *enters rear.*]

RUDY What's going on here?

GWYN I'm about to leave, Rudy ...

RUDY Leave...?

GWYN Just as soon as I can.

RUDY Where are you going?

GWYN It's a secret.

RUDY [*As she starts for door left*] Wait a minute, I want to talk to you.

GWYN Not now.

RUDY When?

GWYN Never. [*She exits.*] [RUDY *turns to* ELLIOTT.]

RUDY Connie's downstairs, getting angrier with every sip; she says you've forgotten all about her.

ELLIOTT I did.
[*He hurriedly exits rear.* RUDY *locks at the door left. He turns to the door; puts his hand on the knob, then hesitates and changes his mind. As he turns* , HAVENS, *carrying the tea tray, is about to exit rear.*]

RUDY Did you go to that meeting Thursday night?

HAVENS [*Turns, holding the heavy tray*] Yes.

RUDY Like it?

HAVENS I was amused, being the first political meeting I've been to in years— but these Communists don't know what they're talking about... heavy talking and thin thinking; in the old days in London it was different.

RUDY You're still living in the nineties, Havens.

HAVENS I never talk to anyone... I admit, I haven't been active since the nineties... I read everything, I follow the course of events... I exercise my brain thinking about social changes, but I don't like violent talk; I've become attached to the present order.

RUDY [*Lazily, lying on his back on the chaise lounge*] I'm getting attached to it myself.
[HAVENS *smiles, turns to door, as* CONNIE *enters followed by* ELLIOTT. HAVENS *stands aside for them to enter.* CONNIE *is flushed. She has been drinking more than she should.*]

CONNIE Will you bring some more cocktails, Havens?

HAVENS Yes, miss. [*He exits.*]

CONNIE Where is this woman? Must I pursue her all over the house? Is she hiding in the attic?

ELLIOTT I'm sure she'll be here in a moment.

CONNIE I really don't want to see her... I'd much rather talk to Rudy... [*Sitting beside* RUDY, *affectionately*] You walked out on me just when I was getting divinely sentimental.

ELLIOTT Are you tight or pretending?

CONNIE Why should I pretend? You believe in frankness and I'm try-ing to live up to it. [*She turns to* RUDY, *cheerfully.*] Frankly, Rudy, I think you could sweep me off my feet— [RUDY *rises.* GWYN *enters left. She stops short, evidently really surprised at seeing* CONNIE. *She had forgotten her.* CONNIE *faces* GWYN *with malice in her smile.*]

Hello, Mrs. Ballantine... you'd forgotten all about me, hadn't you?

GWYN [*Simply*] I've been horribly rude.

CONNIE I don't mind at all, I'm easy to forget.

GWYN I've been so anxious to have you come and see me. Why didn't you come before?

CONNIE I didn't want to come today... but now that I'm here and you've ignored me so charmingly, I feel rather happy about it. I admire you, Mrs. Ballantine, you get such beautiful devotion from men... I wish I could have some platonic friends! I'm afraid I'm physical. [*Sweetly to* ELLIOTT] Am I physical, Elliott?

ELLIOTT I guess so.

CONNIE Isn't it a shame?... I want to be soulful but I can't get away with it. I'm a pushover for ideals but nobody cares. [HAVENS *is serving the drinks.*]

RUDY [*To* HAVENS] How long have you been overhearing idiotic conversations, Havens?

HAVENS Nearly thirty years.

RUDY Any change?

HAVENS There's more profanity nowadays. [*He exits.*]
[CONNIE *gulps her cocktail at a single swallow and goes to the shaker for more.*]

CONNIE The only place for a butler like that is Hollywood.

GWYN Rudy likes him; he spent an hour in the basement with him the other day.

ELLIOTT What on earth did you talk about?

RUDY Politics. [*Everybody laughs.*]

ELLIOTT [*Tactfully, sipping his drink*] What do you think of inflation, Rudy?

RUDY [*Explosively*] For God's sake— everyone in this room is feeling sick and murderous, and you want to make small talk about inflation. [*Pause*]

GWYN [*Smiling, to* RUDY] What are we to do? Wait in stony silence for the millennium?

ELLIOTT It's cozier to cackle while waiting.

CONNIE [*Innocently*] What are we waiting for?

GWYN The rattle of tumbrils and the bloody music of the carmagnole!

CONNIE What's the carmagnole?

RUDY It's a dance.

CONNIE [*She shakes the cocktail shaker, which is empty.*] Let's have a drink.

GWYN Of course.

RUDY [*Taking the cocktail shaker away from* CONNIE.] You don't need any more.

CONNIE [*Looks up at* RUDY *dreamily*] My hero ...

ELLIOTT [*Hastily, glancing at his watch*] We must run, Gwyn, just time for dinner and the theater.

CONNIE I don't want to go yet, I want to talk to Mrs. Ballantine.

GWYN Please stay.

CONNIE [*Approaches* GWYN.] Elliott talks about you all the time... He worries about you... he thinks there's something mysteriously tragic about you... Of course there's a lot of mysteriously tragic things about me, but he can't see it... [*Her voice is becoming more intense, a stran-gled hoarse note.*] He can't see anything, because you stand between us...

ELLIOTT [*Desperately*] Don't, Connie—

CONNIE You're part of my life, you're the biggest part of it... why shouldn't I tell you?

GWYN Of course, you should tell me.

CONNIE [*Wildly*] Go on, be forgiving... you're so damned smooth it makes me sick.

ELLIOTT [*Trying to stop her*] Come away—

CONNIE Not till I've finished— [*Turning on* GWYN *more violently than ever*] You're a faker, you're lazy and clever and as sweet as vinegar— you coil around people and choke them.

ELLIOTT [*Interrupting angrily*] Have some decency—

CONNIE [*Pushing him aside*] Why should I? None of us has! She gets away with murder, she wants to be surrounded and petted and prayed to, and she gets away with it. You all think she's something on a stained— glass window— any woman would know what she is! [*She picks up an almost empty cocktail glass, drains it, drops it weakly to the floor, and speaks in a dazed voice.*] I want to get out of here. [*She turns blindly to the door.*] [ELLIOTT *stands completely lost.*]

GWYN Go with her, Elliott.

ELLIOTT [*To* GWYN] I'll come back; I'll take you to the station.

CONNIE [*In her most social voice, as* ELLIOTT *joins her at door*] Good— bye, Mrs. Ballantine.

GWYN [*Casually*] Good— bye... see you soon. [CONNIE *giggles as* ELLIOTT *leads her off left rear.* GWYN *and* RUDY *look at each other*]

RUDY [*Mutters after a pause*] Damned interesting girl ...

GWYN Yes. [*Pause*] Can we say good-bye without another scene?

RUDY [*Quietly*] Where are you going?

GWYN [*Definitely*] You can't follow me.

RUDY You're not coming back?

GWYN Not to this.

RUDY What else do you think you can find?

GWYN I wonder: this afternoon has been a cross-section of my friends.

RUDY They haven't much to offer.

GWYN You'd be surprised... the offers have been stupendous... marriage... psychoanalysis... money... Monte Carlo... I could have picked half a dozen rosy futures in a single afternoon.

RUDY Why didn't you pick one?

GWYN Because none of them are any good.

RUDY I'm sorry for you... you're in a spot.

GWYN [*With tragic earnestness*] I've wondered about earning my own living ...

RUDY Not a chance in these times!

GWYN I'm not fit for anything. Millions of women have the same problem, but I feel quite alone; I'm at the end of a blind alley, with my head full of epigrams and my heart full of tears.

RUDY You'll be the same till you die.

GWYN I shan't forget you, I shall remember you when I'm gray and sour and wrinkled.

RUDY [*Humbly, with great feeling*] I'm sorry I upset you, I've been up-set myself... I'm in as bad a spot as you are, don't know where to turn: I bluster a lot, but I'm not sure of anything. I used to be sure of myself... now I'm not clear about anything... I thought I was sure of you... I need-ed you badly and I thought you needed me. I was all wrong. Guess my brain's melting. What's the use? [*He turns away.*]

GWYN Where are you going?

RUDY Home.

GWYN What's it like?

RUDY What would it be like? Just a room up six flights of stairs.

GWYN I wish I'd been there just once, to remember it.

RUDY Don't rub it in.

GWYN I'm thinking of us together, in a little room with a skylight.

RUDY There's no skylight.

GWYN One window?

RUDY It's broken.

GWYN Broken furniture?

RUDY Not much of it.

GWYN Covered with the dust of ages?

RUDY Stop being romantic.

GWYN Can you see us in an attic?

RUDY [*Nods*] Wonderful ...

GWYN Awful... [*She hesitates, takes a deep breath.*] I'm going to clean up that place tonight— [*They look at each other. RUDY understands. He is deeply moved. GWYN speaks softly.*] I feel as if I'd been struck by lightning... because you were humble... when you were humble, I understood... [HATTIE *enters.*]

HATTIE Your bags are downstairs... everything you need for the mountains.

GWYN I'm not going to the mountains. [*She suddenly hugs HATTIE and turns away with mocking lightness.*] Good-bye, Hattie... [*As she and RUDY turn toward the door, she is feverishly gay.*] It's good to burn bridges!

CURTAIN

ACT THREE

— SCENE ONE

SCENE: *An apartment on Tenth Street. Six months later. The room is simply but attractively furnished, suggesting* GWYN'S *excellent taste and skill in the use of materials. The mood is modernistic, and in complete contrast to the rather ornate style of the previous acts.* GWYN *has exercised considerable ingenuity in furnishing this apartment economically, and she may well be proud of the result; the room is unusual and interesting, without indicating that comparatively little money has been spent on it.*

There are three windows in the rear wall. Two doors at left, the front one leading to a kitchenette, the rear one to a bedroom. Right, a flight of three steps leads to a platform with a railing around it. Off this platform is the doorway to the hall. At the foot of the three stairs, a door to a closet, which is used for coats, etc. Under the railing of the platform, a low broad couch, covered in gray and piled with a large number of gaily colored cushions.

CONNIE *lies flat on her back on the couch, smoking a cigarette, blowing smoke rings at the ceiling. Her hat and coat are on a stool near the couch. At a big table, center, sits* RUDY, *pounding away automatically at a typewriter. Papers are scattered in disorderly piles all over the table. Also a jar of tobacco and several pipes.* RUDY *is in his shirt-sleeves.*

A long pause, during which CONNIE *continues to blow smoke rings and* RUDY *continues to pound the machine with methodical unconcern. Finally ,* CONNIE *sits up and stares at* RUDY'S *back.*

CONNIE Rudy...[*He doesn't hear her and goes on typing. She rises, crosses and stands behind him*] Rudy!

RUDY [*Turns*] Yeah?

CONNIE What time will Gwyn be home?

RUDY Dunno. [*He turns back to the typewriter, and starts to write again.* CONNIE *stands behind him, annoyed, wanting attention. Finally he realizes that she is standing there and turns again.*] If you want to stay around, why don't you get yourself a drink?

CONNIE I don't want a drink.

RUDY [*Who is evidently preoccupied, gloomy and nervous*] Well, read a magazine... read a book... I'm sorry but I promised this article for to-morrow and I'd like to finish it.

CONNIE Do you think Gwyn will be home soon?

RUDY Somewhere around five or six.

CONNIE Where is she?

RUDY She had lunch with the old lady— they went somewhere this af-ternoon.

CONNIE Mrs. Stoneleigh's quite pleased about you and Gwyn, isn't she?

RUDY [*Nods*] She wants us to spend the summer with her at Southampton.

CONNIE Are you going to?

RUDY Not me... Gwyn may go for a few weeks.

CONNIE Funny, it all turns out very conventional and very dull, doesn't it? [*He shrugs. Gives her a look and remains gloomily silent*] Well... don't you think it's funny?

RUDY Sure, everything's funny.

CONNIE And yet it's sad too—

RUDY Sure, everything's funny and everything's sad... that's a cinch— got any other ideas?

CONNIE I've put in a lot of grueling work on you... after months of effort, I achieve a little... intimacy? Is that a good word? And there you are. You sit down at a typewriter and pound the keys and forget all about me! A woman who's just met a fate worse than death wants a little attention.

RUDY [*Good-naturedly*] Let's have a drink.

CONNIE I don't want a drink— I want to talk. What do you really think of me, Rudy?

RUDY [*Good-naturedly*] I'd like to break your neck.

CONNIE [*Softly, putting her arms around his neck*] Why don't you?

RUDY [*Pushes her away, rises.*] Stop it.

CONNIE [*Angrily*] Well, you can't ignore me... you can't act as if I didn't exist...

RUDY [*Seriously*] Let's get this straight, Connie... there's no sense in kidding ourselves...

CONNIE You don't want to see me again?

RUDY No.

CONNIE [*Shrugs*] There's not much point to it... I'd like you to be crazy about me...

RUDY For what? You're not interested in me.

CONNIE [*With bitter feeling*] On account of Gwyn!... It's gratifying to get a man away from her even for a few minutes... every time I see her, I'll laugh because you and I have a private joke.

RUDY It won't be as private as all that.

CONNIE [*Looks at him startled, gasps*] Oh... you're going to tell her?

RUDY What do you think this is? A dainty little intrigue, with everybody lying to everybody else? Get yourself in a mess—

CONNIE Oh, I like messes... won't telling Gwyn be a little messy? [*She laughs.*]

RUDY You don't know a thing about Gwyn.

CONNIE [*She looks at him maliciously.*] Are you still in love with her?

RUDY [*With embarrassed sincerity*] Don't be funny.

CONNIE [*Surprised and touched*] You really mean it, don't you? [*He nods.*] And another lady, now and then, just stimulates this marvelous emotion?

RUDY No... I haven't done anything like this—

CONNIE That's doing rather well... being faithful for six months must have been an awful strain on you. And why did you let me break up this eternal constancy? Just absentmindedness? [*They both laugh.*] You're not even a little upset about it?

RUDY [*Quietly*] Yes... I am.

CONNIE She'll make a model husband out of you before she's through. Once you're married, it's going to be the end of you, Rudy... I mean, as far as the wild jackass side of you is concerned. [*He laughs. She looks around the apartment.*] You and she started in an attic... how long did that last? Two weeks... then you moved here. In a few months you'll be in a duplex... then you'll go back to the old Ballantine house and Mrs. Stoneleigh will come to live with you.

RUDY I happen to have different plans...

CONNIE [*Lightly*] Your plans don't matter... you haven't a chance...

RUDY Don't be so bitter about it.

CONNIE If you were much of a man, you wouldn't let Gwyn run your life for you. [*She turns, upset, ashamed of herself for having said so much, picks up her hat and coat.*] I'd better get out of here... I wanted to see Gwyn and gloat over her... I can't see her now. [*As RUDY helps her on with her coat*] Thanks for being so nice, Rudy.

RUDY Thank you.

CONNIE So it goes... a moment of abandon and a lifetime of tears! [*As CONNIE turns away from him toward steps, the door of apartment right opens, and GWYN enters on landing above. She carries a number of packages, and several bunches of flowers wrapped in paper. Her arms are full, as she stands looking over railing into the room.*]

GWYN Hello, Connie... I'm glad you're here. [*As she starts down the steps*] Come and take some of these things, Rudy... [*He meets her at steps and takes packages.*]

CONNIE I waited for you, Gwyn, but I gave you up.

GWYN Don't go.

CONNIE I must.

GWYN [*To RUDY as he takes packages from her*] Hello, darling... [*She gives him additional packages.*] Put the steak and the butter in the ice box— leave the other things on the table. [*He nods, crossing with the packages, and exits left front.*]

CONNIE Rudy's been trying to throw me out for an hour— I've been interfering with his work.

GWYN Good, he works too hard. [GWYN *has placed the several bunches of flowers on the table.* CONNIE *peeks at them.*]

CONNIE Spring flowers... they're lovely.

GWYN I can't do without them... it's my one extravagance.

RUDY [*Who has reentered left, overhearing this*] Everything Gwyn buys is her one extravagance.

GWYN [*Carelessly, opening the flowers*] Well, I'm learning.

CONNIE Learning to be economical?

GWYN [*Nods*] Why don't you stay for dinner, Connie? I'll call up Elliott... I bought a steak that's big enough for four.

CONNIE I can't. Good-bye, Gwyn... perhaps I'll phone you later.

GWYN [*At steps*] Do. [CONNIE *stops on platform, stands by railing a minute, looks across mockingly at* RUDY.]

CONNIE Good-bye, Rudy. [*She exits right.*]

GWYN Rudy... [*She hesitates*] I've had a very exciting day... I'll tell you about it in a moment— [*As she speaks, she gathers up two vases and starts for the kitchen with them*] Did you finish the article?

RUDY No, I haven't finished the first sentence.

GWYN Then you'll want to work tonight, won't you? [*She exits into kitchen with vases.* RUDY *looks after her, troubled, crosses to typewriter, looks at the sheet in the machine.*]

RUDY [*Angrily*] Got to work... three thousand words of tripe for thirty dollars...

GWYN [*Reappearing with vases filled with water*] It's not worth it, Rudy, it takes you away from your other work— why don't you give it up?

RUDY Because thirty dollars every two weeks is worth worrying about.

GWYN [*Starting to fix the flowers at table*] Of course it is... but the novel is much more important.

RUDY [*Laughs*] When you come right down to it, I think it's old stuff and not very good of its kind... if I had any sense, I'd tear it up and begin over again.

GWYN Well, why don't you? It's better to tear it up a dozen times as long as you express yourself in your own way.

RUDY [*Derisively*] Self-expression! What's so sacred about self-expression?

GWYN [*Laughs*] You're in a dreadful temper, darling!

RUDY No, I'm not... I'm serious. I'm not sure I can write a novel that's worth writing. Self-expression is just an excuse for putting a lot of words on paper... books and poems and plays and pictures... neurotic people rushing to express their starved souls.

GWYN You're not one of the starved souls, are you?

RUDY Why not, what's so different about me?

GWYN [*Turns to him vigorously*] It's really up to you, isn't it? You're able to write living words if you want to— it might take a long time... but you can do it... you can find the essence of life and put it in words.

RUDY [*Laughs*] The essence of life! That's a wonderful phrase, it's so brave and so meaningless!

GWYN [*Glances at him and returns carelessly to fixing the flowers*] It happens to mean something to me...

RUDY Love, I suppose?... That's all there is to it— that's simple, isn't it?

GWYN No, it's very complex and difficult.

RUDY Did you borrow from your aunt today?

GWYN Well, yes, I did, but only for a special reason—

RUDY There's always a special reason— how much did you get today?

GWYN Does it matter?

RUDY Yes, it matters— if I'm kept I want to know what the price is.

GWYN [*Shocked*] Rudy!

RUDY How much? Five hundred? A thousand?

GWYN A thousand... I'll explain it to you later— but money's not important— why make a fetish of it?

RUDY You're the one that makes a fetish of it... this apartment and every stick of furniture in it has been handed us by a diabolical old woman.

GWYN We'll pay her back.

RUDY How do you know we will? What makes you think I can ever earn a thousand dollars?

GWYN I didn't know you felt so strongly about it—

RUDY You don't listen to what I tell you.

GWYN It's on your account— so you can have leisure and a chance to work—

RUDY I don't want leisure at her expense— or yours either.

GWYN I've always said it didn't matter. I don't mind being poor—

RUDY You don't know what it means, you call *this* being poor—

GWYN I'm fond of this apartment, because I did it for us... I worried about every detail of it.

RUDY Don't you see the trouble, Gwyn? You've tried to fit me into your own design... I don't fit... I don't want to live this way... it's not right for me.

GWYN There's something very wrong between us: you're angry... you're bitter against me?

RUDY No... not against you.

GWYN [*Worried*] What is it?... please tell me.

RUDY Connie spent most of the day here. She telephoned shortly after you left, and I told her to come over.

GWYN Oh, I see... [*She turns to fixing the flowers again.*] You made love to her?

RUDY Yes. [*A pause. She continues to arrange the flowers.*] I've hurt you, Gwyn— I'm sorry. I love you and I don't want to hurt you; I can't make an abject apology because I don't feel abject.

GWYN Of course not: why on earth should you be abject? I don't know why I'm so surprised... I suppose I should have expected something of this sort, but it never entered my head. I don't want to scream and yell and have tantrums. All that really matters is how you feel. Do you feel about her as you do about me?

RUDY [*Shocked*] Gwyn! [*Laughs*] You get it all wrong. There's nothing of that sort—

GWYN Then what is it?

RUDY I never promised eternal constancy. I simply say that each of us has a fundamental right to choose his own conduct.

GWYN There's something wrong between us. This wouldn't have happened a month ago, or a week ago... it couldn't... you've changed.

RUDY Yes, perhaps I have.

GWYN Why?

RUDY You and I have been living in a regular Turkish bath of emotion... a deadly wonderful concentration on each other. Isn't it time to wake up from this dream and look at ourselves?

GWYN It never occurred to me to doubt... even our worst quarrels have been illuminated by something... haven't they, Rudy? I've packed more feeling into this place than all the rest of my life.

RUDY That's your side of it... emotion. Love is the essence of life and there's nothing else! Talk about self-expression: you express yourself all right, you express yourself in me.

GWYN [*Brokenly*] What else could I do?... It's meant so much. I've tried to make it perfect.

RUDY What's your idea of perfection? Money?

GWYN No.

RUDY Well, it's based on that.

GWYN We've argued so much about money—

RUDY You don't make the slightest effort to spend less—

GWYN Oh, I have, Rudy, I've been careful.

RUDY You scrimped and saved and suffered: Curtains for five dollars a yard, chairs for sixty-five dollars each.

GWYN And because these chairs cost sixty-five dollars, you made love to Connie Blane this afternoon? Is that what you're trying to tell me?

RUDY I'm not making any excuses— it may have been casual and stupid, but it shows we're drifting along in a casual, stupid way.

GWYN If I want you to be faithful to me, we must live in a cave in Central Park?

RUDY You have no intention of getting along without your aunt's money, have you?

GWYN I want to please you, but it seems so trivial.

RUDY Money's not trivial, it's the root of everything. You know where the old woman gets hers— from cotton mills in the South, from mines in Pennsylvania, from munitions too.

GWYN You can't go into that.

RUDY You've got to; got to get under the surface. Money's controlled every move we've made from the night we met. You've created the atmosphere in which we live, Gwyn, out of your own past.

GWYN You think I haven't changed... to me I've torn myself up by the roots and made myself over...

RUDY You keep just as close as you can to the things you thought you ran away from: You visit with your aunt— you confide in Elliott— you run to Dr. Golden like you would to a confessional—

GWYN [*Her voice strained, tense with emotion*] I tell you, it's not easy to adjust myself... you're a difficult person—

RUDY We've gone along in a sort of mystical excitement— poetry and ecstasy and quarrels. Every fight we have is a courtship, you don't want to give yourself, you're insanely emotional and you're afraid of it... half demon and half Puritan... the Puritan part is always making you deceive yourself, making you hide away from your own emotion...

GWYN [*Desperation in her voice*] I can't help being what I am... I'm faithful to what I feel.

RUDY I don't know what you feel.

GWYN You... only you... [*A pause. He stands beside her, deeply moved. She looks up at him wearily.*] I'd die to *please* you. [*Pause*] I can't change all of a sudden and be a different woman— I don't even know what sort of woman you want me to be.

RUDY I don't know... I'm blinded because I love you.

GWYN Yet you can turn away from me— you can turn casually to someone else! That's a strange kind of love! Don't talk any more— [*She turns toward bedroom.*]

RUDY [*Stopping her*] I'm going to take a walk. [*He gets his hat from closet by stairs right.*]

GWYN Will you come back for dinner?

RUDY Sure. [*He runs up stairs and exits right. She stands quite still for a moment. She picks a flower out of a vase, stares at it as if she had never seen it before, then throws it on floor. She picks up telephone beside couch, and dials.*]

GWYN [*Over telephone*] Hello... Dr. Golden?... I'm sorry to disturb you... I know it's late, but I thought perhaps you'd let me come to your office for a moment... Oh, I see... well, in that case, I shall have to wait until tomorrow... [*She laughs*] Could you? If you have time to stop in I'd be very glad... [*The front doorbell rings.*] Please do... as soon as you can. Good-bye. [GWYN *rises and goes up steps right to front door. She opens the door and admits* CONNIE.]

CONNIE Hello.

GWYN Hello... did you pass Rudy as you came in?

CONNIE No. Do you mind my coming back?

GWYN I'm glad.

CONNIE I'm a little vague, Gwyn, I've been sitting at the Brevoort brooding over a drink... have you any rye?

GWYN [*She opens a cellaret, containing bottles, glasses, etc., front left.*] I'll get you some ice.

CONNIE I don't want any ice... [*As she pours*] I'm not supposed to drink, I'm on a diet. I've lost eight pounds in ten days.

GWYN I must try it.

CONNIE I'll copy it for you; it's a schedule: meat every day, no liquor, of course. [*She takes a large swig from her glass. Looks across at* GWYN *nervously*] Better have some, Gwyn, you look white.

GWYN [*Pours herself a drink.*] I will have a little... Rudy and I had a fuss.

CONNIE Did you?

GWYN It's horribly embarrassing, isn't it?

CONNIE [*Harshly, her voice a little hysterical*] Do you know why I came back here? Because I knew it was the nastiest thing I could do... because it seems terribly exciting to butt in on your private emotions...

GWYN You're not in love?

CONNIE With Rudy? I should say not.

GWYN I should be much less puzzled if you were both desperately in love with each other.

CONNIE I'd prefer it myself... if I had half a chance to take Rudy away from you, I'd do it.

GWYN Why?

CONNIE I hate you... I told you once; you've forgotten, but I haven't.

GWYN I'm not important enough to be hated as much as that. I haven't done anything dishonest... I'm very confused and very miserable.

CONNIE So am I. All I do is run around in circles... I'm casual about sex, I'm casual about everything, I'm so casual I'm dizzy.

GWYN What about Elliott?

CONNIE I expected too much of Elliott... I was insane about him and I wanted him to feel the same way... The first time we were ever together he telephoned to you and asked you how you were feeling... do you remember? Now it's simmered down to one of those semi-permanent affairs... and I cheat him all the time. You'll find out before you've been with Rudy much longer... this will happen again and again, and every time it will be a little worse—

GWYN What's the end of it?

CONNIE [*Sings in a thin heartbreaking voice*]
"I'm ready for the river,
The slithery river,
So get the river ready for me!"

GWYN That's not a good answer.

CONNIE Don't worry, I shan't do it... you're much more likely to die than I am, because you care about things. I'm content to reel in and out of taxicabs, in and out of beds— I won't end in the river, I'll end in a cozy cottage in Westchester... I'll get a good-natured husband, I'll torture him by being frank about my past.

GWYN If that's the only point in living, it would be better to give it up right now.

CONNIE Of course, it's better to give it up. You're confused because you want perfection— you like dizzy talk about revolutions— you want a lot of things that don't exist outside your own head... you and Rudy will end right across the road from me, in a farmhouse, quarreling and drinking and being attractively bitter. [*Doorbell rings*]

CONNIE Is that Rudy?

GWYN I don't think so. [*She opens the door. DR. GOLDEN enters, wearing a dress suit, looking very spruce and important.*] Hello, Doctor, I'm glad to see you. Do you remember Miss Blane?

DR. GOLDEN Of course, how do you do, Miss Blane?

CONNIE A bit manic-depressive, Doctor.

DR. GOLDEN [*Politely*] Really.

CONNIE I'm a dandy case— do you want the sordid details?

DR. GOLDEN [*Coughing*] Not just at present.

CONNIE Mother's promised to treat me to an analysis whenever I feel I've reached the end of my rope... it probably won't be long. [*She ascends steps to door.*] Good-bye, Gwyn.

GWYN Good-bye. [CONNIE *exits.*] I'm sorry I telephoned you in such wild haste— it was a foolish impulse.

DR. GOLDEN [*Chuckles*] One can't call on a psychoanalyst as one would on a fireman, to slide down a greased pole and rush to the scene of the trouble.

GWYN [*Laughs*] Well, perhaps it would be a good idea to turn the hose on me.

DR. GOLDEN Are you as desperate as that?

GWYN Yes, you've helped me a great deal, Doctor.

DR. GOLDEN I hope so.

GWYN Rudy wants to leave me. He said so... he won't do it this time...

but sometime he'll do it. I can't look forward to that... I don't want to go ahead... I want to go back... the past is secure... [*Hysteria in her voice*] I should like to die... in the house where I lived safely... Shut myself up in a musty old house with ghosts... shut out the sunlight, shut out the air... lie in state, aching and very quiet, till I turn to dust.

DR. GOLDEN [*In a dry, vigorous voice*] I don't believe you.

GWYN I want everything to stop. I've been drunk on moonlight, and I want the moon to stay fixed forever.

DR. GOLDEN [*In the same dry manner*] You express yourself hysterically, but I know what you mean... We all feel the need of security.

GWYN I'm in love with a man who's been unfaithful to me this afternoon and has every intention of repeating it.

DR. GOLDEN Well, that's unfortunate... but a great many people are in the same boat.

GWYN I know— I'm hopelessly romantic—

DR. GOLDEN You *must face facts.*

GWYN So you've told me.

DR. GOLDEN But you don't do it... you indulge in flights of mystical idealism... you turn love into a sort of religion... you ought to translate all this energy into some other useful activity... go to work or paint pictures... [*During this speech*, RUDY *has entered above right.*]

RUDY [*Looking over the balcony*] Pardon me, Doctor, did I interrupt a speech?

DR. GOLDEN Not at all— I was just leaving.

RUDY Don't go on my account.

DR. GOLDEN [*Indicating his dress suit*] As you observe, I'm on my way to a banquet. In fact, I'm the guest of honor and I can't be late. [*To* GWYN] Will you telephone me in the morning?

GWYN Of course.

RUDY [*Sarcastically*] She couldn't get through the day without phoning you, Doctor. [DR. GOLDEN *chuckles and goes to door right.*]

DR. GOLDEN I'm not trying to take her away from you, Mr. Flannigan. [RUDY *grunts rather ominously.*]

GWYN [*Seeing* DR. GOLDEN *to the door*] Thanks for coming. [DR. GOLDEN *exits.*]

RUDY [*As* GWYN *turns back into the room*] Did you send for that fool?

GWYN Yes, I did.

RUDY Haven't you any common sense on your own account, without sending for a witch doctor in a dress suit?

GWYN He told me I ought to stop worrying and find some useful work.

RUDY That's all right— but is that the measure of your helplessness? Don't you see it's cockeyed that you have to be told to stop worrying by a money-grubbing pathologist?

GWYN Rudy... perhaps we're not much good together.

RUDY We've been trying to make a compromise— but we're pulling in opposite directions— we've got to follow your path or mine— we can't combine them.

GWYN I wish I could see your path.

RUDY [*Quietly*] I saw it just now— a flash of it— I've been walking over by the docks— the stevedores are on strike— there was some sort of a meeting and the cops broke it up.

GWYN You went out looking for that, didn't you? [RUDY *nods.*] To me that's a sentimental idea!

RUDY It's got nothing to do with your lily-white soul.

GWYN It's got nothing to do with you either.

RUDY You're damn right it hasn't... in the streets and on the docks and in the fields, people are carrying burdens in the night and in the heat of the sun...

GWYN Do you expect me to go out and carry a burden?

RUDY No, I don't— but it's better than what you and I are doing— you sit at the feet of a psychoanalyst while I indulge in coy infidelities.

GWYN I don't want that— I'm as anxious as you are to find a way to live— a way that means something, that touches reality—

RUDY But those people with burdens are not real to you?

GWYN I know that terror and starvation are all around us— I want to do what I can— but it's not a solution for us, Rudy... I can't become a part of the struggle—

RUDY But the struggle's right at your doorstep— you're either in it or you're out of it. You can't shut the world out— you can't seal love up in a vacuum.

GWYN That's what I thought we'd done... I thought you and I were so close together that nothing could touch us— I thought we were in a castle, with walls six feet thick and a moat around it... pretending we were Tristram and Iseult! All we are is Mr. and Mrs. in the funny papers!

RUDY I've got no illusions about myself, Gwyn— I'm lazy and soft— but I went to a school of muscle and sweat and I know what it means. You're figuring on a future built out of Mrs. Stoneleigh's bonds... you'll see workers shot to protect those bonds and you'll run to a psychoanalyst and pay him fifty dollars to tell you not to worry.

GWYN You're not fair.

RUDY Yes, I'm fair, because it's one thing or the other— you can't play both sides against the middle, not in the year nineteen-thirty-four. You know which side you're on— you're on the side where the bonds come from!

GWYN I don't see—

RUDY Of course, you don't— that's why it's hopeless.

GWYN It's hopeless to try to keep you because you've made up your mind against me— I don't want to hold you... Connie saw the reality of it... marry and retire to Westchester and drink ourselves to death... [*Turning on him with deep feeling*] I don't want it... All around us there are little broken people— I thought we could be different, but we can't... I don't care anything about the future... I love you and hate you and pity you— I want to take you in my arms and hold you like a mother, wrap you in my arms and never let you go— that's deadly and destroying— [*She cries out violently.*] Go away then— freedom is better! [*Doorbell rings.* RUDY *opens the door.* ELLIOTT *enters.*]

ELLIOTT Hello!

RUDY There's no more to say. [*He exits abruptly ,* GWYN *stands quite still for a moment.* ELLIOTT *looks at her sympathetically, now realizing that something is seriously wrong.*]

ELLIOTT What's the matter? You look as if you'd been run through a wringer.

GWYN Rudy and I are finished.

ELLIOTT [*Gasps*] Why?

GWYN Incompatibility!

ELLIOTT [*Trying to be very firm*] You can't do this— I won't permit it—

GWYN [*Gaily*] Won't you? That's sweet of you!... [*She starts toward door left.*] I'm packing. [*He holds her back.*]

ELLIOTT Stop and think.

GWYN Can one think, when one feels as if one were going over Niagara Falls in a barrel? [*There is hysteria in her voice*] Help me, don't let me be maudlin.

ELLIOTT Don't mind me— it might do you good— go ahead, scream, smash things!

GWYN [*Smiles*] Not I! It's an old story... let the dead bury their dead, each man kills the thing he loves— I'm full of old dead words out of books... Do you know any new words? Words that haven't been invented yet? [*He is silent. She hesitates, still smiling.*] You haven't heard the really funny part of it... I'm going to have a child— this afternoon I went to the doctor to make sure... I came home singing...

ELLIOTT Did you tell Rudy?

GWYN How could I? I planned it deliberately, to make him settle down— I didn't want a child— I deserve to be put on a rack and tortured... [*She controls herself, speaks calmly, well in hand.*] Come and help me pack. [*She takes his hand, pulls him reluctantly toward door left.*]

CURTAIN

SCENE TWO

SCENE: *Same as Act One. The following morning. When the curtain rises, the stage is empty, and dimly lighted. A little light filters through the heavy white cloth which has been curtained across the windows right. All the furniture is covered with white sheets. Through the bare arch left one can see the shadowy further room. All the lamps and knickknacks have been dismantled. There is the bare ghostly outline of furniture under sheets. The ship's model is still on projecting shelf left under a white cloth. HAVENS enters right rear. He is unshaven, wearing shabby trousers, his shirt open at the neck, and an old coat, in marked contrast to the immaculate figure of previous scenes. He takes a kitchen chair, carries it to windows right and gets on it, carefully pulling down the cloth which is draped over the windows. Through the leaded panes comes bright sunlight.*

The front doorbell is heard buzzing off-scene. HAVENS *gets down from the chair and exits center rear, leaving the door open. Voices are heard in the hall.*

COLONEL FOWLER'S VOICE How are you, Havens? Is everything all right?

HAVENS' VOICE. Yes, sir. [COLONEL FOWLER *enters the room followed by* HAVENS]

COLONEL FOWLER I dropped in to tell you I concluded the sale of the house this morning, the people who were here on Monday.

HAVENS Foreigners?

COLONEL FOWLER [*Nods*] Unsatisfactory terms... but we've waited so long that any offer seems like a miracle. [HAVENS *nods.*] If contractors come here, show them through... Any prospects for yourself?

HAVENS No, sir.

COLONEL FOWLER Hard times... By the way, I notice there's a window broken in the parlor.

HAVENS It's being fixed today.

COLONEL FOWLER Good... I'll get in touch with Mrs. Ballantine later.

HAVENS [*With obvious hesitation, not sure whether he should mention the fact or not*] As a matter of fact... [*He hesitates again.*] she's here!

COLONEL FOWLER Here? She can't be here? What's she doing?

HAVENS Sleeping in her own room. She came last night.

COLONEL FOWLER Anything wrong?

HAVENS Not that I know of: I haven't heard her moving about yet.

COLONEL FOWLER I'll wait and see her. [*Front doorbell rings again.*]

HAVENS One moment, sir. [*He exits center.*]
[COLONEL FOWLER *stands by window right, takes a slip of paper and a pencil from his pocket and starts figuring on it, muttering to himself*]

COLONEL FOWLER [*Under his breath*] Eighteen thousand... twenty-one thousand... taxes... forty-one. [*He shakes his head.*]
[MRS. STONELEIGH'S *voice, brisk and emphatic, is heard in the hall.*]

MRS. STONELEIGH'S VOICE Go and get her, Havens, she can't be asleep at this hour.
[*She enters the library, followed by* ELLIOTT. ELLIOTT *looks rather dejected, but* MRS. STONELEIGH *is beaming.*]

MRS. STONELEIGH [*As* COLONEL FOWLER *pockets the slip of paper and comes forward*] Heavens... I thought you were Jack's ghost... you look like him, Richard.

COLONEL FOWLER What are you doing here?

MRS. STONELEIGH That question was on the tip of my tongue.

COLONEL FOWLER Business, the place is sold.

MRS. STONELEIGH For nothing, I suppose.

COLONEL FOWLER Not much. It's the only offer we've had.

MRS. STONELEIGH It's dreadful to see it go! If this house had been built a year earlier, I would have been born in it. [*Looking around and sniffing*] Stuffy, isn't it?

COLONEL FOWLER I'll open the window. [*He turns to window right.*]

MRS. STONELEIGH [*Lifts up corner of the sheet over big couch center*] Take the other corner, Elliott.

COLONEL FOWLER [*As he opens the window, speaking over his shoulder*] Is anything the matter with Gwyn?

MRS. STONELEIGH A minor tantrum, nothing of the slightest consequence.

ELLIOTT [*Annoyed, to* MRS. STONELEIGH] I wish I'd kept you away from here.

MRS. STONELEIGH [*Disregarding this*] Things are going to turn out much better than we expected, Richard.

COLONEL FOWLER I'm glad—

MRS. STONELEIGH You'll be amazed when you hear the news—

ELLIOTT Gwyn doesn't want you to tell everybody about it.

MRS. STONELEIGH One can't call Richard "everybody"— and after all, we three are closer to her and love her more dearly than anyone— [*Turning to* FOWLER *triumphantly*] It's been miraculously settled... a little child shall lead them!

COLONEL FOWLER Lead them?

MRS. STONELEIGH Gwyn told me yesterday... I took her to my doctor and arranged about everything.

COLONEL FOWLER But the legal angle?

ELLIOTT It's been straightened out.

MRS. STONELEIGH The divorce was granted in Chicago. I had my own lawyer go out there to look into the matter... the child rounds the whole thing out like a bit of fiction.

COLONEL FOWLER [*Dubiously*] Gwyn knows what she wants—

ELLIOTT There's only one hitch... she's left Flannigan.

MRS. STONELEIGH That's why I'm here... As soon as I heard of this tiff, I knew it was up to me to take charge—

ELLIOTT You'd better be careful—

MRS. STONELEIGH Poppycock! I think I'll go and wake her myself!

ELLIOTT I suppose you intend to shake her and shout "poppycock" in her ear.

MRS. STONELEIGH Certainly. [HAVENS *enters center rear.*]

HAVENS She'll be here in a moment, madam.

MRS. STONELEIGH Thank you, Havens, how often do you shave?

HAVENS Only twice a week under present conditions. I'm sorry, I meant to do it this morning.

MRS. STONELEIGH [*Vaguely*] I would... I really would. [*Rubbing her finger along the mantelpiece*] The dust is an inch thick.

HAVENS I go over everything with a damp rag—

MRS. STONELEIGH [*Interrupting*] Twice a week?

HAVENS Yes, madam. [*He exits right rear.*]

MRS. STONELEIGH [*As HAVENS disappears*] Something's the matter with that man: he's gone to pieces.

ELLIOTT Maybe it's just the dust.
[GWYN *enters center rear. She wears a delightfully frilly negligée and doesn't seem to have a care in the world.*]

GWYN Hello... Hello, Richard... I'm amazed at seeing you all— And Elliott...

MRS. STONELEIGH Kiss me, dear.

GWYN How did you know I was here?

ELLIOTT It's my fault— I told her—

MRS. STONELEIGH I phoned you this morning and there was no answer... I felt something was wrong and I called Elliott.

ELLIOTT And she insisted on rushing over here to take charge of the case!

GWYN [*To* MRS. STONELEIGH] What do you want, Aunt Kate?

MRS. STONELEIGH Obviously I want to know what's wrong and what's to be done about it: Yesterday we understood each other, and everything was settled; now I learn that you have an inconsequential quarrel—

GWYN [*Interrupting her gently*] I don't need your help, Aunt Kate, I'm all right.

MRS. STONELEIGH [*Forcefully*] You are *not* all right, and there's no time to waste. Any child in my family *must* have a name.

COLONEL FOWLER [*Helpfully*] In Spain they call them after their mothers.

GWYN You're a mine of useless information, Richard.

MRS. STONELEIGH It's all so simple, Gwyn... it's natural and lovely for you to have a child... I've always said you should have six—

GWYN [*Smiles, trying to keep the flippant tone of the conversation*] All right. By different fathers.

MRS. STONELEIGH I insist on a name— if you've really broken with Rudy, find someone else— for instance, there's always Elliott!

ELLIOTT [*With a sigh*] Always...

MRS. STONELEIGH Elliott wouldn't hesitate for a moment— you'd rather enjoy it, wouldn't you, Elliott?

ELLIOTT [*Angrily, much upset*] Do you have to stick pins in *everyone*, Aunt Kate?

MRS. STONELEIGH [*Interrupting, reasonably*] So sorry... I didn't know you were in such an emotional state.

ELLIOTT Well, I am.

GWYN It doesn't help to argue about it. [*She turns to the others.*] It's sweet of all of you to worry about me, but please go away—

ELLIOTT [*To* MRS. STONELEIGH] There you are—

COLONEL FOWLER Gwyn, before I go... this has disturbed me so much that I almost forgot what I came for— I've sold the house, furniture and all, eighty thousand cash, to some Roumanians.

MRS. STONELEIGH I don't believe it— Roumanians don't have eighty thousand dollars.

COLONEL FOWLER I've investigated that.

MRS. STONELEIGH What do they want with it?

COLONEL FOWLER A club.

ELLIOTT What sort of a club?

COLONEL FOWLER Well, I'm not very clear... a night club, or gambling club.

GWYN How quaint! [*She goes to ship's model left, carefully takes the cloth off it.*] I think I'll save Jack's ship. It carries a very curious cargo.

ELLIOTT Apes and ivory... from Cathay?

GWYN [*Smiles*] No, broken dreams from New England! [MRS. STONE-LEIGH *grunts.*]

ELLIOTT Aunt Kate is one year older than this house.

MRS. STONELEIGH In another year, they'll turn me into a gambling club!

COLONEL FOWLER Unfortunately you won't get any money out of the sale, GWYN

ELLIOTT Why won't she?

COLONEL FOWLER You see the first mortgage is forty-one thousand, the second mortgage is eighteen— there are back taxes, commission to the agent and other obligations— it comes out even almost to a penny—

ELLIOTT Well, what's the good of that?

COLONEL FOWLER Every day Gwyn holds onto this house she runs further into debt.

MRS. STONELEIGH What's to become of you?

ELLIOTT Gwyn asked us to leave her alone— I think it's only fair to do as she wishes.

MRS. STONELEIGH I've tried to be close to you, Gwyn... I've tried to understand! Perhaps you're trying to see your way, but thumbing one's nose doesn't help one to walk in darkness.

GWYN [*Wearily*] That's true.

MRS. STONELEIGH Your child will be rich some day, I haven't changed my will, I don't intend to change it.

GWYN I don't want your money—

MRS. STONELEIGH Tell her what it means, Richard.

COLONEL FOWLER [*Sincerely*] What can I tell her? Everything's changing... you see corporations crumble and die: people change even more profoundly.

GWYN People can't change fast enough: one's blood and brain change slowly...

MRS. STONELEIGH [*Pleadingly*] I've been very patient, Gwyn... I'm bitterly tired, but I've watched and waited—

GWYN You don't see what's at issue, Aunt Kate... Rudy and I have our own problem... I want you to stay away from us— I don't want you to tell him things— if he knew about the child, he'd be under an obliga- tion— I don't want that— if there's anything worth saving between us, we must save it ourselves—
[*As* MRS. STONELEIGH *turns to leave, door center rear opens and* RUDY *enters in his shirt-sleeves. His hair is disheveled. He has such a hangover that he can hardly stand. He has one black eye, and an ugly scar on his forehead.*]

RUDY Where's the party?

MRS. STONELEIGH Thank God.

ELLIOTT Where have you been?

RUDY Asleep.

MRS. STONELEIGH [*To* RUDY] It's a relief to see you.

ELLIOTT [*To* RUDY, *who looks as if he were about to drop in his tracks*] Sit down, old man, before you fall down.

RUDY [*Sinking on couch*] Old man is right, what a head! [*He lies down flat on his back on the couch.*]

MRS. STONELEIGH We shall leave you in Gwyn's capable hands.

COLONEL FOWLER [*Starting for door*] By all means... good-bye, Gwyn.

RUDY [*From the couch*] Any Scotch in the house?

GWYN [*As she leads* MRS. STONELEIGH *and* FOWLER *to door rear*] If you stay there long enough, a Roumanian will bring you a drink.

RUDY [*Composing himself*] All right, I'll wait.

GWYN [*Puts her hand on* ELLIOTT'S *arm as he starts to leave with the others*] Stay for a moment, Elliott. [ELLIOTT *nods and turns back into the room.*]

COLONEL FOWLER [*At door*] Take care of yourself, Flannigan. [RUDY *raises his head and peers over the couch at this suggestion.* FOWLER *exits.* MRS. STONELEIGH *and* GWYN *exit rear.*]

ELLIOTT [*To* RUDY] Don't pass out on us, Rudy, you're the corpus delicti and we need you.

RUDY How did I get here?

ELLIOTT You phoned me at two A. M. and drooled like an idiot. I told you where she'd gone and you promised to let her alone.

RUDY What's the old lady excited about?

ELLIOTT She thinks you can be turned into a solid citizen. I think a little pick me up would do you good... I'll ask Havens. [*Rings bell.*]

GWYN [*Reentering*] How do you feel?

RUDY [*Hand to his head*] Words... oceans of words... a Bacchic souse... a haze... a stupor... a frenzy... an escape! You have a different way of escaping, Gwyn, you have a deep soul and you hide yourself in it... I take my soul out on a jag... deaf, dumb and blind, walking around on air, one foot on Tenth Avenue and the other foot in Jersey... and everywhere I was looking for *you!* It was confusing because you were everywhere... you were a statue on a monument... the tinkle of ice in a glass was your voice... I'm sure I was out on the river. I was in a boat; what was I doing in a boat? [HAVENS *enters right rear. He has now shaved and is fairly presentable.*]

HAVENS You rang, madam?

RUDY [*Sitting bolt upright*] Havens! It was you—

HAVENS [*Nods apologetically*] Sorry, I thought you were a burglar because you came through the window— once we started fighting, there was no stopping!

RUDY You beat me to a pulp! I congratulate you, Havens, I didn't know you had the strength.

HAVENS [*Modestly*] You weren't yourself.

ELLIOTT Anything to drink in the house?

HAVENS No. I'm sorry.

ELLIOTT I'll step out and buy you a pint, Rudy.

RUDY Thanks. [ELLIOTT *exits.*]

RUDY What are you doing with yourself, Havens?

HAVENS Reading.

RUDY Any new books?

HAVENS I don't buy anything new: "Looking Backward" by Bellamy, Ingersoll, Henry George, Owen, Kropotkin...

GWYN This is news to me, Havens.

HAVENS [*Smiles discreetly*] Begging your pardon, madam.

RUDY Talk to him, he's very interesting.

HAVENS I live in the past, but I think a great deal about the future.

RUDY Havens, I hate to say so, but there's a lot of gentle Jesus in your make-up... why don't you preach brotherly love and get hung on a cross?

HAVENS [*Cheerfully*] I prefer the pantry. [*He exits.*]

GWYN That's extraordinary, I never knew him.

RUDY He's a hermit. For thirty years his soul has lived in a cave while his hands served cocktails. [*A pause.* GWYN *sits beside him, takes his hand.*]

GWYN Here we are, darling.

RUDY What did I say to you last night... when I found you?

GWYN There was blood on your face and you cried like a child. Last night I knew you loved me, I understood... how much it means to us both. If you and I are any good together—

RUDY What's good about it? We're both what we've always been; we fight each other and learn a little but we don't change.

GWYN That's not enough for me— we must change.

RUDY How?

GWYN What you told me yesterday— the starving people—

RUDY Been worrying about that?

GWYN If that's where reality lies, I don't want to escape.

RUDY [*Seriously*] If you want to go after that sort of reality, you'd have to do it alone.

GWYN And you?

RUDY Me too! Maybe you want it, but we'd never find anything like that together.

GWYN Why not?

RUDY Too tied up in each other...

GWYN Could you find it alone?

RUDY [*Rises, deeply troubled*] I'm not much good... might get somewhere in ten years if I had the nerve—

GWYN [*In a frightened whisper, searching his face for the answer*] Why not with me?

RUDY No, I'd go on doing this sort of thing, get in an emotional mess and get drunk to settle it. As long as I'm with you, I have no courage... I feel responsible, worry about you whether you want me to or not... worry about money and write books. Books are all right if you can make 'em spit fire and lead... I don't know how to write, don't know enough. I don't want to sail over the battle on a pink cloud pounding a typewriter.

GWYN Suppose you were alone? What would you do? Where would you go?

RUDY Iowa City.

GWYN What's special about Iowa City?

RUDY Nothing... it's like a hundred other places. I met an old friend last night... down by the docks... he took me out in a boat with two quarts of gin. He didn't drink but he listened... I told him about my soul and it made him laugh. He doesn't have any time to search his soul— he's going to Iowa City today; business for the Farmers' League... out there the farmers live on dirt and rotten pumpkins... there's plenty stirring, propaganda, stopping foreclosures, picketing the roads—

GWYN [*Half to herself*] That's more important...

RUDY [*Cheerfully*] It's better than staying in New York waiting for the town to blow up— I don't want to blow up in a boudoir!

GWYN Neither do I!

RUDY That's what it amounts to— hide away in a corner of chaos and

315

play a pornographic game!

GWYN It's a clear choice... between me and Iowa City.

RUDY Sure, that's a place where I could be useful... if I mixed up in a strike in an industrial town, I'd be a joke— I couldn't get close to the workers and they wouldn't trust me. But Iowa's different— I know the people out there, I know what they're up against.

GWYN Do you know what time your friend leaves?

RUDY Sure.

GWYN Then you must be on the train... and don't think about me, don't come back...

RUDY If you say so—

GWYN That's what you wanted me to say, isn't it?

RUDY [*Gravely*] I didn't have the courage... I had to come back and get it from you.

GWYN I'm glad you did... if we're better alone, we must both go on alone.
[ELLIOTT *enters rear, carrying a package containing a pint bottle.*]

ELLIOTT Here you are, Rudy.

RUDY What's that?

ELLIOTT Whiskey.

RUDY I forgot... I don't need it now... thanks just the same. [*He looks at GWYN searchingly and turns abruptly to the door.*] I better get out of here. [*He exits.*]

ELLIOTT What's the idea?

GWYN [*Smiles*] You seem to be on hand whenever Rudy and I say good-bye.

ELLIOTT You're not going through that farce again? [*She nods*] I never heard such nonsense.

GWYN It's divinely sensible if you only knew... I'm rather relieved because it's final... he'll never come back.

ELLIOTT I know you're able to paddle your own canoe... but if I could help you... that is, without rocking the boat?

GWYN No.

ELLIOTT If there's any hope for me, I'd like to know it.

GWYN Today is the end of a number of things, Elliott; I want it to be the end of our fictitious brother and sister relation.

ELLIOTT [*Meekly*] Angry at me?

GWYN No. For years I've used you mercilessly as a prop for my ego... I've encouraged you and petted you and put my feet on your neck.

ELLIOTT You're being cruel.

GWYN It's not half as cruel as what I've done: You're in love with Connie and you've made hell for both of you, because you can't break away from me! There's no sense in it, I can't give you anything.

ELLIOTT. Does Rudy know about the child?

GWYN No.

ELLIOTT You don't have to go through with it, you know.

GWYN I must. I shall probably be a very bad mother, but it's my only chance to be anything.

ELLIOTT Why go through this agony?

GWYN I must.

ELLIOTT [*Deeply troubled, pleadingly*] Sooner or later, you'll stop re-
belling, you'll grow old, fighting all the bright new confusion just the
way Aunt Kate has fought you, always losing and smiling,
because bitterness wins in the end ...

GWYN You're looking in the wrong crystal ball, there's nothing but
the past in yours.

ELLIOTT There's nothing but the past in the future.

GWYN Even the child in me knows better than that.

ELLIOTT Why should anything be different? He'll go through the mill,
tapped for bones, at Yale, the Stock Exchange and an assortment of
women.

GWYN Our children won't play at life in boudoirs and offices: they'll
face something different whether they like it or not. If you and I could
look in the crystal ball we'd turn to stone; we're not fit for the future,
we're little people, we comfort ourselves with little passions, we waste
ourselves with little fears, we walk in a funeral procession— towards a
red horizon; we can't see the cities burning and the marching
armies— there's blood in the sky.

ELLIOTT You're guessing at another war.

GWYN I'm not guessing, civilizations don't die in bed.

ELLIOTT Why go through the pains of labor?

GWYN I'm afraid... perhaps I can make a child who won't be afraid,
he'll take sides and die— but there's always a chance, he might live
and make a new world.

ELLIOTT [*His voice almost breaking*] I don't believe there's anything
like that... I don't believe there's any chance for a new world— I wish I
could see it— [RUDY *enters.*]

RUDY [*Carelessly, to* GWYN] I can't find my tie, it doesn't matter.

ELLIOTT [*Glancing from one to the other*] Hello, Rudy... Good-bye,
Gwyn. [*He exits.*] [*A pause.* GWYN *and* RUDY *smile at each other.*]

GWYN [*Quietly*] It's silly to tell you how perfect it's been... I can look
back and see the perfect rightness of it. People don't fall in love blindly... they think it's blind but they need each other... we each gave what
the other needed... you dragged me out of a dead house into a new
bright world— I gave you balance and perspective and a chance to
think.

RUDY Wherever I go from here, Gwyn, you've done it. It's a rough
road for people like us— we get tangled up with our own crazy problems— it's different for people who work and fight hunger and death—
all we fight is our own shadows.

GWYN We've come a little way on the road.

RUDY I'll go away carrying your brain and your heart—

GWYN I'll carry yours, Rudy. [*He looks at her a moment and exits.*
GWYN *is alone. She hears the front door slam.*]

CURTAIN

John Howard Lawson

Though John Howard Lawson's career as a professional playwright was relatively brief, lasting less than 15 years, he nonetheless demonstrated remarkable range and exerted considerable influence. Throughout the 1920s, he was a key player in the burgeoning avant-garde theatre scene in the United States, writing plays that drew on and advanced non-realistic forms such as expressionism, dada, and surrealism. Then, in the 1930s, he was a significant contributor to the practice of socialist realism in the United States, writing both plays that model that approach as well as a widely used critical study on the form. Thus, though now he and his accomplishments are often little more than historical footnotes in the annals of theatre history, Lawson's role in the development of theatre in the first half of the twentieth century is noteworthy.

Born in New York City on 25 September 1894, Lawson graduated from Williams College in 1914. Following a brief stint with Routers News Agency (a post secured for him by his father, who was the executive managing editor), Lawson served as a volunteer in the Norton-Harjes Ambulance Corps stationed on the French front during World War I. In the years immediately following the war, Lawson lived as an expatriate in Europe, primarily residing in Paris through the end of 1922. While there, he wrote drafts of *Roger Bloomer* and *Processional*, scripts that would eventually develop into his first major successes in the New York theatre.

First produced in March 1923, *Roger Bloomer* centers around its title character, a restive young man who, in the course of the play, journeys from his small Midwestern town to New York City, persistently drawn on by his resolute conviction that only on his own will he discover a life worth living. The script marks an important moment in the development of expressionism in the United State theatre. Prefiguring Lawson's work with this mode, both Eugene O'Neill with *The Hairy Ape*, *The Emperor Jones*, and *The Great God Brown* and Elmer Rice with *The Adding Machine* had experimented with expressionism. However, whereas the protagonists in the works of O'Neill and Rice ultimately succumb to the pressures of an unforgiving world and die in defeat, Lawson's Roger triumphs over overwhelming odds, laughing in the face of the furies that haunt him. Initially and briefly produced by the nascent Equity Players and, in turn, picked up by noted independent producer Marguerite Barker, *Roger Bloomer* received numerous positive notices. More importantly, both critics and audiences were keenly interested in seeing what Lawson would do next.

Lawson followed the success of *Roger Bloomer* with *Processional*, which was similarly well received by both critics and audiences. It was produced in January 1925 by the celebrated Theatre Guild, arguably the most important art theatre in the United States at that time. In *Processional*, Lawson ingeniously combined a variety of modes of expression – including devices and ideas drawn from vaudeville, jazz, and the European avant-garde (specifically, dada) – to tell a story of a bloody labor conflict in a West Virginia coal-mining town, and its central figure, the anti-hero Dynamite Jim. Because of his bold experimentation with dramatic form – as well as his biting critiques of American racism and violence, puritanical ideology, and big business greed – *Processional* came to be viewed as Lawson's most significant achievement in the theatre and was often the standard by which his other scripts were measured.

Much less successful was *Nirvana*, produced independently in New York in 1926. Though *Nirvana* does indeed fall short on a number of levels, with it Lawson once again demonstrated a willingness to tackle difficult and controversial subjects, as well as an ability to experiment boldly with dramatic form. In it, Lawson sought to highlight the limits of the Judeo-Christian belief system in the post-Einstein world. While a few critics and a handful of audiences saw possibilities in his poetic rumination on this complex issue, as well as the odd fusing of the well-made play structure and surrealism, most found it bewildering. Thus, savaged by most critics and largely ignored by the public, *Nirvana* closed after only four performances.

The following year, Lawson, along with John Dos Passos, Michael Gold, Francis Faragoh, and Em Jo Basshe, founded the New Playwrights' Theatre. Through relentless self-promotion (including a number of brash manifestoes penned by Lawson), the New Playwrights' audaciously claimed that theirs would be a theatre without compromise, focused on pressing topics, and aimed at working-class audiences. While the group of young artists set themselves up as iconoclastic, saviors of American theatre, in the end the New Playwrights' lasted just three seasons, rarely finding favor with critics or their target audience. Though the New Playwrights' valiant attempt to reimagine theatre in the United States was marred by near-constant infighting, often exasperated by dire financial problems, Lawson nonetheless managed to write and see through to production two of his scripts. The first was 1927's *Loudspeaker*, a cartoonish, fast moving and, ultimately, pessimistic satire of American politics, big business, and yellow journalism, that looked to the method Russian Constructivism for inspiration. The second was 1928's *The International*, a sprawling, musical-dance piece that tells the story of a future world war between the forces of capitalism, communism, and fascism by way of the odd union of realism and choral odes that recall Greek tragedy. In the end, however, Lawson's attempts, as a member of the New Playwrights' Theatre, to continue experimentation with form and address difficult topics was met with indifference if not hostility; the productions of both *Loudspeaker* and *The International* were, largely, condemned by critics of all stripes and ignored by audiences.

After the unceremonious failure of the New Playwrights' Theatre in 1929, Lawson spent most of the next four years in Hollywood, working as a staff screenwriter, first with MGM and later with RKO. While Lawson had above average success working in the studio system, contributing in substantial ways to a number of projects, he nonetheless longed to return to the theatre. His wish was granted in late in1932, when he arrived in New York for the Group Theatre's production of *Success Story*. Lawson's tale of the tragic consequence of sacrificing conviction for mammon and love for lust, manifest in the starkly realistic portrayal of Sol Ginsberg, received considerable commercial and critical acclaim. Indeed, many critics counted *Success Story* as evidence of Lawson's return to top form, and held out hope that he would be from that point forward be a major contributor to the American stage. Unfortunately, however, though Lawson had hoped that the triumph of *Success Story* would jump-start his theatrical career, the deepening depression, which resulted in a dearth of theatre work in New York, forced his return to Hollywood and MGM once again in late 1932.

Soon after arriving in Hollywood for the second time, Lawson became involved in the recently formed Screen Writers' Guild. Flush with the possibility of improving the working conditions for screenwriters, Lawson quickly rose to a position of influence within the group, and was elected its first President, an office he held from mid-1933 through mid-1934. Though Lawson's time as president of the SWG is often glossed by theatre historians, the year he spent lobbying for fair treatment of the group's members (both with studio heads and with representatives from the Roosevelt administration) afforded him a potent education in the shape and scope of American politics and its relation to art, and led him to view with great skepticism the undue power afforded big business, particularly in relation to the United States' political process. So profound was the experience that Lawson would later claim that his time as President of the SWG led directly to his adopting a more ardently revolutionary political stance.

In the spring of 1934, the siren call of the theatre led Lawson to return once again to New York and the theatre. Soon after arriving, he saw staged concurrent productions of his scripts *The Pure in Heart* and *Gentlewoman*. The former, which was independently produced by Richard Aldrich and Alfred de Liagre Jr., uses many of the avant-garde modes of expression central to Lawson's work in the 1920s. Conversely, the latter, produced by the Group Theatre, relies on realism and the well-made play structure, devices central to the playwright's work in the 1930s. Despite their formal differences, both scripts deal with contemporary individuals acknowledging and reacting to the perceived ruin of spiritual and emotional life in the modern world. Significantly, in both pieces the protagonists live lives of compromise, and, in the end, fail to rise above their own individual introspection and neuroses. While the simultaneous production of these scripts on New York stages was initially viewed as a triumph, it soon became one of the more difficult episodes in Lawson's life. Both *The Pure in Heart* and *Gentlewomen* were brutally condemned by critics, including those writing for the left-wing newspapers. As these revolutionary critics' opinions were the only ones Lawson cared about by this point, their charges of "ideological confusion" were particularly upsetting.

In part in response to these charges, as well as due to his now years' long journey to understand more fully the artist's relation and responsibility to society, in late 1934 Lawson joined the Communist Party. In turn, he spent the better part of the next two years participating in various left wing and progressive causes. Concurrently, he worked on the manuscript for *The Theory and Technique of Playwriting*, a study that was and continues to be cited as instrumental in forwarding the influential ideas that all dramatic conflict is social in its orientation, and that realism is the preferable mode of theatrical expression.

On the heels of these experiences, Lawson wrote and saw produced his script, *Marching Song*. As he had with *Gentlewoman*, with this piece Lawson drew on the elements of the well-made play structure, this time dramatizing the tale of a strike in an automotive plant. Significantly, the central character in *Marching Song*, Pete Russell, who in some respects is Lawson's analogue, struggles with the choice and consequences that accompany commitment to a cause, but in the end finds peace though an allegiance to justice and belief in the power of collective action. Produced by the leftward leaning Theatre Union in March 1937, *Marching Song* garnered many positive notices (particularly from the left-wing press) and modest commercial success.

Despite this achievement, Lawson was growing increasingly dissatisfied with his abilities to rectify his newly recognized revolutionary political principles with his ideas regarding the theatre. Thus, in late 1937, he left New York and the theatre and returned to Hollywood, this time for good. In turn, he would spend the next ten years of his life serving as a leading member of the Hollywood cell of the Communist Party, all the while writing numerous screenplays while under contract with various studios. Lawson's political activism did not go unnoticed; in 1947, he was one of the infamous Hollywood Ten, called before the House Un-American Activities Committee, and labeled an "unfriendly witness." Unwilling to cooperate, Lawson was cited for contempt of congress, convicted, and, in turn, served a two-year term in federal prison. Once he was released, and though he never completely abandoned the theatre – as is evidence by the handful of scripts that he worked on at various times during the balance of his life – Lawson's focus was on advancing revolutionary ideology. As such, his principal writings over the course of the final decades of his life were Marxist analyses of United States history and culture.

By the time Lawson died in San Francisco on 11 August 1977, his career in the theatre had been largely forgotten. Though his contributions are, perhaps, modest, especially when compared to figures such as Eugene O'Neill or Clifford Odets, the mark Lawson left on theatre in the United States is nonetheless consequential. In the end, then, though the work of John Howard Lawson is rarely read or produced today, many of his scripts written and produced between 1923 and 1937 stand as important contributions that influenced, sometime profoundly so, the development of theatre in the United States. As such, it behooves the contemporary theatre scholar, the theatre artists, and the theatre audience to be aware of how he influenced the shape and scope of theatrical expression.

Jonathan Chambers

Bowling Green State University

For a more detailed account of Lawson's career in theatre, see *Messiah of the New Technique: John Howard Lawson, Communism, and American Theatre, 1923-1937*, by Jonathan Chambers and published by Southern Illinois University Press.

AFTERWORD

I've been greatly impressed with Allie Mulholland and his Re-Group Theatre and in the way they've brought forward and given life to the forgotten Group Theatre plays. Two of those plays, brought to light by Allie and his fellow Aladdins, were written by my father, John Howard Lawson, and published in this volume. Allie is a man with a strong commitment to quality theater and due to his wide reading of plays, brings insights relevant to theatrical history. The thirties was a time of great turmoil, suffering and change. Out of that struggle, the decade produced extraordinary creative activity and new ways of expression in the arts, especially in theater.

I was born in 1926. Growing up as a child in the 30s and into the 40s, I was greatly influenced by those times. That was especially so since my parents and their friends were involved in many significant political and artistic events and constantly talked about them. When I lived in New York City for two years, I was exposed to an even wider panorama of cultural and political variety: political rallies at Madison Square Garden, plays, foreign films, novels, newspapers, and highly creative people.

I remember the freezing Saturday mornings in January of 1937 when I'd go with my father to spend the day watching the rehearsals of his play, "Marching Song". Dressed in heavy winter clothing, we'd take the subway to Times Square and walk down 44th Street to the Bayes Theater, taking a wide elevator up to the lobby. Walking into the dimly lit auditorium and down the aisle, I could see it was empty except for the first two rows where the actors and production people sat.

As we arrived, a thing that impressed me was how so many of the actors called out, "Hi, Jack! How are you?" It was a big cast, and as Father was taking off his coat, a number of them got up and made their way to the aisle to greet him. Smiling, they shook his hand and asked all kinds of questions. What I saw was the huge respect they showed him. I'd seen novelists, screen writers, and people at political rallies show respect for my father, but this was different. It is true that in theater, the author is looked upon as the true creator of the work. I believe this was more than that. As happens with actors, by necessity, they become deeply immersed in the dialogue and actions of a play. "Marching Song" is a stirring drama. Called a proletarian play, it is about working people caught in the jaws of the depression. Having lost jobs and homes, they are struggling to solve their problems and to survive. In the end, they find a way to join together in unity. I think those actors were giving my father recognition for all they felt about the play, all he'd put into it, it's characters, it's dialogue and it's structure. It was the only play my father wrote where almost all the New

York critics praised it. Audiences responded to it.

Naturally, having spent those days at the rehearsals, I have a special feeling for the play. But the real point I want to make is that, as well written as "Marching Song" is with interesting characters and excellent dialogue, I think "Success Story" and "Gentlewoman" are far more interesting plays. The writing of "Marching Song" had been influenced by Mike Gold, the critic for the Communist Daily Worker. He had dismissed "Success Story" and "Gentlewoman" as too bourgeois, that term for middle class used so often in those times. He characterized "Gentlewoman" as a "Bourgeois Hamlet", meaning a play about middle class people with inner conflicts.

In my view, those plays absolutely represent my father's true métier. He was bourgeois and knew middle class people, especially middle class intellectuals. The two plays published here are, for me, fascinating studies of the complexities of certain types of bourgeois people and their inner conflicts. I'm happy to say that the director of the Group Theater, Harold Clurman, in his book *The Fervent Years* agrees with my view. He had great respect for my father and believed in his talent, but thought he should write about characters he knew. Sol Ginsberg in "Success Story" and Gwyn Ballantine and Rudy Flannigan in "Gentlewoman" are types he knew. More than that, they are characters which reflect the very inner conflicts my father had within him at the time.

He was bourgeois, for one thing, in the sense of having come from a wealthy New York family. His father, my grandfather, had run away from home at fifteen and went out to the wild West. After a number of adventures involving gunmen and gamblers, he went to Mexico City and started an English language newspaper. He became a highly successful, wealthy self-made man in the newspaper business. I doubt that my grandfather was a model for Ginsberg. But I believe that, when my father first went to Hollywood in 1928, one of the things that interested him was it being a world of corporate power.

It was the important MGM producer, Irving Thalberg, a self-made, driven man who valued good writing, that brought my father to Hollywood because of his plays. In turn, my father had respect for Thalberg's creative instincts in film and found his career fascinating. Obviously, F. Scott Fitzgerald also admired Thalberg when he made him the basis for the character Monroe Starr in his unfinished novel, *The Last Tycoon*. I assume that Thalberg was connected in my father's mind, in some way, to Sol Ginsberg.

From when I was six, I have a clear memory of driving in our Packard touring car, with my father, from Mastic Beach, where we lived, out to Montauk Point at the Eastern tip of Long Island. It was a bright, sunny, blue-sky day. As we stood on the dock, a white ship appeared out in the blue ocean. When the ferry from Providence, RI arrived, my father's best friend, John Dos Passos, stepped off. They'd know each other since serving together in the Ambulance Corps during the First World War. Since that time, they'd had a big influence on each other's politics and writing. At the time he came to visit us, Dos was working on his great trilogy, *U.S.A.*

Dos fascinated me, not because he was a novelist and avant-garde experimental writer, but because I thought he was a strange looking man with his bald head and somewhat bug eyes. It always amazed me how, when he read, he held the page an inch or so from his eyes. My mother told me he'd thrown away his glasses based on a theory that that would improve his vision. As usual, after greeting each other, the two men began to argue. In the car, they continued to argue all the way back to Mastic Beach. Whatever it was about, books, plays or politics, I knew what they always did when together—they argued.

I liked Dos, and I wasn't usually afraid of him. One night it was different. I sat in the living room after dinner on a footstool. Dos was on the couch and my father in a chair. This time, when they began to argue, it became highly intense. Dos stood to storm up and down the room. As he did so, he wildly waved his arms as he screamed and yelled to make his point. Sitting on the low footstool, looking up as this large man rushing back and forth in such a violent way, I got frightened. I was so upset, I ran to the library where my mother sat crocheting. Showing my fear in fast, emotional talk, I explained how scary Dos looked, and how afraid I was about what he might do. My mother just smiled and said, "There's nothing to worry about, honey. They're just arguing."

I don't really know what the argument was about, but I like to think it had to do with the letter my father had just received from Harold Clurman concerning the script of "Success Story". From my father's unpublished autobiography and other papers, I know now that the Group Theater was at their summer camp at Dover Furnace, NY. They were rehearsing "Success Story", under the direction of Lee Strasberg. The letter my father got disturbed him and also disturbed Dos who'd had a disagreement with the Group and didn't trust them. Dos said the script was just right, and whatever they suggested should be fought against. My father didn't have that extreme a view and greatly valued his relationship with Clurman and Strasberg and the company.

What the letter said was that Clurman and Strasberg believed that the character of Sarah Glassman was not clear enough and had to be changed. They'd decided that the right solution was to make Sarah into a committed Communist. My father reacted strongly against that idea. In his mind, it was wrong in that it went totally against what he saw as the central meaning of the play. Sarah does have the sensibility to see and understand injustice around her and comes to see how corrupt Sol Ginsberg is. But, in my father's view, she is a thoroughly bourgeois woman. Though she sees that Sol is corrupt, that isn't why she rejects him. She rejects him because he's the only thing she's ever believed in—and has always loved.

As a strong woman, she can be a character out of a typical bourgeois novel. Though not the same, an example might be, Tolstoy's

Anna Karenina. As if it is all she believes in, Anna follows her feelings of love to the end, even in violation of the rules of society, and ends in tragedy. Sarah is like Anna, a product of bourgeois society who believes totally in love. If she was a Communist, she'd have a completely different relationship to Sol.

As an ambitious, angry, driven man willing to destroy anything in his way to get what he wants, Sol Ginsberg can't escape what he's become. In his drive to outwit the Capitalist system at its own game, he does corrupt things and harms people. In my father's view, he isn't all bad, but a product of the system by which he was created. Also, he has the ability to see his own corruption and know what it is. That's the real tragedy, that it matters to him. He realizes that to have achieved everything he wanted means he's ending with nothing of real value. That is underscored when he sees that Sarah, the only one who has truly loved him and believed in him, now sees through to the destructive person he is. She can't help still loving him, but she knows she has to reject him because he will only destroy her. He knows he's lost the only thing of value that means anything to him. He has failed in every way.

Though my father could see the point that Clurman was making about giving clarity to Sarah's character, he strongly believed his own view was the correct one. He began writing heated letters to Clurman. For a week they carried on an intense correspondence, each holding to his belief. Finally, my father went to Dover Furnace and gave a speech passionately defending his view before the whole company. Seeing the intensity of my father's feelings, Clurman and Strasberg came to the conclusion that, in the best interest of the play, they had to accept his view.

What the above story shows me is a demonstration of the seriousness and passion that the entire Group Theater, Clurman, Strasberg, the actors and all involved, and my father brought to the productions they mounted.

-Jeffrey Lawson

Suggested Additional Reading:

Adler, Stella, *The Technique of Acting*. NY: Bantom Books, 1988.

Clurman, Harold, *The Fervent Years*. NY: Knopf, 1945.

Hethmon, Robert (editor) *Lee Strasberg at the Actors Studio*. NY: Viking Press, 1965

Kazan, Elia. *Elia Kazan: A Life*. NY: Knopf, 1988.

Lewis, Robert. *Slings and Arrows*. NY: Stein and Day, 1980

Meisner, Sanford. *On Acting*. NY: Vintage, 1987.

Smith, Wendy, *Real Life Drama*. NY: Knopf, 1990.

Notes on the ReGroup Theatre Company

According to the dictionary, to 'regroup' is "to become reorganized by determining what is wrong with the current system in an effort to make a fresh start." THAT idea is where we got our name.

As a company comprised of actors, we want 'to act' in great plays, and we use the Group's definition of a great play as "one that is propaganda for a better life". Yet, sometimes you have to take action in order to reinvent the structure of a broken system. That is what we are trying to do.

Instead of being disillusioned by the seemingly constant decline of the Theatre, we attempt to capture a piece of the spirit that once made Theatre the premiere American art form. If we can find those sparks, perhaps we can get the fire burning again. In this plugged-in, tuned-out era, what better way to bring people together than to recreate a truly communal experience between the actors and the audience. The audiences is as much a part of the true Theatre as the actors, and they deserve that respect. They buy a ticket for an experience; one that will make them participants with this particular Theatre Company now and in the future. Purchasing a Theatre ticket should be a totally different experience than just buying a movie ticket or some commercially packaged product.

We began by studying our Theatrical legacy, trying to find where it went off course. The starting point for this study was the plays. Who better depicts the struggles of life than our great dramatists? Working backward through the American canon, we found that the characters once embodied more depth and size. Though it is a generalization, the older plays focus more on large, challenging life struggles which, no matter how specific they might be, they have universal appeal. These are not little people who are jilted and bickering, they are people torn apart and fighting to make something better out of this world. We were onto something, we just didn't know what.

The next step in our search was to turn to the great 'masters' of the American Theatre, primarily all the members of the Group Theatre. Besides learning from them, it raised questions: "Where are the greats of the Theatre community now? Where *is* the Theatre community now? Who could be called the Elder Statesman of the American Theatre?" Modern Theatrical artists have become so involved in the individual pursuit of a career, that they have left the Theatre to fend for itself.

Eighty years ago, the members of The Group Theatre were in the midst of a terrible economy, were competing with trivial fare, and had an audience that was losing interest in the power of the Theatre. They chose to 'act,' and we hope to capture some of that same spirit. W are using the Group's amazing "lost" plays in an attempt to reeducate audiences as to what great Theatre can be as well as teaching actors and playwrights what power the Theatre can have. Through exposure to these gems, we hope to provoke modern playwrights to provide us with work that is as relevant as the Group's plays.

As the original Group realized, our current Theatrical structure in this country is designed to fail. After every play, companies disperse and go on to start from scratch with a new group of artists. But imagine what momentum could be gained from a permanent company or companies that have a common language, a database of experiences and history. In just over a year, we have seen how helpful it is for our growing company to be able to reference a moment from a previous production. Not only is it timesaving, but we can build upon the past foundation. This permanent company also provides the artists with security. How safely can you explore a project when you are forced to worry where the next job is coming from? The community we started in a closet in January 2010, has grown to working with over 2 dozen actors. They are equal part soldiers, family members, community leaders and teachers. Currently dependent on a handful of individual donors and our own personal contributions, the ReGroup Theatre Company, like its role model, has learned to be thrifty and creative. Our growth potential is unlimited if we can find like-minded people and corporations to collaborate with us.

The United States is one of the only leading countries in the world that does not have a national theatre. For a relatively young country, the USA has an amazing Theatrical Legacy. The words of Albee, Hellman, Howard, Kaufman, Lawson, Miller, O'Neill, Odets, and Williams document our journey as a country. Dated? No. They have the power to bring to life past generations and to let us see our connections and roots with those that came before us. By reviving these amazing works and presenting them as they are written -not as dull historical pieces- we aim to inspire new dramatists to continue in their footsteps. Despite popular belief, American Theatrical history did not begin or end with the brilliance of Tennessee Williams or Arthur Miller. With a focus on the Group, we can see the influence their plays had on these master dramatists, and it shows us that American Theatre is an ongoing process with brilliant roots. By tapping into that greatness, we are not actors or playwrights existing in a vacuum. We are part of a continuing legacy, neither the beginning nor the end.

The ReGroup Theatre Company

Allie Mulholland
Artistic Director

Emily Ciotti
Assistant-Artistic Director

Charter Members
George Bartenieff
Linda Glick
Gary Hilborn
Kelsey Moore
Maurya Scanlon
Aleksandar Ristov
Gregory Victor

Honorary Board of Advisors
Austin Pendleton
Molly Regan
Susan Rowland
Ally Sheedy

www.ReGroupTheatre.org

This book would not have been possible without the graciousness of:

Jeffrey & Susan Lawson, Susan Rowland
and John, Sam, & Toby Sifton

Thanks to all those who made the first year of the
ReGroup Theatre Company a remarkable one:

Harold Baldridge, Ted Bessen, Charles Black, Jeane' Blazic, Elyse Brandau, Tyler Burke, Rachel Casparian, Paul Cereghino, Jonathan Chambers, Gail Cohen, Libby Collins, Michael Collins, Meredith Collins, Joshua Coleman, David Cromer, Stephen Dexter, Selena C. Dukes, Jamie Effros, Robert Ellermann, Michael Ellis, Adam Feingold, Eugene Fertelmeyster, Peter Filichia, Susan Finley, Jack Gilbert, Roger Gindi, James Grissom, Swann Gruen, Logan James Hall, Marcus D. Harvey, Michael Jefferson, Laura E. Johnston, Annie Keefe, Kevin Kolack, Ben Leasure, Alastair Lumsden, Karen Malpede, Marsha Mason, Jan Maxwell, Pete McElligott, Jill & Lance Miller, Charlotte Moore, Ross Nathan, James Naughton, James Patrick Nelson, Michael Oberholtzer, Scott O'Brien, Patricia Palermo, Walter & Sompit Oerlemans, Tim Page, Dana Panepinto, Estelle Parsons, Christopher Pennington, Porter Pickard, Briana Pozner, Ronald Rand, Antonia Rey, Nicole Romano, Ryan Roth, Jose Angel Santana, Julian Sapala, Patricia Scanlon, Marc R. Sklar, Martha Wade Steketee, Kent & Sharon Stites, Anna Strasberg, Lindsay Teed, Emilio Tirado, Shelley Valfer, Tony Vellela, Laura & Don Victor, Chris Walls, Kate Warren, Shaun Bennet Wilson, Hardy Winburn, Sylvia Zensen, The Dawn Powell Estate, The Barrow Group, The Irish Rep, The Neighborhood Playhouse, Shetler Studios, St. Luke's Theatre, The Field , The Jerome Robbins Foundation

....and our amazing audience.

Made in the USA
Charleston, SC
01 October 2012